CONTINUING BONDS WITH THE DEAD

STUDIES IN AMERICAN LITERARY REALISM AND NATURALISM

CONTINUING BONDS WITH THE DEAD

Parental Grief and Nineteenth-Century American Authors

Harold K. Bush

The University of Alabama Press
Tuscaloosa

The University of Alabama Press
Tuscaloosa, Alabama 35487-0380
uapress.ua.edu

Typeface: Meridien

Manufactured in the United States of America
Cover art: iStockphoto (dried flowers © Cecilla Bajic; picture frame © nipastock)
Cover design: Erin Bradley Danger / Danger Design

∞

The paper on which this book is printed meets the minimum requirements of American National Standard for Information Sciences—Permanence of Paper for Printed Library Materials, ANSI Z39.48-1984.

Cataloging-in-Publication data is available from the Library of Congress.
ISBN: 978-0-8173-1902-1
E-ISBN: 978-0-8173-8954-3

To my parents, Harold K. Bush and Mary Lyon;
my stepparents, Ione Bush and Stan Lyon;
and my son, Daniel Bush

Contents

Illustrations

Acknowledgments

Nothing is done alone, and so here I make known publicly my personal thanks for all the help over many years.

I dedicate this book to those closest to me, who have preceded me into that undiscovered country, the ones with whom I have daily sensed a continuing bond: my son, Daniel Bush; my parents, Harold K. Bush and Mary Lyon; and my stepparents, Ione Bush and Stan Lyon. In many ways the book began on my life's worst day, in June 1999; almost uncannily, the bond has continued, and probably will forever.

I also owe just about everything surrounding this book to my dearly beloved wife, Hiroko. I wouldn't have made it this far without her, as I reminded her in the chapel at Mont Saint-Michel, and neither would this volume exist without her. I also thank warmly the Hara family, in Tokyo, Japan, together with our extended families sprinkled over two continents.

My personal debt is just as wide-ranging. Our many close friends are the reason we have persevered; I simply cannot name them all here, but will give very special mention to the Frankos, the Johnsons, the Victors, the Leiboviches, the Middekes, and more general recognition to all our beloved New City family.

My list of work-life co-conspirators is quite long. Professionally, I owe much to all my colleagues at Saint Louis University as well as to the excellent research assistants who helped me get this project done: Stephanie Wallace, Colin Pajda, Kyle Crews, Jonathan Lux, Aaron Belz, Joe Webb, and Matthew Miller. Keith Wilhite helped get it all going, over a decade ago. At SLU, I owe much to Dean Barber and to the chairs of my department, who have generously provided funding and time to work: the late Thomas Moisan, Sara van den Berg, and Jonathan Sawday. I also have great friends among the faculty at SLU. I'd like to start listing all the names, but at the risk of neglecting someone—thanks to all my generous colleagues.

I am profoundly aware of the extent to which very little of what I say is original with me. At some point or another, I take it that most readers of this statement have also sensed what Mark Twain called the "unconscious," plagiaristic tendencies of their own creations.Thus, I want to thank all those who have contributed—directly or unbeknownst to them (or me)—to the development and maturation of the thoughts and ideas in this book. Foremost of these are the minions of the Mark Twain scholarly community: the folks working at the Mark Twain Project at Berkeley, beginning with the director Bob Hirst, all the editors who have welcomed me, and the wonderful staff; and the many friends in the Mark Twain Circle, who have counseled me and encouraged me along the way: especially Shelley Fisher Fishkin, Joe Csicsila, Chad Rohman, Bruce Michelson, Peter Messent, Linda Morris, Kevin MacDonnell, Tsuyoshi Ishihara, Barbara Schmidt, Susan K. Harris, John Bird, Steve Courtney, Jeanne Reesman, and Jerrod Roark. Besides those named: well, the list is just too long. If you've been to Elmira more than once, and/or if you've ever sat upon the porch of Quarry Farm at sundown, and sung along to the old songs with a cold drink at your side—well, you know who you are.

The Lincoln scholarly community has been similarly generous and willing to help in my work on this project. It's deeply humbling to be welcomed by the who's who of a scholarly community, as one of its own. In particular, I would like to mention the help of Michael Burlingame, Douglas Wilson, Allen Guelzo, Gabor Borritt, Mark Noll, Richard Wightman Cox, Robert Bray, Stephen Mansfield, and Barry Schwartz—all of whom corresponded with me, answered my questions, and suggested all kinds of things along the way. Thanks for those thousands of hours, all devoted to a single life!

More generally are all the various scholars in the at-large community of American literature and culture; many have given gracious attention to my work or parts thereof. I count it a true blessing that some of the top names in the field would find anything I do of interest, and among that stellar company who have helped with this project are the following: David Reynolds, Susan Belasco, Patricia Ward, Edward Blum, Paul Harvey, Joan Hedrick, Roger Lundin, John Crowley, Thomas Wortham, Ryan Schneider, Gary Scharnhorst, David Nordloh, and more—truly, so many more that I find it hard to create a short list. I also recognize, and thank profusely, the late-in-the-game encouragement of my stellar agent, Jill Marr of the Sandra Djikstra Agency.

Finally I applaud the staff at the University of Alabama Press; they have been a joy to work with: special thanks to Dan Waterman, in particular, and to his many helpers, including especially the two anonymous reviewers of the manuscript, whose wise and very thorough comments helped make a better book. Their wisdom and professionalism, along with that of everyone else listed here, I attribute to the "Father of lights, the giver of all" (James 1:17), and of course I confess that with the greatest of thanks as well.

CONTINUING BONDS WITH THE DEAD

Introduction

"Continuing Bonds" and Nineteenth-Century American Authorship

While gazing at the grisly images on CNN of the Virginia Tech slaughter, my wife and I had multiple reactions, as most Americans did during the frenzied, initial stages of the media coverage in April 2007. As a college professor, I certainly thought about my own students and the devastation that such an event would have on my campus. My wife, a Japanese citizen, noted the likelihood of cultural stereotyping that might result from the fact that the murderer was of Korean descent. But most poignantly, the Virginia Tech murders, like the news about the deaths of any children, evoked our deepest sympathy for the surviving parents, whose great hope for the future had been summarily crushed on what would forever remain one of their lives' darkest days—if not the darkest.

They say that losing a child is life's greatest tragedy. Much recent psychological data confirms this generalization; for most survivors, the death of a child becomes the crucial event for the remainder of their lives. Parental grief is grueling, long lasting, and can lead to all sorts of mental hell. Worst of all, and what is often misunderstood until much later, is how for many grieving parents the loss becomes not only *the* crucial before-and-after moment of adulthood, but also it usually has a lifelong effect.[1]

Sometimes, out of the rubble of lost lives, something redemptive emerges. One of the most amazing and uplifting aspects of the aftermath of the Virginia Tech disaster was the hopeful response among some of the survivors. A testimony to the deeply felt need to commemorate the dead was the massive response of Virginia Tech students, who quickly created their own temporary, public memorial site, filled as is now common with flowers, candles, stuffed animals, university mascots and logos, or whatever else a particular deceased person invokes for the survivors. Almost immediately plans began for constructing a physical memorial on the campus to remember the dead permanently; it was dedicated prior to the beginning of the new school year, only four months later. Digital tributes became widespread: the website that Virginia Tech produced to memorialize those who were murdered was the most prominent, but there were many on other sites as well, especially Facebook.[2] As the poet Nikki Giovanni, a professor at Virginia Tech, stated at the memorial service one year after the episode: "We will continue to invent the future through our blood and tears and through all our sadness." Suffering must yield to hope, she reminded her listeners, and in the end, hope wins out.[3]

Perhaps most compelling were the comments, often in tandem with specific actions, that the bereaved parents made regarding the children they lost at Virginia Tech. These shocked parents talked poignantly about the legacies of their lost children in constructive terms. The testimony of the father of a young woman named Reema Samaha was especially moving. As Joe Samaha was being interviewed on CNN about his beautiful daughter, a creative dancer, haunting images of Reema dancing on stage were being transmitted over the airwaves. Mr. Samaha emphasized how he and his family would keep Reema alive forever in their hearts, and that her life would continue to have meaning. "She did not die in vain," he insisted. He promised a national audience that Reema's life committed to art and beauty would continue to reap redemptive benefits, for as long as he and his family could keep her values and memory in mind. Eventually, a scholarship fund and a website were created to continue Reema's legacy in support of dance and the arts.[4]

In these moving comments, Joe Samaha recognizes that the bonds with his daughter must continue even after her untimely death. His insistence is a common feature of parental grief, and it reminds us that bereaved parents believe it is their task to insure that the legacy of their child must never dwindle away into oblivion. Although some friends or family might dismiss such sorrow and sentiment as mere wishful thinking, and often try to dislodge these impulses so that the grieving parent might "move on" or "find closure," these feelings and promises derive from deeply held metaphysical beliefs about the power of suffering and the motivational memory of the beloved. "I keep her in my mind," Joe Samaha said. "Her face is in my mental vision. It keeps me going."

The beautiful image of his lovely daughter Reema, dancing away into eternity, is a telling feature of the way that Joe Samaha chose to memorialize that horrible day in April 2007. His insistence that Reema "did not die in vain" is precisely the phrase that has been used over and over again by parents trying to deal with life's greatest horror. I doubt if Samaha knew it, but that exact phrase appears in America's most celebrated speech: Abraham Lincoln's address at Gettysburg in 1863, where Lincoln urges his listeners that they should "highly resolve that these dead shall not have died in vain."[5] Variations of the phrase have appeared in countless letters and diaries throughout American history. Long before the Civil War, Harriet Beecher Stowe wrote in 1852 to a friend that her own son's death need not be "suffered in vain."[6] And well into the twentieth century, Martin Luther King wrote that the children killed in the Birmingham church bombing of September 1964 "did not die in vain. God still has a way of wringing good out of evil."[7] Indeed, a redemptive view of suffering permeates the Christian faith. The idea that our lives are not futile is rooted in the Bible, which reminds us that we do not suffer tragic circumstances in vain, as in I Corinthians 15:58: "Therefore, my beloved brethren, be ye steadfast, unmovable, always abounding in the work of the Lord, forasmuch as ye know that your labour is not in vain in the Lord."

Such a redemptive hope in the face of unspeakable evil and suffering, as illustrated by Joe Samaha's promise to "keep [Reema] in his mind," has also been a major theme of American cultural history and has been vindicated time and time again by the tales of survivors. Samaha believed that Reema's memory alone could "keep him going," as countless other grieving parents have believed. Samaha's convictions are that something uniquely meaningful and redemptive can emerge from life's greatest tragedies, that somehow survivors are able to maintain bonds with the dead, and that those bonds can help the survivors generate some of the most meaningful accomplishments of their lives. Similar convictions have had a powerful influence in American culture. Historically, such a view is commonly linked to a romantic, antebellum worldview. In nineteenth-century America, Christian frameworks of redemptive suffering enabled and sanctioned bereaved parents to transform their grief into constructive acts carried out in memory of the dead, and many key writers were guided and influenced to varying degrees by these concepts. But by the time the new century commenced, a perfect storm of changes in culture and belief had moved many Americans away from these religious frameworks. By then, what Charles Taylor has called the "nova effect" of new options for belief—or unbelief—had exploded onto the scene: a myriad of new options for constructing meaning and purpose.[8]

As a result, and within just fifty years, more "modern" authors were facing a much more openly contested, cross-pressured, and confusing world where God and transcendence were no longer the key features of an epistemological "default position." And yet to varying degrees they continued to yearn for modes of reattachment to the dead, despite what science and liberal religion seemed to be telling them. A symptom of the epistemological nova effect, according to one dominant scholarly narrative, was the manner by which an "American way of death" gained ascendency from the end of the Civil War through the dawn of the twentieth century. The new way of death featured increasingly new ways of thinking about death and was marked by rapid shifts in the funeral industry. This account has focused on what has been termed the "death of dying": the ways that death had become more remote, less concrete, and thus less metaphysically "present" in the lives of middle-class citizens. The American experience of death changed dramatically from a religious, sentimental and intimate event to a much more scientific and business-oriented transaction.

This narrative of the changing way of death is illuminated by numerous cultural phenomena: perhaps none so telling as the way ministers sermonized about death at funerals. As Lucy Bregman has shown, funeral sermons from the pre–Civil War period through World War II demonstrate "a change, a momentous shift from what Christians used to say about death, and what they say now. The older language, ideas and images, had a long history, and persisted in full force for the early decades of the 20th century. Then this language faded, losing its hold over the collective religious sensibility of American Protestantism. . . . what grew up was the belief that prior to the 1970s, 'nothing' had been said about [death]. American society's denial of death was a vacuum, one that our current, recent language and understanding has now filled. The conventional way to label this is to say that 'American society denies death,' and that only now are we emerging from the era of silence and denial."[9] As Bregman goes on to show, however, and despite this denial, preachers said a great deal about death prior to that time—but especially throughout the nineteenth century, as the sermons revealed. In particular, Bregman's analysis is provocative in suggesting that in those days, "for a Christian funeral, the primary purpose is to worship God. So say at least five generations of clergy writing 'how-to' manuals for other clergy about Christian funerals. . . . The underlying and most basic purpose of the Christian funeral is worship of God. The role of the minister is to turn the congregation's attention away from anything less than this, and neither the dead person nor the pastor is to take center stage. Comfort is the aim of [a] funeral, but this is achieved when our hearts touch God, and not through direct psychological consolations. From this starting place, it is clear why pagan practices, such as viewings, may be a part of American life, but potentially subvert the authentic Christian aims of a few." In addition to worship, these funeral practices had a specific point to make about those in attendance: "Preaching death is where a Christian funeral must begin. The congregation is, above all else, the future dead. . . . Definitely before silence and denial, the whole point of a funeral sermon is to lay out explicitly and publicly Christian doctrines of salvation, eternal life, divine judgment."[10] As such, Bregman argues that formerly, the funeral was a sacred space focused on worship of God, with the redemption of all things through the grace of God a key. One can easily recognize how different these practices are from the funerals of the twenty-first century, which focus more on the deceased and less on the dogmas of the church. The worship of God has by now also been replaced, generally speaking, with a frightening absence: where was God? And why was this tragedy visited upon this innocent victim? Anger and bitterness often replace worship and veneration of a deity, particularly when the dead person is young. This change is detectable among the later writers covered here—especially Mark Twain.

Besides preaching, this shift is also notable in somewhat less conspicuous practices; for example, the bureaucratic and anonymous routines of the funeral business, the medical practices of embalming, and the promised security of life insurance all reflected and fostered a transition from intimacy and community throughout the death experience to one of anonymity and denial—and away from facing the fact that each of us is, in effect, the future dead. The consolation found in the presence of God has given way to a fear of death becoming enervated by entertainment and distraction; religious belief has come under attack; and rural forms of Christian worship and religious practice have diminished as more and more Americans have moved to the cities. These rapid changes also added to the draining of the grief experience of its mystery and its supernatural elements. Even as popular belief in God's final judgment and the threat of eternity in Hell dwindled, new ways of reading the Bible proliferated (along with new, less artful translations of Scripture), further demystifying the text. Meanwhile, biological death became more and more subsumed by the rise of science and medical expertise, where a more naturalistic approach gained prestige and credence.

All these shifts are extremely significant, because together they reflected and exacerbated the growing detachment between the Christian believer and God. The disconnect with God is mirrored in a growing chasm between survivors and lost family members, calling into question whatever continuing bonds might hold them together through eternity, which may or may not even exist. As Bregman writes, "Among the more optimistic preachers on death, there was also the assurance that a dead child strengthened the Christian's existing link to heaven, the world to come. . . . Those whose children have gone before them into heaven . . . feel themselves connected more closely to God, since the child becomes a link."[11] But by the end of the nineteenth century, that link was being severed, and thus, so was the connection with God. Moreover, it is plausible that a candid, unmediated encounter with death and our unrelenting recognition of ourselves as the future dead may in fact be crucial components of our humanity, insuring as they do a full and permanent bond with the departed and an increased seriousness about the project of being human. A regular, frank encounter with our mortality, in other words, was formerly understood as essential to our humanness and our dependence upon God and the life of faith, and was a predictable feature of funeral sermons. But as dependence on God is called into open question, and as death is tamed or domesticated by modern business practices, perhaps humanity loses a crucial aspect of its identity. Furthermore, as worship is displaced from the center of the funeral event, a culture of hopelessness and "weightlessness" is fostered.[12] While some commentators have viewed the "death of dying" as a liberation from the fear of death, it may well be that, besides being a cognate symptom of a default secularization and loss of faith, the American way of death has had untold negative repercussions. Perhaps the death of dying even leads inevitably to desecrations of human sanctity. But one obvious by-product of this massive shift was its effect on the way survivors understood their relationship with both their Maker and the dead. By the turn of the twentieth century, a powerful sense of the "continuing bonds with the dead" had become for many Americans a far less compelling possibility—as had the sense that the best response to pain and suffering was to worship God, not flee from Him.[13]

Nevertheless, as much recent clinical research has shown, and as such tragic events as the Virginia Tech massacre illustrate, a redemptive view of suffering and death has not disappeared, despite a century-long siege informed by secular science and demythologized religion. Indeed, some scholars are documenting a comeback in the memorialization of the dead. One cultural historian even speaks of a growing "memorial mania" among westerners, some of it increasing after the almost wild exhibition of spontaneous grief after the death of Princess Diana.[14] Today, pockets of American religious culture are intent on returning to some of these older forms of grieving and on recognizing that perhaps we can learn much from our earlier forebears about the nature of death. Within the church there is now a thriving movement attempting to recover some of the older forms of belief and funereal practice, such as burial (as opposed to cremation) and graveyards next to church buildings. Mourners are demanding more extended physical contact with the dead by embracing older concepts like wakes and graveside rituals. Many churches still center their attention on God at funerals and often incorporate worship in the services, especially music. Meanwhile, clinical practitioners increasingly report that concepts of the continuing bonds with the dead are not only commonplace but also deeply comforting and consoling among survivors—especially in the context of a Christian view of redemption and grace. Researchers are also showing how continuing bonds can be extremely empowering.

These continuing bonds—certainly part of what Abraham Lincoln once referred to as the "mystic chords of memory" that bind together families, communities, and nations—are the subject of this book. And so, to begin with a representative case, we might consider one man's response to the death of his young adult son in the days when American Romanticism was under sustained attack, and seemed to be dying: the height of the Civil War.

A great man unknown to most Americans today is Henry Bowditch, a Harvard professor of medicine, who was in Boston in March 1863 when he was told that his beloved son, Nathaniel, had been severely wounded in the Battle of Kelly's Ford in Virginia. He promptly boarded a train for Virginia, to see for himself what had happened and whether he could be of any assistance. When he arrived, hopeful that he might help Nathaniel recover, he was summarily informed that his son was dead. His surviving son, Vincent, later recalled, "my father had to endure the agony of learning that, having been left for hours upon the field, my brother was at last painfully and slowly removed to the camp upon a horse's back by a fellow soldier, who found him suffering and alone, no ambulance having been provided for the wounded."[15] After hearing of his son's brutal death, Bowditch was taken to the army camp, met with his son's comrades, and was told what a fine a soldier Nathaniel had been.

Overcome by profound sorrow, Bowditch undertook pragmatic actions to express and relieve his grief, as well as to ensure Nat's continuing

Henry Ingersoll Bowditch. Frontispiece to his son's book *Life and Correspondence of Henry Ingersoll Bowditch* (1902). Courtesy of the Massachusetts Historical Society.

presence in memory. He arranged for Nat's body to be embalmed so that "it may be seen on my return to Boston" by Nat's mother, fiancée, siblings, and friends "who were also in need of solace." "You have not lost him," the Reverend James Freeman Clarke's sermon informed them; Nat was "not dead but alive with higher life"; he was now on "just the other side of the veil," where "he says . . . I wait for you all." Despite all of this consolation, Henry Bowditch struggled emotionally for the rest of his life. But he was a professional man not used to emotion. The struggle became so extreme that he didn't know how to handle it. Watching him go through that period of mourning and trying to come to terms with Nathaniel's death was very moving and difficult for all of those around him. Bowditch "kept a careful record of his experience of loss, from his physical reaction—'like a dagger in my heart'—to the news of his son's injury, to the consolations that ultimately liberated him from a world of pain. . . . Bowditch 'broke fairly down' when he was told of Nathaniel's death." He kept apologizing for his emotional outbursts, and tried to find ways to channel his passions and to turn his loss into something he could use. But "almost immediately," he reported, "the divine influences of such a loss began to strive for mastery . . . & I thought that never was there a nobler cause for which he could have died."[16]

The key cause he was referring to was, of course, the preservation of the Union, which the Civil War was testing. Bowditch was an ardent abolitionist whose work for the cause of ending slavery went back several decades and probably began to flourish when he attended the funeral of William Wilberforce in England in 1833. But the more specific cause that emerged from the death of his son, Nathaniel, and which he associated with his dead son for the remainder of his life, was the need for better ambulance services on the battlefields. Bowditch was "distressed by the lack of ambulances and more general provisions for the wounded in the Union army, [and] now saw the direct results of this lack of system in the death of his son, who had lain unattended on the field. His son's death, he recognized, gave him 'greater moral influence' to pursue his cause. The state, he insisted in a pamphlet published in the fall of 1863, had an obligation to its soldiers. 'If any government under Heaven ought to be *paternal*, the United States authority, deriving, as it does, all its powers from the people, should surely be such, and should dispense that power, in full streams of benignant mercy upon its soldiers.' Bowditch's arguments not only contributed to the establishment of a comprehensive ambulance system by the following year but articulated a logic of obligation that applied not just to the wounded but also to the dead."[17]

Bowditch had previously witnessed great suffering among injured soldiers at battlefields such as Centreville, but now he believed that his son's suffering had been exacerbated by the lack of an organized ambulance system in the Union army. And so he began a lengthy campaign for such a system, writing *A Brief Plea for an Ambulance System for the Army of the United States; as Drawn from the Extra Sufferings of the Late Lieut. Bowditch and a Wounded Comrade* (1863), which was also delivered as an address to the Harvard Medical School and contained a passionate call on Congress to act. Bowditch was eventually successful in helping create such a system, thanks in no small part to the influence of *A Brief Plea*. There, he begins by claiming that his experiences were brought about by God's hand: "Providentially, as I deem it, I have been twice brought to know the wretched want of system now existing in the arrangements for taking care of the wounded on the field of battle, viz: —during my visit to Centreville, in September last, and from the dying statements of my son."[18]

After his visit to the Centreville battlefield, Bowditch commenced his campaign for better ambulance systems. Little did he know at that time that within months his own son would die as a result of an insufficient medical response. This disastrous loss, he believed, made his own arguments in favor of better services even more powerful. "Since his death, I think that I stand in different, and, may I not say? somewhat wider relations, than those I enjoyed from the teacher's chair. Resting as I now do under the solemn cloud-shadow of a great but benignant sorrow, I hope that some words I may now write, will reach beyond the confines of my profession, and touch other human intellects and hearts." The image of his dead son is clearly etched into his mind as he makes his final plea. Bowditch proclaims his hope, "when in sight of the mangled dead body of a darling, first-born son, that *such enormities, as are now liable to happen, under the present want of any proper ambulance system in the United States army, shall not be permitted hereafter*."[19]

Bowditch's insistence on better ambulance services had a lasting effect, and his efforts touched perhaps hundreds of lives in the final years of the Civil War. Although statistical numbers are hard to come by, it seems clear that the death of Nathaniel Bowditch—and the powerful effect the ensuing grief had on his father—saved the lives of many of his Union comrades in later years. And beyond the war, Bowditch continued to be involved in public health matters throughout his life, including the establishment of the Massachusetts State Board of Health in 1869, of which he was president until 1879. His influential book *Public Hygiene in America* was published in 1877, and eventually Bowditch became president of the American Medical Association. His work on the causes and treatment of tuberculosis, in particular, was well known and long lasting.

When he died in Boston on January 14, 1892, many of the greatest accomplishments of the final decades of his life were in his own mind associated directly with that fateful day in 1863 when a stranger informed him of his son's painful demise on the battlefield, waiting in vain for medical help to arrive. In 1902, his son, Vincent, recalled tenderly how his father described the effects of Nat's death: "[it] summoned me like the notes of the bugle to the charging soldier. It stirred me to the depths of woe, but at the same time seemed to me to be the harbinger of victory over all. I determined, a stricken father as I was, to lay aside all thought of self, save as a means of stirring the whole people in such a way that the Government would be forced to do something to prevent thereafter such vile treachery, as I deemed it, to every soldier of the Northern armies. . . .

But how much has all the beauty of life gone from me."[20] Nat's death was both a deprivation and a motivation in the life of the surviving father.

The story of Henry Bowditch is a powerful illustration of what some psychologists have lately been calling the "continuing bonds with the dead."[21] Continuing bonds theory describes the ways that survivors can continue to be motivated and inspired by the dead, especially those whose deaths are seen as untimely and premature, as in the case of children. If understood in a religious frame of mind, the dead are commonly perceived as not being dead at all, but as "still alive," having gone on to a better world in the direct presence of God. Thus, according to this account, the bonds do in fact continue, since the soul of the dead continues perpetually. Henry Bowditch, for example, found great comfort in a poem published before the war titled "My Child," by John Pierpont, a fellow abolitionist, a Unitarian clergyman, and a friend. The poem, like so many other works of consolation in those days, focused on the ongoing memory of the lost and the ultimate reunion with the dead: "Those whose children have gone before them into heaven . . . feel themselves connected more closely to God, since the child becomes a link," according to Bregman.[22] The poem also represented the hopeful possibility that his own powerful bonds with his dead child could continue, and even empower him in the future, as in the final stanzas:

> He lives! In all the past
> He lives; nor, to the last,
> Of seeing him again will I despair;
> In dreams I see him now;
> And, on his angel brow,
> I see it written, "Thou shalt see me there!"
>
> Yes, we all live to God!
> Father, thy chastening rod
> So help us, thine afflicted ones, to bear,
> That, in the spirit-land,
> Meeting at thy right hand,
> 'Twill be our heaven to find—that he is there![23]

Bowditch, a man of deep faith, accepted the premise of the ongoing reality of his dead son in the next world, beyond the veil. In addition, he found real hope and inspiration from remembering the dead and embracing the ongoing bonds with his lost son.

Bowditch's response to Nat's demise was not unusual, and neither was parental grief. "The club," as some bereaved parents have darkly called it, the one nobody wants to join, was actually well populated by literary greats in nineteenth-century America. It is well known that in the nineteenth century, the loss of children was not uncommon—especially for those under the age of five; in the preantibiotic world of medicine, often the deaths occurred due to simple problems such as impure food or water, or the spread of contagious airborne disease. Cholera, for example, killed Charley Stowe, and typhoid fever proved the demise of Willie Lincoln in the White House. Often our most famous authors lost multiple children: Harriet Beecher Stowe, Abraham Lincoln, and Mark Twain, for example, all suffered the loss of not just one but of multiple children over the course of their lives. The others covered here, W. D. Howells and W. E. B. Du Bois, suffered the death of a single child. Howells and his wife desperately tried everything they could think of to help their poor sickly daughter, Winifred, who died a painful death at the age of twenty-five, but the medical science of that day was powerless to help (and indeed, probably made matters worse). Similarly, Du Bois's son Burghardt died in 1899 due to a lack of medical help—but in that case, largely exacerbated by the racial prejudices of the medical community in Atlanta.

Many other great American authors are not studied here, but they were all part of the "club" and suffered mightily as well: Ralph Waldo Emerson, for example, who had dug up the coffin of his dead first wife Ellen in 1831 to look inside, suffered extreme depression when his beloved son Waldo died in 1842. Again, many years after the fact, Emerson opened the coffin to view Waldo's corpse. Out of the horror of his son's death emerged one of Emerson's most important works: "Experience," an essay filled with regret and perhaps even trauma. "In the death of my son, now more than two years ago, I seem to have lost a beautiful estate, —no more. I cannot get it nearer to me . . . it does not touch me: some thing which I fancied was a part of me, which could not be torn away without tearing me, nor enlarged without enriching me, falls off from me, and leaves no scar. It was caducous. I grieve that grief can teach me nothing, nor carry me one step into real nature." It is surprising, as has been noted, that this passage has been so often misread or misunderstood. From a clinical view, it seems clear that, two years later, the traumatized Emerson is still suffering from latency, an inability to realize his son's death, to get nearer to it (about latency and "realizing" a death, more later). But most of all, as Jay Grossman has argued, the famous, odd word "caducous" fits perfectly with an Emersonian conceit about the transmigration of the soul and the permanence of a bond with Waldo. While the caducous nature of a leaf or limb means it is only temporary and it will fall away, a leaf also represents "the desired culmination toward which the striving in Emerson's essays repeatedly directs its readers: '*That* is morning, to cease for a bright hour to be a prisoner of this sickly body, and to become as large as nature.'"[24]

Emerson's case is surely one of the century's most famous, but other examples of authors losing children and writing about it abound. Fanny Fern's novel *Ruth Hall* (1854) describes the death of the heroine's daughter, about which the author had firsthand experience as well: her oldest daughter Mary died of meningitis in 1845. "Eight years since the little Daisy withered! And yet, to the mother's eye, she still blossomed fair as Paradise. . . . Still, the little hymn was chanted at dawn, the little prayer lisped at dew-fall; still, that gentle breathing mingled with the happy mother's star-lit dreams. . . . Blessed childhood! The pupil and yet the teacher; half infant, half sage, and whole angel!"[25] Similarly, Louisa May Alcott's novel *Little Women* (1868) features the "good death" of the angelic Beth March, and while Alcott never had children, she was a firsthand witness to the throes of her parents' grief when her younger sister, Lizzie, died in 1858. In 1867, Herman Melville's eighteen-year-old son, Malcolm, shot himself in the head on the second floor of the family house in New York. Ambrose Bierce suffered the deaths of two sons: the oldest named Day committed suicide in 1889; the other named Leigh died a sickly alcoholic in 1901. Many more could be added; the list is so long it might make my choices for detailed study seem somewhat arbitrary. And yet despite such sad experiences, these literary stars managed for the most part to forge ahead and to live steady, productive lives that helped shape the rise of a mighty nation.

Several common elements help form a coherent narrative. First, my primary subjects—Harriet Beecher Stowe, Abraham Lincoln, William Dean Howells, Mark Twain, and W. E. B. Du Bois—are among the most important American writers in our nation's history, especially in terms of this era. Second, there are similarities in the ways all these authors harnessed their suffering in constructive ways to produce their landmark achievements. And yet the constructive uses of grief clearly became strained and diminished as time went on. And so third, the changes in the responses of these authors are emblematic of the religious and social changes at work in the general culture. In the midst of the "dying of death" and the rise of a more secularized public sphere, these radical shifts included the loss of a solid grounding on a Christian version of the bonds with the dead, and responded to the rise of cultural awareness of the theological problem of evil and suffering, along with the challenges of discovering a compelling theodicy for the modern world. The effects of these philosophical and religious challenges become more prominent in the later writers studied here (especially Twain and Du Bois), and they increasingly influenced grief patterns well into the twentieth century. The sheer anger toward God in Twain's work, for example, as well as the more symbolic and liberalized account of continuing bonds in Du Bois's masterpiece *The Souls of Black Folk*, suggest the decline in the explanatory abilities of the Christian faith. This deterioration is often associated with the age of realism and the rise of modernism in America.

In terms of plan, *Continuing Bonds* narrates each individual's experience of parental grief and shows how the burdens of grief triggered transformation, rejection, and (sometimes) a sense of redemption. In terms of the redemptive work that emerged from each author's experience of grief, and not coincidentally, it is intriguing to consider that each of these five major figures had a direct involvement in the struggles of African Americans to attain civil rights in America. Furthermore, my accounts suggest how these writers undertook a social justice agenda partly as a memorial of or legacy to the dead. Thus a subplot of my study is how the loss of a child often and even crucially drove the surviving parents, white and black, male and female, to work for social justice and equal rights for all Americans—especially for the rights of African Americans, but also (in the cases of Howells and Twain, and eventually Du Bois) for the rights of all oppressed or subjugated peoples around the world, as best illustrated in these writers' vitriolic attacks upon American empire. One might even suggest that Howells and Twain, upon their reunion during the presidential campaign of 1900, constructively formed what I will call an "Anti-imperial friendship": their common cause speaking out against imperialism. This crusade was borne partially out of the shared grief experience of two despondent fathers who missed their talented daughters—each had died in excruciating agony in her early twenties, just a few years apart, and just as America commenced its overseas imperial adventuring.

In all these cases, *Continuing Bonds* describes how heroic encounters with loss, aggravated grief, and sometimes trauma led these authors to a profound awareness of "the continuing bonds with the dead." Each author responded by composing at least some works they considered worthy of the memory of the departed dead—in effect, works they hoped might alleviate the suffering of humanity. Of course, some of them—perhaps, again, most notably Mark Twain—simultaneously penned angry screeds against God and faith. Less well known is how Twain still found ways to channel his grief into constructive work. Perhaps Lincoln stated the book's central theme most powerfully, at Gettysburg: "It is for us the living, rather, to be dedicated here to the unfinished work which they who fought here have thus far so nobly advanced. It is rather for us to be here dedicated to the great task remaining before us . . . that from these honored dead we take increased devotion to that cause for which they gave the last full measure of devotion." Lincoln's concept of the power of continuing bonds echoes the book of Hebrews, which urges us to remember that we are always "surrounded by a cloud of witnesses" (12:1). Thus there is a deeply spiritual impulse at work in this narrative. But as I've mentioned, this biblical imperative was in the process of breaking down for many intellectuals in the wake of the horrific Civil War in America. Despite the ravages of time, the continuing devotion to our bonds with the dead, as Lincoln's beautiful summation suggests, has been urging survivors onward for a very long time, and in much more profound and constructive ways than we have generally recognized. *Continuing Bonds* is about those sacred motivations—how grief changed in a relatively short amount of time, and how those sacred motivations continue to resonate for us in the twenty-first century.

Continuing Bonds also explicitly challenges Sigmund Freud's conceptions of grief by insisting on the importance of lifelong mourning and of our perceptions of one's connections with the dead. In place of Freud's developmental model of coherent selfhood (the reassertion of a healthy individualism following traumatic loss), this study connects Victorian practices of mourning with recent developments in postmodern grief studies. Much recent clinical data underscore the lack of coherence and unity that follows parental bereavement, the parent's sense of "amputated" being, and the failure of developmental models or stage theory to account for all parental response to the death of a child. Instead, much evidence shows that different people respond in radically different ways to the loss of a child. On the surface, the lack of a coherent model of grief is a serious blow against Freudian concepts. Alternatively, many similarities do exist among grieving parents. One crucial similarity has had profound consequences in American literary history: the manner in which parents ultimately might achieve wholeness not by moving away from the deceased but by forging even deeper connections with their dead child.

This, of course, is precisely the approach many parents took in the nineteenth century, and herein lies the logic of *Continuing Bonds*. Nineteenth-century author-parents (here represented most robustly by Stowe and, to a lesser extent, Lincoln and Howells) conceived of their deceased progeny as present, spiritually alive, and just "beyond the veil," held securely in the caring arms of a loving God. Today, more clinical workers are affirming such beliefs among twenty-first-century bereaved parents. It's almost as if a more natural form of grieving, long denied or even banned by the Freudian models that reigned throughout the twentieth century, has been given new life and credence under the umbrella of a postmodern theory of grief. In other words, secularization and the death of dying have ultimately failed to erase the spiritual claims and desires of religious believers committed to a supernatural vision of human life.

In these regards, nineteenth-century bereaved parents may have important things to teach their contemporary counterparts about how to process and accommodate (while never fully overcoming) the loss of a child. Such a view challenges psychoanalytic theories of grief and the sort of advice that originally grew out of the modern theories of grief of the early to middle twentieth century, all of which built upon Freud's view that extended and grueling grief patterns are harmful, perhaps even "pathological." In *Mourning and Melancholia* (1917), Freud makes a distinction between "mourning," which is the normal reaction to the loss of a loved one, and "melancholia," which he considered a form of mental illness. According to Freud, grieving people need to break free from the deceased, let go of the past, and reassert their individualism by forging ahead and charting a new course for life. A healthy grief experience, according to Freud, is one where the deaths of loved ones will not leave traces of any gross change in the bereaved.

But clinical practice and data all indicate now that the deaths of children leave very intense and never-ending changes in almost all parents. Bereaved parents almost always think about the dead child every day for many years, and refuse to let go. Clinical workers are now discovering that this is not only predictable but also probably much healthier for the bereaved. For decades, counseling and therapy for survivors has urged them to let go of the dead and get on with their own lives, an approach that has been called the "breaking bonds" or the "severing ties" hypothesis.[26] In reality, a vast amount of research has consistently shown that lifelong grief is normal in cases of the loss of close family members, and many psychologists recognize the importance of the continuing bonds with the dead, particularly in the case of parental loss of children.

Rather than breaking bonds with the dead, as many Freudian psychotherapists have advised for much of the twentieth century, grieving parents of the nineteenth century often found redemptive ways to draw upon the continuing bonds with the dead. This redemptive model did not bring "healing" per se, but it did help the survivors to endure and persevere in meaningful ways. Most interesting of all is the way that this older model conforms with a growing body of contemporary clinical study that supports the embrace of continuing bonds with the dead and the standard view that now expects parental grief to be lifelong, rather than viewing it as "pathological" after some period of time (often a year or even less), and if progress and some sense of "closure" are not suitably attained.

This grim approach to advising the bereaved has been largely dismissed by recent theorists, however. Instead, today's psychologists often speak of postmodern, constructivist theories of grieving as including a "continuing bonds" subfield, essentially a new model of grieving. Dennis Klass coined the term, and he and his coeditors of the influential 1996 collection *Continuing Bonds: New Understandings of Grief* popularized it. By 2008, one researcher could argue as follows: "[Continuing bonds] has now replaced 'severing ties' [a model associated with Freudian grief theory] as the dominant academic discourse."[27] Variations on these themes have been advanced in other works by Klass, as well as by such researchers as Robert Niemeyer, Christine Valentine, and many others.

Some researchers have located the perceptions of the dead as completely within the minds of the bereaved, and thus as merely imagined. Similarly, dismissive views of these bonds became standard according to secular models of grief. Valentine notes that many bereaved persons "expressed surprise at discovering the extent to which their deceased loved ones continued to influence and form part of their ongoing lives," suggesting that their views of the domain of death had been altered by their experience of loss.[28] The question of afterlife and the "reality" of these bonds is a fascinating one, but it is beyond the scope of this study. However, in terms of practice, it is crucial that researchers are not dismissive of these questions, or of the biblical view of the promise of afterlife and reunion. For many bereaved parents, in the nineteenth century and today, the bonds with the dead are real, as scores of in-depth interviews suggest. It is a historical commonplace that as the nineteenth century progressed, the issue of the biblical "reality" of life after death came more and more into play, thus affecting profoundly the sense of continuing bonds with the dead. In other words, as American authors and intellectuals began questioning the nature of death and the promises of

Scripture, the power of a continuing bonds model began to dissipate. For now, we can suspend the debate about the "reality" of such bonds—a debate revolving around the metaphysics of death and the existence of an afterlife. But Valentine does provide an intriguing insight: even as Freud dominated twentieth-century grief therapy, the vast majority of sufferers held onto various forms of continuing bonds with the dead. It may be that academic discourse about parental grief has been most influenced by the ever-expanding evidence of clinical work, most of it calling into question the Freudian models. In particular, there have been vast numbers of laypersons rejecting the "severing ties" model and insisting on continuing bonds with the dead. This sensibility has also been reflected in a proliferation of continuing bonds motifs in popular culture. In other words, the real life experiences of grieving persons who were theistic or spiritual may have trumped the psychological theories of secular science. Another key development has been extensive data showing that grieving parents struggling four years or more with traumatic recurrence is not abnormal or pathological, but quite predictable. And so, as this book will suggest, perhaps there is something important we need to learn, and recover, from our earlier forebears in America, like Henry Bowditch. To begin, some theoretical concepts used throughout this study will be described in somewhat more detail.

"Continuing Bonds" Theory, Generativity, and "Posttraumatic Growth"

Many mental health professionals consider the death of a child to be life's most tragic and traumatic experience. Clinical research provides much evidence to support this common belief. It is indeed a horrific experience. The death of a child typically commences a lengthy period of religious and moral crisis, a crisis profoundly affecting the work and thought of the surviving parent from that moment onward. Data provided by clinical psychologists can help us understand several important facts. First, surviving parents have to work through multiple myths about the loss of their children. They say, for instance, that time heals all wounds. But today it's becoming common to challenge the metaphor of "healing" and the extent to which it is useful in talking about the deaths of loved ones. Can one be "healed" of loss? Perhaps in the case of children, amputation is a better metaphor: rather than getting a new leg or arm, one must instead simply learn to adapt and figure out ways to deal with the permanent loss of a limb. Trauma theory is helpful since the root of the term *trauma* is the Greek word for wound. Traumatic wounds are permanent, and like anyone who loses an arm or a leg, no real "healing" is possible, and the wound will affect the wounded for the rest of her life.[29] Trauma stays with the wounded, and this element is now considered the crucial component of trauma; one's inability to "get over it" is the primary evidence that one has been traumatized. In fact, clinicians have recognized that the idea that one can or should "get over" the death of a child is one of the key myths about parental loss, and many psychologists now admit that it has been abused and is probably one of the most destructive as well. Thus it is now considered common sense that it is very bad advice to tell grieving parents to "let go of the dead child and get on with your lives," although many well-intentioned friends of the bereaved will do so.

Second, intense, even nightmarish, mental and physical reactions are normal and predictable, often for many years. Since at least the 1800s, the term *trauma* has also been associated with the German word for *dream*, suggesting the ways that horror can visit a survivor even during sleep, or how normal sleep routines are easily disrupted. Besides sleeplessness, the majority of bereaved parents will experience some combination of a growing and powerful sense of confusion, lethargy, disillusionment, or even of losing their mind. The physical feelings of numbness, shortness of breath, dizziness, sleeplessness, laziness, forgetfulness, and incoherence in thought patterns are very common. Looking around and expecting the dead child to run in at any moment, many grieving parents have discovered, should not be considered a sign of mental illness. Feeling irrational attachment to so-called linking objects (such as the dead child's favorite book, stuffed animals, or hairbrush) is not a sign of pathology. Such emotional and physiological responses are now recognized as all quite predictable.

Third, parental bereavement brings about a crisis of meaning. Losing a child challenges one's view of the world, leading frequently into a kind of despair and hopelessness. Seriously questioning the nature of God is not unusual for people of faith. A child evokes a connection with the past, an investment in the future, and an extension of self. To say it another way, a child is a concrete expression of hope in the future, and when a child dies, much of a person's hope dies as well. One disturbing clinical study showed that this psychological state of "overwhelming life meaningless" does not necessarily change with time.[30] In other words, there is clinical evidence that the adage "Time heals all wounds" really does not fit parental bereavement. Actually, the opposite might be more accurate: there may be an intensification of pain, especially in the third or fourth year after the loss. Numerous studies show that parental grief may actually get worse with time.

Fourth, one oddity of the research on parents who lose children is the huge differences in spiritual reactions, and the unpredictability of those responses. A single, satisfactory model of grieving behavior is no longer thought to be plausible, since so many ways of responding have been documented. Some parents turn completely and permanently away from church, God, and belief of any sort. Others become even stronger in their trust of God, and find their religious faith rejuvenated and strengthened. And then there are some who experience a bit of both versions. The responses of these "divided" subjects seem to be torn in two—they seemingly must deal with increasing doubts about God as well as increasing faith, however strange that might sound. So we must beware of telling grieving people to look for positive outcomes—for it is never that simple. And we should be prepared for grieving parents to have their faith commitments severely challenged, if not (as is often the case) completely abandoned. In addition, it is common for married parents to experience very different responses and patterns from each other, and this dissonance between responses can become a source of unendurable tension within the marriage. An adage is that bereaved parents commonly see their marriages fall apart. It's just too difficult and painful for the spouses to deal with the wildly incompatible reactions of their partners, according to this myth, but recent studies indicate that this phenomenon has been wildly exaggerated.[31] In fact, it may be true that in many cases, the death of a child can strengthen a marriage in the long run, since the relationship facilitates a deeper attachment to the dead child through shared memories and even physical attributes.

Fifth, and of some importance for the purposes of this book, research indicates that neither mothers nor fathers seem more inclined to sustain powerful bonds with the dead child. The gender myths of our culture, and to some extent the cultural practices of grieving, have led some people to assume that mothers are more susceptible to profound grief and trauma than fathers. But studies indicate that survivors of both genders commonly hold the dead in loving memory for long periods, often forever, and both are visited equally with profound grief. Bereaved parents often go to their own graves cherishing deeply the memory of the dead child, treasuring and cultivating the child's legacy, and remembering the child almost as if he is still with them. This is usually because, on some level such as a metaphysical belief in the afterlife, the survivors believe the child really is still "alive," somewhere, somehow, and they truly expect to reunite with the dead child on the other side. Grieving parents also often perceive the lost child as an active participant in aspects of their continuing life work. The bonds with the dead often are conceived to generate deeper sympathies and good works, and an ongoing memory of the dead is considered to contribute to the good of society, as many of the stories told here will demonstrate.

I do not advocate, nor do I expect, that every grieving parent can or should become a stout soul in the face of the sheer horror they've faced, and I'm not naive enough to expect that they will each discover constructive and redemptive energies on the order of the American authors discussed here. Indeed, it is precisely the psychological hindrances that writers like Stowe, Lincoln, or Howells overcame that make their stories heroic and inspiring. The trauma of parental grief is horrific and long lasting, to be sure, but glib talk about "the power of positive thinking" or "finding the silver lining" is hardly the point. Nevertheless, it is a crucial fact of American history that many survivors, like Dr. Bowditch, have managed to continue the journey of life and to find redemptive meaning in their losses—miraculously, it might even seem. As in the moving cases of Bowditch's son, Nat, and Samaha's daughter, Reema, the presence of the dead child is always there to keep the survivor going and to motivate real change in a real future.

In the religious terms that were the norm when this story begins in the 1840s, many survivors found consolation in their faith in God. Believers like Stowe and her family took comfort in verses assuring them that God "holds all things together by the word of His power" (Hebrews 1:3), that "the spirit will return to God who gave it" (Ecclesiastes 12:7), that survivors are always "surrounded by a cloud of witnesses" (Hebrews 11:2), and that eventually He will most assuredly "wipe away every tear" (Revelation 21:4). Most importantly, at the end of one of the most crucial chapters of the New Testament regarding the defeat of death, Paul writes that because of this profound victory, our works "are not in vain" (I Corinthians 15:58). And so whatever trials we encounter, Stowe believed and wrote, redemption is always possible. In these and many other verses, in which bereaved parents have found consolation and hope, Christians were continually taught to remember the dead with honor and wisdom and were inspired to complete the work they began.

In these frames of reference, a final myth that needs to be questioned is the concept that all outcomes of traumatic experience are harmful. But they are not. For example, the loss of a child is frequently a catalyst in surviving parents of what the psychologist Erik Erikson has called "generativity." By generativity, Erikson refers to the complex choice middle-aged and older adults must face between stagnation in life and a creative means of affecting positively the younger generations that will follow. Generativity "is the adult's concern for and commitment to the next generation, as expressed through parenting, teaching, mentoring, leadership, and a host of other activities that aim to leave a positive legacy of the self for the future." It is the strong need to "give back" to the next generations, or to have some positive impact upon the world, a desire to promote the welfare and well-being of future generations.[32] This generative spirit, inspired and motivated by the death of a child, is precisely what we see in the life of Henry Bowditch: all to honor his dead son. As historian Drew Gilpin Faust puts it, "[Bowditch] made Nat's death, and the long abandonment on the battlefield without medical care that preceded it, a cause célèbre in the effort to establish adequate ambulance service in the Union army, a goal that was achieved in the last year of the war. Bowditch transformed Nat's suffering into the salvation of others."[33]

Similarly, in his volumes *The Stories We Live By* (1993) and *The Redemptive Self* (2006), psychologist Dan P. McAdams has shown that generativity is a key theme in American autobiography, and that Americans are particularly prone to seeing redemptive aspects come out of tragic circumstances. He claims that in the American construction of self, redemptive struggle and generativity are central. McAdams describes the common themes in the stories of "highly regenerative" adults describing the "transformation of bad life scenes into good outcomes." Such stories highlight how "extremely bad events (e.g., death, loss, failure, frustration) are followed by good outcomes (e.g., revitalization, improvement, growth, enlightenment)."[34] Some major expressions of these themes are the often repeated desires "to give something back" to family, friends, schools, organizations, or society in general, and he detects a variety of clichés to sum up this concept: from "it's always darkest before the dawn" to "turning lemons into lemonade" to "finding the silver lining of a dark cloud." Counterintuitively, something constructive and lasting emerges out of life's worst tragedies. In spiritual terms, this good can be called the redemptive. The key feature of the stories survivors tell, as documented by McAdams, is redemption, which he defines as the ability to see something positive come out of tragic circumstances. Over two decades, McAdams has built on Erikson's important earlier work by studying the ways that survivors of disaster and misfortune tell their stories, envisioning the ongoing effects of the dead, and commonly sensing the presence of the deceased. Redemptive stories or "sequences" are told when brave people, faced with tragedy, find ways to turn the pain into something powerful and perpetual. According to McAdams, "Research findings suggest that highly generative American adults are statistically more likely than their less generative counterparts to make sense of their own lives through an idealized story script that emphasizes, among other themes, the power of human redemption. In the most general sense, redemption is *a deliverance from suffering to a better world*. Religious conceptions of redemption imagine it as a divine intervention or sacred process, and the better world may mean heaven, a state of grace, or some other transcendent status. The general idea of redemption can be found in all of the world's major religions and many cultural traditions."[35]

Another way of thinking about this legacy is now being documented by social scientists, following earlier work by Erikson, McAdams, and others. Psychologists are now giving increased attention to what is called *posttraumatic growth*. Posttraumatic growth is an emerging area that records instances of resilience in the midst of life's pain and suffering; it is the study of whatever constructive outcomes result from the experience of trauma and grief. Obviously, there are very negative aspects of trauma, and the well-known concept of posttraumatic stress syndrome (or disorder) has become common shorthand in our culture for these negatives. Much less widely understood, however, is the fact that trauma can also produce constructive effects, and some psychologists are now giving increased attention to posttraumatic growth. A term Richard Tedeschi coined, posttraumatic growth is the study of resilience in the midst of life's pain and suffering, and the constructive outcomes that result from the experience of and struggle with trauma and grief.[36] And so, as some theorists in the largely secular field of psychology are now suggesting, the relationship with a deceased child frequently can also have an energizing effect on the cultural work and spiritual life of a surviving parent. Among other things, traumatic pain of this nature can produce within the subject a much more thorough awareness of the suffering of humanity, and thus can engender sympathy. Also, the dead are perceived to become supervisory, in the sense that their continued "presence" shapes the survivor's identity and life purpose in significant ways. Survivors often carry out central life projects as a means of honoring the deceased, oftentimes working toward the alleviation of injustices, illnesses, or other negative features of life that they associate with the lost person. Again, it is striking how the secular social science seems to be meshing with more spiritually inclined approaches to grief.

Continuing Bonds builds on and contributes to all of these findings by documenting how leading Americans who lost children managed to maintain a profound belief in the possibility of progress and betterment, even in the face of life's worst tragedy. In other words, generativity, redemption narratives, and posttraumatic growth are all manifestations of hope that suggest a deep and abiding faith in the fundamental value of the human enterprise. Theologically, the lives covered demonstrate the sheer power of human hope: hope allows us to go on, even in the midst of the worst events of our life. The influential American authors here all share in this deep hopefulness and belief in the human species. Indeed, the case studies to be narrated include some of the most poignant examples of famous Americans whose generative responses to the loss of children affected the entire nation. In general, their stories illustrate (to varying degrees) three elements that are common in many similar instances: (1) a desire that the dead child would continue to have a meaningful legacy in the world; (2) a willingness to understand the tragedy within the context of the superintendence of God in the world; and (3) the achievement of a constructive outcome that illustrates how calamity and trauma can be beneficial for future generations, and how suffering and tragedy can generate redemptive fruit. But these elements waned as a new century began.

Given this model's efficacy and its ability to bring solace and comfort, it might seem natural for it to continue to hold cultural sway. But as the century wore on, that hopefulness and redemptive spirit was powerfully tested—a testing best illustrated in the experiences of Twain and Du Bois: they both push back, though in somewhat different ways. By 1900, it is clear that the deeply felt gestures toward our sentimental bonds with the dead had come under sustained attack, and we might naturally be led to ask why such dramatic changes had occurred—and how the cultural conditions of the era both reflected and contributed to those patterns of change.

The "Spiritual Crisis of the Gilded Age" and the American "Death of Dying"

The positing of a growing "spiritual crisis" during the post–Civil War period in America has been a stock element in any attempts to answer these questions. This crisis was influenced by various sustained attacks against conventional evangelical accounts of Christianity that had held sway in America for almost a century. Such attacks came on several fronts: the widespread impact of Darwinian theories of evolution; the popularization in America of the German Higher Criticism of the Bible and of liberal forms of Social Christianity; the growing interest in theories of the unconscious and human psychology; rapid advances in astronomy; the lingering grief and trauma from the Civil War, which spawned widespread epistemological doubt about God, providence, and the American mission; and the widely publicized scandals of several leading clergymen, most famously Henry Ward Beecher in 1874, scion of America's most illustrious religious family and brother of Harriet Beecher Stowe.[37]

The story of the "spiritual crisis of the Gilded Age" is well known, but beyond this more predictable cultural account were other somewhat less obvious (and perhaps more surprising) social phenomena that reflected and contributed to the full emergence of ongoing spiritual crisis. I will briefly augment this account by discussing some symptomatic developments in science, business, and funereal practice that reflected and contributed to the rise of a cultural mood that historians have labeled the "death of dying." Theologically, we might begin by noting that in biblical terms, it is God alone who abolishes death and fully attains that victory only at the very end of history. But that has not kept humans from trying desperately to annihilate their archest enemy. By 1899, the quest of the modern soul to conquer death, or at least to alleviate the fears humans held toward death, had grown to such an extent that one British author could even write of "the practical disappearance of the thought of death as an influence bearing upon practical life."[38] The "cultural circumvention of dread of death" had become a topic of widespread cultural opinion in England and America, and evidence of the dying of death, and of spatially placing death "elsewhere," were commonly listed as contributing to this mood. Historian Philippe Ariès has narrated the cultural shift from collective social rituals of mourning to a less visible individualized appearance of death, which took place from the eighteenth century to the mid-twentieth century. In the West, death became largely disenchanted and invisible, elsewhere, not a proper topic for public discussion, a "tamed death" as one that was open and expected and prepared for to a forbidden death—almost a social taboo. By the beginning of the twentieth century death is hidden, reversed; mourning dress disappears; tears and crying are not considered proper; the illusion of happiness and "letting go" becomes predominant; familiarity with funeral rites and customs greatly diminishes.[39] As Ariès describes it, "[modern death was] no longer death, it [was] an illusion of art. . . . In life as well as in art and literature, death [was] concealing itself under the mask of beauty."[40]

Perhaps the most influential account of these phenomena for cultural historians in America was Jessica Mitford's *The American Way of Death* (1963), a powerful, best-selling journalistic account of the rise of the funeral and life insurance businesses and the profit motives attached to them. Among other things, Mitford's account told her horrified readers in explicit detail about the practices of morticians, including a graphic, blow-by-blow account of embalming. These and other depictions of a "modern" way of "American" death, one that is characterized by scientific, medical, and business expertise—as well as the sheer commodification of the process and of the body itself—had contributed, according to Mitford, to a growing, pernicious disenchantment of death and dying, resulting in the alienation of individuals from their former communal ritualizations—and from their God.[41] In general, the secularization of society, the rise of science, the emphasis on modern individualism, and the liberalization of the churches have together been considered the main culprits in distancing Americans from the existential dilemma of death, as in Ariès's influential account. In light of his analysis, however, little has been mentioned about numerous other material and cultural phenomena that were symptomatic of, and certainly contributed to this spiritual malaise and its coincident "forgetting" of, death. Earlier, I mentioned funeral practice, especially preaching, as exemplary of such changes. I will mention a few more practices, including the expanding popularity of cremation, the disappearance of hell from popular theology, the human search for pleasure and entertainment, the growing popularity of suicide, the duration and security of life, and the quickening pace of modern life that left much less time for meditating on death. But according to some historians, it was the rise of science and its various forms of "expertise" that proved most insidious, and trumped all these conditions: "After 1850 scientific naturalism was the crucial catalyst of the dying of death."[42]

America's ever-increasing embrace of a scientific ethos involved the implicit redefinition of death, one that increasingly considered the phenomenon of death as belonging strictly to the natural, and kept any supernatural or religious elements out of the discussion. In 1854, the *Encyclopedia Americana* defined the term in this manner: "death, in common language, is opposed to life, and considered as the cessation of it. It is only, however, the organic life of the individual that becomes extinct; for neither the mind nor the matter which constituted the individual can perish. That view of nature which considers the whole as pervaded throughout by the breath of life, admits only of changes from one mode of existence to another."[43] Here, the breath of life phrasing comes from

Genesis chapter 1, referring to the human vitality as a direct inheritance from God. The 1854 definition also assumes the continuation of some sort of life after organic death. As such, this encyclopedia definition from before the Civil War assumes a supernatural view of human life. Jumping forward to 1904, however—exactly fifty years later—the newest edition of the same *Encyclopedia Americana* presents a drastically different, much more scientific definition: "death, in common language, a state opposed to life, and considered as the cessation of it. Strictly speaking, we can trace only the cessation of organic life. The matter of which the body is composed does not perish on the death of an organized being; it undergoes various changes, which are known by the names of decay and putrefaction, and which are the preparation for its being subservient to new forms of life. What becomes of the mind, or thinking principal, whether in man or animal, is a matter of philosophical conjecture or religious faith. The investigations of science do not throw the least light upon it."[44] The divorce between religion and science, and the assumption that religious elements are unnecessary in defining death, is complete. Thus in the span of less than sixty years, the naturalistic interpretation of death forced any supernatural explanations to the wayside and assumed direct control of how educated people should talk about death. Scientific dominance over matters of medicine and vitality now extended into the realms of death, including any so-called supernatural explanations or concepts, now simply labeled as matters of either conjecture or faith, about which science has no opinion.

We might well ask: How does such a naturalization of thinking on a subject like death affect the everyday encounters with death, which are the normal course of events in our lives as human beings? There is a matter-of-factness about the scientific view that should be interrogated here. Perhaps surprisingly, the rise of the American life insurance industry may be one of the most telling responses to the scientific takeover of death. Historian James Farrell suggests that by drawing conclusions from Darwinian accounts of evolution, especially a species-orientation toward life and death, American business created one of the most profitable and long-lasting institutions symbolizing the death of dying: life insurance, which profoundly "modified the meaning and management of death for the Americans," especially among the wealthy and middle class.[45] Before 1830, there was virtually no such industry. During the period described earlier by the two competing definitions of death, roughly 1830 to 1900, explosive growth in the purchase of policies made life insurance one of the most financially powerful institutions in American life. This growth was concretely expressed in the emergence of Hartford, Connecticut, as one of the cultural and business capitals of the United States. By 1900, approximately eighty-four companies held over fourteen million policies, about one policy for every five Americans. By 1920 there were over 335 companies, holding over sixty-five million policies, roughly two policies for every three Americans. Rarely has an industry seen such rapid growth allowing the collecting of literally billions of dollars into the hands of major corporate entities.[46]

As James Farrell explains, "the empirical basis of life insurance implied acceptance of a naturalistic cosmology. Life insurance assumed the uniformity and continuity of natural occurrences. Insurance actuaries viewed death as a predictable natural event and not as an arbitrary exercise of divine will. The supernatural might yet have a supervisory role in the universe, but in general, life insurance replaced divine providence with human prudence." As such, the life insurance industry can tell us much about the American attitude toward death in this era. After the Civil War, Farrell claims, "the financial security of the statistical community replaced, to some extent, the emotional security of personal communities—the family, the neighborhood, the town. . . . Life insurance replaced the informal aid of family and friends with a formal system of financial compensation for death. . . . It made a profitable business out of the prospect of death."[47]

In the context of a description of the death of dying, life insurance played a prominent role insofar as it distanced neighbors and extended family from the direct encounter with death. The financial burdens of death are no longer a community affair and an act of trust in God; they are handled by nameless bureaucrats in an office in Hartford or any of the other emerging insurance centers. Life insurance also allowed individuals to trust in some large unseen corporate entity, as opposed to trusting in the community surrounding them or the God in whom they lived and breathed and had their being. Now faith in the provision of God could be replaced by the certain knowledge that financial support would come from a silent, benevolent, and trustworthy entity: the life insurance company. Life insurance, in short, reduced the fear of death to the extent that it provided much-needed financial help in the time of crisis. By wisely spending a few dollars every month, one might achieve some victory when death's shadow crossed the door. It was a way of domesticating death; insurance agents could circumvent the fearfulness, especially of widows, when the breadwinner was taken from them, which happened the vast majority of the time. The care of widows, mentioned a number of times in the New Testament as a community-oriented Christian duty of special significance, quickly had become the profitable territory for faceless underwriters in Connecticut.[48]

Concurrently with the rise of the life insurance industry, Americans underwent vast changes in the disposal of dead bodies, the practice of funerals, and the rise of the funeral industry. Before the Civil War, funerals were mainly homegrown affairs: families gathered, members often built the coffin itself, the body was displayed in the home or the nearby church or chapel, and then the coffin was picked up by the mourners and carried directly to the gravesite (usually right next to the church), at which time it was interred. Often members of the family both carried the coffin and took physical heaps of dirt in their hands, to throw into the grave. If a professional of any sort were involved at all, besides the preacher, it would be the undertaker, whose responsibilities were minimal. Instead it was the work primarily of those closest to the deceased. In such a situation, family and friends stared directly into the face of the dead: preparing the body quickly due to the rapidity of decay, and transporting it to the open grave itself. Then every Sunday (often for the rest of their lives), they would pass the family plot on their way to and from the church meeting, as a weekly reminder of where they would themselves end up one day.

By the turn of the twentieth century, such practices had become uncommon for the vast majority of middle-class Americans, especially in urban centers, which were increasingly where more people were living. By then, the term *undertaker* had been supplanted by the much more friendly *funeral director*. The term of one "directing" a funeral suggests the idea of the professional in charge as a sort of "stage manager" whose job is to create an appropriate atmosphere and to escort the grieving family and friends "through a drama in which social relationships are stressed and an emotional catharsis or release is provided through ceremony."[49] If the one in charge is the director of the funeral, then clearly the starring role in the production of the modern American funeral is the occupant of the open casket (not coffin). The worship of God and the presentation of biblical doctrine are both displaced by the sentimental memorialization of the deceased. As exemplified by the concept of the more ornate "casket," a less abrupt euphemism opposed to the older concept of a coffin, commonly cobbled out of a cheap wood like pine, the modern funerals produced a whole new terminology, also ornate and euphemistic.

Corpses became loved ones, or were called by their names (Mrs. Jones, Mr. Smith), and they were now housed in "slumber rooms" until prepared for the funeral, rather than just sent to the morgue.

Even the body became much more ornate in the modern funeral than in the days before and during the early nineteenth century. The practice of embalming dead bodies grew rapidly during the course of the Civil War, since hundreds of bodies needed to be shipped north. Science provided a solution: draining the blood and then injecting certain chemicals into the arteries could slow decay considerably. The corpses of soldiers were often eviscerated and filled with substances like sawdust, charcoal, or lime. And so an underreported result of the Civil War was the widespread practice of a new form of preservation, one that the public would eventually come to accept. Before the war, embalming was almost unheard of in the burial of the dead. It was only in 1840, with the translation into English of the first major book, *The History of Embalming* by the French scientist Jean Nicolas Gannal, that the US medical community became familiar with the concept. And yet before the war, and for decades afterward, embalming seemed unnatural for most Americans. Often clergy led the way in criticizing such practices. Some were prophetic in noticing how these practices emptied death of its profound metaphysical substance, so that they in fact were wary that these practices might drain death of its metaphysical weight. Henry Tuckerman spoke out against embalming as a "superstitious homage, to rescue the poor human casket from destruction, [it is] grotesque and undesirable."[50] For others, embalming was a pagan act diverting attention away from the sovereign God who had formerly been at the center of the ceremony. Worship was replaced by fond memories of the dead.

As historian Gary Laderman writes, the Civil War not only introduced the public to the viability and usefulness of embalming, it also helped to determine which professionals would be associated with dead bodies in the future. As a result, during the Civil War, "undertakers familiar with the operation of embalming began to travel with the very soldiers who could end up on their embalming tables. Because there were few Northerners to sell to in and around Virginia, at least one entrepreneur targeted the man who could be both consumer and commodity in his transaction." Laderman describes one case where a brigade of men passed by two undertakers advertising their services, and he records the negative response of the brigade's commanders: "The officers did not appreciate his resourcefulness in drumming up business: the chief of the medical staff pointed out their demoralizing influence; and the general sent the embalmer a civil order to desist from this method of advertising."[51] But by the end of the Civil War, embalming dead bodies had become so common that it was performed famously in an upstairs room of the White House on the murdered body of President Abraham Lincoln. Doctors from the Army Medical Museum performed an autopsy, in which they sawed off the top of Lincoln's head and removed his brain. Reportedly, the bullet fell to the floor at that moment. Then, after the autopsy, the embalmer, Dr. Charles D. Brown, took over, draining the blood from Lincoln's jugular vein. The body was being prepared for what turned out to be one of the most famous funeral train trips in American history: the return of Lincoln's corpse to Springfield, Illinois. As such, people are often surprised to discover that an embalmer accompanied Lincoln's body throughout the two-week trip back to Illinois, his job being to maintain the body for public viewing. Newspapers along the way always commented on the appearance of the deceased president, but there were variations in these reports. Generally, Lincoln was described as peaceful or placid, or as natural. But some reviews of his appearance were critical; the best embalming techniques at that time were simply powerless to eliminate the strange discoloration of Lincoln's skin, or the hollowness of the cheeks. One journalist "questioned whether it was appropriate or prudent—despite the 'cunning workmanship'—to 'tempt dissolution much further.'"[52] In this remark we can note the author's reservations that there is something spiritually dubious about the whole enterprise of embalming and keeping the corpse from decaying—as if it were somehow tempting the fates, or going against the natural order of things.

Although after the war the practice of embalming continued to seem exotic and even grotesque for most Americans, slowly public opinion changed over the next twenty years. Eventually, what was good enough for the Civil War dead and for President Lincoln, many Americans considered good enough for themselves and their family. The first convention of the National Funeral Directors Association met in Rochester, New York, in 1882. Rochester was important because it was home of one of the largest manufacturers of caskets, the Stein Company, and also because it was the home of Auguste Renouard, the most famous pioneer of embalming science in America. Thus began what became called *mortuary science*, and the rise of professional training and credentialing process. One leader was S. R. Lippincott, who explained at the first convention that morticians everywhere needed "to plant our standard in the Army of science. What we need now and what we must have is greater scientific inquiry."[53] As speakers gave their lectures rhapsodizing the rise of the funeral industry, Renouard gave demonstrations on the correct procedures for embalming in an adjacent room.

Embalming followed by public display for several days or even a week afterward became the standard American way of dealing with the dead in the decades after about 1890. Along with it grew a morbid curiosity for mementos of the dead—locks of hair in particular. Photos of the reposeful dead became almost mandatory for middle-class Americans. The desire to keep the dead among the living as long as possible propagated a new area of commerce: rings, brooches, lockets, and other mementos. Artists built whole careers on their ability to render the portraits of corpses, generally rendered in a moment of life but based on the embalmed body and whatever pictures were at hand. This genre of portraiture transformed the dead body back into a thing of beauty and vitality, with an intention of bringing much consolation and relief to survivors. After 1840, with the rise of photography, paintings began to be supplanted as photographs representing the dead body in a placid state of rest and peace became popular. Sometimes these photographs showed the body in bed, surrounded by family and flowers, and often displaying religious elements such as crosses or Bibles. They represented what's been called the "good death": the saintly believers, having succeeded in living a good life, achieve their full and final reward, having gone on to be with the Lord. But ironically, these acts of preservation failed to maintain what had previously been considered most important: the spiritual bond with the dead. These were merely cosmetic, temporary alleviations of decay, and were powerless to relieve the grief of survivors. The earlier consolations were afforded by faith in God and the community of the saints. By the end of the nineteenth century, the home settings of the good death were no longer prevalent, replaced by the looming presence of the embalmed body. The harmony and peacefulness of a family gathered around their beloved dead had been transformed by the rise of an impersonal funeral industry, whose minions immediately took possession of the body to hide it away from the family members until presented in its final embalmed form for public gaze—a mere token of its former self.

The rise of embalming coincided with the rise of the life insurance and funeral industries. Altogether, these rapid changes, along with many other material practices and cultural beliefs, reflected and fostered the distancing of death, and the dying of death in American culture. They are among the many symptoms of the secularization of death and the ostensible removal of death's ultimate power over us, and thus a kind of denial of death. All these practices worked to circumvent fear and to domesticate death, to hide it away and to place it elsewhere. Further, these new practices were symptomatic of the intrusion of science and management practices: "What strikes the historian is the totality of the Mid-Victorian impulse to contain the life experiences of the individual from birth to death by isolating them as science."[54]

As one of America's best social and cultural commentators of the period worried, Americans were learning to forget about death and were becoming distanced from the metaphysical realities of death and their mortal natures. This phenomenon was most acute in New York City, which for this observer represented modern America more than any other city. New Yorkers, he wrote, were learning to forget about death, but meanwhile, all hell seemed to be breaking loose. The protagonist of this writer's greatest novel had recently left the life insurance industry, where he had been the editor of one of the largest life insurance company's house organ. But his wife finds New York much too alarming: "I could never have any inner quiet in New York; I couldn't live in the spirit there. . . . They forget death . . . they forget death in New York." One day driving through a street filled with lower-class immigrants, the husband agrees: they have "no hopes of driving out of it, except in a hearse. I must say they don't seem to mind it. I haven't seen a jollier crowd anywhere in New York. They seem to have forgotten death a little more completely than any of their fellow-citizens."[55]

The author is William Dean Howells, and the novel is *A Hazard of New Fortunes*. The opening lines of Howells's greatest work were written as his daughter, Winifred, was isolated in a sanitarium, trying to overcome a grave medical condition as her exasperated parents waited and prayed. She died just as the first chapters of the novel appeared in print, but Howells's encounter with the grimmest realities of a daughter's death were only beginning, and yet he persevered and managed to complete his masterpiece. If postwar prosperity and fame had encouraged him to forget about death, unexpected hazards suddenly forced him to remember it again. And as I will argue below, Howells learned the hard way that a denial of death is itself futile, and that a fully orbed humanity must recover its proximity to the horror and pain of death, despite whatever worldly successes one might find. This recognition is a key theme of *A Hazard of New Fortunes*: a story I will detail later.

We humans need a consistent recognition of death, Howells's novel insists, in order to understand and value fully this life of ours. And we never discover the fullness while here in this world, try as we might. As Martin Luther King Jr. stated on the day before he died, "I may not get there with you. But I want you to know tonight, that we, as a people, will get to the promised land!" King's eloquent line recalls the end of Hebrews 11, which reads: "Yet all these, though approved because of their faith, did not receive what had been promised. God had foreseen something better for us, so that without us they should not be made perfect" (Hebrews 11:40). Similarly, it is left to those who remain, like the bereaved parents represented here, to accomplish the prophetic, uncompleted tasks of the dead. Without us, the dead cannot be made perfect. Strengthened by their recollections, and energized by what Lincoln described as "the mystic chords of memory," grieving parents have found the courage to continue their own journeys toward a better world. And America has advanced toward that "more perfect union."

And so, perhaps much like Basil March in *Hazard of New Fortunes*, Americans today are rethinking their cultural abandonment of death and their dismissal of the continuing bonds with the dead. This recovery of an older sensibility may be signaled by the widespread mania for memorialization. Perhaps we are rediscovering that we need close encounters with death in order to appreciate fully the beauty and passion of our lives as humans, created in the image of God, and yet limited in our mortality and in our powers of perception. The disenchantment of death and dying, and the attempts to domesticate death, are being interrogated and often abandoned as unnatural and toxic trends in human history. They are toxic to the extent that they have disallowed redemptive views of pain and suffering. When people do not fully confront death, they forget about their own mortality, become distant from their own end, and turn unsympathetic to the suffering of others. The consequences include a liberalizing of death and a reduction of its vast powers of horror, and in turn, the production of weak, romantic theodicies that do not ring true to human experience. People, in short, must know the stain of death; they must touch it, and feel it, and even breathe it, and if not, perhaps they cannot fulfill their own humanness. Likewise, a true theodicy must fully confront the horror; it cannot minimize evil and death with trite sayings and glib responses about someone being "called home to God," or that some tragedy was "God's will." Death must be confronted instead as the last enemy of God, and perhaps our most appropriate response to death is, after all, worship of God—even in the face of the anger and confusion that tragic events produce in us.

The narrative trajectory of *Continuing Bonds* suggests the imperative to reenchant death and dying, and thus to reenchant theodicy with the full mystery of iniquity that our fallen condition on a broken planet necessitates. We humans cannot solve the sting of death by ourselves, but we must confront it fully, as Basil March does in Howells's *Hazard of New Fortunes*. Basil runs the critical and spiritual gauntlet in his confrontation with death and emerges a better person. By first admitting that science or liberal religion or managerial perfection or any other human activity is powerless to overcome the sting of death, or even to define it, we might begin to find a better alternative. Humans, it turns out, must encounter death as mystery, turn to their Maker, and admit that grief is not so easily solved or tamed. Evil and pain are with us always, and death is the last enemy of God, but our hope is that eventually, even death will be overthrown. Meanwhile, we hang onto the mystic chords of our continuing bonds—and hope for a better world. Many great American authors have done so—and their stories are enlightening.

1

Hatty's Grief

Harriet Beecher Stowe and the Death of Charley

In the early years, America's frontier towns faced dire circumstances, not the least of which were contagious diseases like typhoid and cholera. Infant cities along rivers were suddenly teeming with people and the germs they carried, and they struggled to provide an infrastructure for all the new arrivals, including fresh, relatively pure water. Cholera first came to the Ohio Valley in 1832, evidently by way of the state's many new immigrants flowing down the riverways of the Ohio and Mississippi. The city of Cincinnati had very poor sewage systems, and as the rainwater ran through the streets, it accumulated the microbes from the garbage of city residents and the manure of horses, pigs, and other animals. Sewers became like open petri dishes, perfect for the rapid multiplication of germs—especially in the humid days of summer. Stagnant water, commonly found in the newly constructed canals of central Ohio, also festered disease. One result was widespread cholera infection among canal workers. Treatment for the disease before the Civil War was almost as bad as the illness, resulting often in mercury poisoning. And the ailment was not understood to be contagious. As a result, the river cities of America, including Cincinnati, were known to be places of serious health hazards, particularly in terms of infectious disease.[1]

In 1833, when Calvin Stowe was preparing to move from his beloved New England to a new position at the Lane Seminary in Cincinnati, he realized that one of the greatest dangers in moving out West would be widespread contact with disease. He wrote to his wife Eliza, "in more senses than one we may take our lives in our hands when we go to Cincinnati."[2] Calvin Stowe was correct: He was forced to delay his arrival at Lane because of a cholera epidemic. The next year, in summer 1834, the city was again burdened with a huge outbreak of cholera. It struck Lane Seminary. The wife of Lyman Beecher, president of Lane and one of America's most famous preachers, wrote the following sad account to her twenty-three-year-old daughter Harriet in August 1834: "nothing special occurred the ten days preceding your departure among ourselves, but the sickness in the city was dreadful, one hundred & more deaths in one week, & Edwards affecting letter came with the intelligence of the death of his second little boy, which I forwarded to Boston—next came the illness of our dear Mrs. Stowe. . . . She was taken ill of the dysentery the very day you left."[3] She was referring to Eliza Stowe, wife of Calvin, who seemed to recover, but soon enough she entered into her death throes, and died surrounded by family in August 1834.

Harriet Beecher arrived soon afterward and began the task of consoling her good friend Calvin in light of the loss of his wife Eliza. Harriet (known to friends and family as Hatty or Hattie) was gifted at this task of consolation. She knew Eliza well and understood the great loss Calvin had undergone. She also had excellent skills as a counselor of women and over the course of her lifetime wrote scores of letters of consolation to women near and far. According to her biographer, Harriet "pursued a self-conscious lay ministry to the bereaved and troubled."[4] She had learned many of these counseling and pastoral techniques at the Hartford Female Seminary, which her sister Catherine had organized. Hatty resisted the urge of most ministers to scrutinize the spiritual state of the lost. Instead, she fully embraced the pain and confusion and anger that often follow the death of loved ones, as in this letter to one bereaved mother: "When the heartstrings are all suddenly cut, it is, I believe, a physical impossibility to feel faith or resignation; there is a revolt of the instinctive and animal system, and though we may submit to God it is rather by a constant painful effort than by a sweet attraction."[5]

Calvin was greatly strengthened by the arrival and ministry of the young Harriet Beecher, and within a year of Eliza's death he was ready to proclaim his love for Hatty. In 1835 he wrote to her, "I thank God that he has given me a female friend to whom I can open my heart. There are some feelings which a man cannot exercise, and my heart cannot rest in masculine friendship alone. I must be within reach of woman's love, or my own feelings will suffocate me." In May of that year he wrote several more letters proclaiming his fondness for her: "My affection for you is no sudden caprice. . . . It is of slow and natural growth, & true to its object as the needle to the pole star." He felt bonded to this new guiding light: "I have a sort of feeling of the inseparable as though my blood somehow circulated through your veins, and if you were to be torn from me I should bleed to death."[6] Soon, in January 1836, they would make the formal vows of matrimony and begin their lives together—a union brought about to a large extent by the devastating effects of a cholera epidemic.

Calvin and Harriet produced seven children and suffered numerous further heartaches during a long union. Besides outliving three of the children born to her, Hatty also suffered at least two miscarriages. As theologian Serene Jones explains, the loss of "the hoped-for child" must necessarily include loss through miscarriages. Jones argues that we should become particularly sympathetic in the case of women who have suffered the death of their child within them, a trauma that turns the woman's body into a kind of "living grave."[7] Trauma is "an event that continues, that persists in the present. Trauma is what does not go away. It persists in symptoms that live on in the body, in the intrusive fragments of memories that return. . . . Trauma is what is not integrated in time; it is the difference between a closed and an open wound. Trauma is an open wound."[8] Both of Stowe's miscarriages left their scars, and Hatty's extraordinary career continued to be marked by other similarly traumatic wounds. Many of her stories, arising from the "living grave" of her earthly memories of loss, famously depicted trauma as well.

The loss of a child was not the only traumatic experience during these early years of her marriage to Calvin. Her joyful and well-liked brother George also died under tragic circumstances, in June 1843. George had accompanied the Beecher family west to Ohio, when the patriarch Lyman Beecher brought his young brood with him to found Lane Seminary. George married and then set up his household in a town called Chillicothe. He was well known for the care with which he tended to his garden there: "George had just written exuberantly in a circular letter of his completed house and his wish that they would all come and see him that summer, including within enumeration of the flowers and fruits that he was cultivating."[9] But evidently all was not well with George. One fine morning he went to market and then returned to work in his beloved garden. Then George evidently took a shotgun and blew a round into his head, to the great horror of his survivors.

Her brother's apparent suicide threw Hatty into a deep spiritual crisis. She wrote to another brother Thomas: "The sudden death of George shook my whole soul like an earthquake, and as in an earthquake we know not where the ground may open next so I felt an indistinct terror as a father, brothers, husband, might any or all sink next—these deep stunning agonies show us heart secrets before undreamed."[10] She wrote a family circular letter to all of her siblings: "I woke up last night from a troubled dream about funeral processions and accidents and alarms—and it came slowly over me, that it was so indeed, that on earth I had no more that brother—that I never should see his face, or hear his voice or exchange a word with him again. . . . Our circle has begun to break up."[11] Again, it was a wound with teeth, and it left a mark of "indistinct terror" on her view of the world and its evils.

But what may have been the worst of these misfortunes (though by no means the last) began with the reappearance of the dreaded cholera, in the very hot summer of 1849. If anything, the epidemic of 1849 was even worse than earlier ones. Its most famous victim was in Tennessee, where it took the life of former president James Polk. Saint Louis, arguably hardest hit of all, lost at least 10 percent of its population that year to the disease: "Sextons, undertakers, even horses in St. Louis were exhausted in the Sisyphean task of removing and burying the dead."[12] Cincinnati was also one of the hardest hit areas, claiming over eight thousand dead. The city had become so used to such outbreaks by midsummer that life continued almost as usual. Since most of the illness and death was confined to the poorer quarters of the city, populated mostly by African Americans and immigrants, families like the Stowes did not prepare as rigorously as they might have. But as the end of June approached, it became clear to most residents that this visit was an attack of unusual magnitude. Harriet wrote to Calvin on June 29 concerned about the "universal panic" gaining traction throughout Cincinnati: "Those who had talked confidently of the cholera being confined to the lower classes and those who were imprudent began to feel as did the magicians of old, 'This is the finger of God.'"[13] Her reference is to Exodus 8:19, where the magicians describe to Pharaoh what they believe to be the source of the plagues, thus casting the cholera panic into biblical proportions. Earlier that year she had also invoked Exodus, in a letter to her sister Sarah Beecher: "it is all shoreless tideless hopeless unmitigated mud here—mud without hope or end—dreadful to look upon & like the Egyptian frogs it comes into our houses to our bed chambers and kneading troughs—and still the weather is cross and sour and baleful and everyone is sleepy and has the headache my own poor self among the number."[14] Her mood is tied directly to the horrid weather as symbolized by mud—and the mud itself is seen as a living organism carrying the plague sent by God into the homes of the city's citizens, to judge those in the land of the living. A view of the cholera epidemics as a judgment of God was commonplace, as in the comments by the governor of New York State at about the same time: "an infinitely wise and just God has seen fit to employ pestilence as one means of scourging the human race for their sins, and it seems to be an appropriate one for the sins of uncleanliness," he proclaimed.[15] Her brother Henry Ward later wrote that he remembered "very long sermons [proving] that the cholera did not depend on natural agencies, but that God held it in his hand, and dropped it down upon the world."[16]

Henry's account stressed his misgivings with the Calvinist tendencies of his famous father. Lyman Beecher's version of Calvinist theology during Henry's and Hatty's childhood and young adulthood sought to develop a model society based on strict discipline and a "moral sense" enforced by the terror of an eternal Hell. From a Calvinist perspective, it was also typical to see pain and suffering as the natural wages of our sinful nature as fallen humans, and also as our faithful teacher in the way of all flesh. According to such a view, cholera was a just recompense for the rampant sins of newly sprawling urban areas, and since it struck mainly the poor and the destitute, it reflected particularly on their vices. Lyman Beecher's sermons represented for Henry and Hatty a version of old-school Calvinism that both came to regard as dark, unemotional, judgmental, and guilt ridden: "The monstrousness of a deity who allows the undeserved suffering of the innocent and who shows his love by wrath, the visceral conviction that the mass of men are irredeemably predestined to destruction, the gross popular abandonment to belief in miracles and special providences, and the final bind that man is responsible for his actions even though not free to determine them."[17]

Harriet and her maverick brother Henry became important voices of protest against the severity of Calvinism, and both began searching for ways of mitigating "dark Calvinism's" extraordinarily painful emotional effects.[18] This conflict comprises a common understanding of this era that emphasizes a "rejection of Calvinism," as seen for example in the ways some writers of fiction protested aspects of Calvinism such as predestination.[19] But as Thomas J. Davis claims, these writers, such as Catharine Maria Sedgwick, tended to "adopt uncritically the negative attitudes toward Calvinism that were common in the nineteenth century."[20] In fact, the religious changes at work during this era were far more complex than such an account can suggest, and additionally, a growing schism within Presbyterianism indicates how even the most Reformed denominations were debating the legacy of Calvin.[21] For starters, as one historian sees it, "the term Calvinism is profoundly unhelpful. It was coined as a polemical tool for tarnishing the reputation of the Reformed, and it is of no real use to modern intellectual history . . . so-called Calvinists were not those who look to Calvin as the major theological authority but rather those who look to the tradition of reformed confessions."[22] Another agrees: "Calvinism became virtually synonymous in the minds of its critics with the enigma of predestination and the bondage of the will."[23] In addition, some scholars of Calvinism argue that these tensions of the nineteenth century were inherent in Calvin's thought from the very beginning: "the deep division over religion and national identity did not originate with the New England Puritans, however much they exhibited the division. Rather, that ambivalence is at the root of the Calvinist tradition of which they were apart, going back to the founder, John Calvin himself. . . . In many ways, American Puritanism exemplifies conflicting propensities within Calvin himself."[24] Finally, as Charles Hodge, one of the great theologians of the era, proclaimed in 1851, these clashes certainly predate the Reformation by many centuries: "from an early period in the history of the church, there have been two great systems of doctrine in perpetual conflict. The one begins with God, the other with man. The one has for its object the vindication of the divine supremacy and sovereignty in the salvation of men; the other the rights of human nature."[25]

Hodge labels these contesting parties the Augustinian and the Pelagian—a common vocabulary among educated Christians of the period, but one that unfortunately pits one system, fully and completely, against the other. Stowe's theological vision attempts a middle ground, and so in many ways remains highly dependent upon Calvinism. Rather than viewing her as merely a staunch critic of Reformed theology, as many critics do, we should recognize Stowe as a well-read and astute believer who is powerfully drawn to major aspects of Calvin's thought, while at the same time strongly critical of others. Mark Valeri writes, "Calvin modeled for his followers a highly disciplined moral method grounded in the Bible. His vision for social order was breathtakingly rigorous and demanding in such terms. Calvinists applied the Bible to everything."[26] The same could be said for Stowe. The beauty of Calvinism remained very real to her and was evident in many of her own remarks. For example, she writes, "Calvinism, in its essential features, will never cease from the earth, because the great fundamental facts of nature are Calvinistic, and men with strong minds and wills always discover it."[27] Peter J. Thuesen ingeniously recognizes Stowe's idealizing of aspects of Calvinism as suggestive of famous concepts in the work of sociologist Max Weber: "[Stowe] lauded the industriousness of the New England Puritans and their heirs even while critiquing the harsher aspects of their theology.

She also anticipated Weber in annexing the notion of the 'Protestant ethic' to nationalism, in her case by identifying Calvinism as the source of the Yankee propensity for hard work and moral clarity."[28] What emerges in Stowe's novels is "an alternative to the negative ideogram of Calvinism that so often prevailed in American culture and even, at times, in her own writings. On Stowe's reading, the term Calvinist was synonymous with the sober, virtuous Yankee yeoman—the sort of citizen whose industry built the American Republic."[29] Of course, Stowe also sharply criticizes the New England Calvinist obsession with the evidences of conversion—as we shall see. But as Charles H. Foster argued many years ago, "Stowe said both yes and no to Calvinism."[30]

Significantly, these ongoing debates about the true legacy of Calvinism and Reformed thought within the Beecher household were at their most intense during seasons of grief and mourning. A turning point came during a period of tension between the father Lyman and the children when the oldest daughter Catherine suffered the loss of her fiancé. Catherine Beecher's fiancé, Alexander Metcalf Fisher, was a very fine, handsome, and charismatic young professor who drowned at sea while traveling to Europe in 1822. Fisher, who perished in a shipwreck off the coast of Ireland, and as with Henry, never showed any of the prescribed signs of regeneration as a Christian believer, a troubling circumstance for reformed New Englanders of this time. During her lengthy struggle with grief, Catherine suffered greatly, both emotionally and physically, including chronic pain, symptoms that may have been the outcome of traumatic stress. The pain and suffering due to the death of Fisher also caused Catherine to begin questioning the nature of God, the purposes of pain, and the meaning of her faith. The helplessness of not knowing the spiritual fate of Fisher after his death was augmented by the stoic detachment of Catherine's stern father. All of this was witnessed closely by her younger sister Harriet, who looked up to Catherine almost as a second mother, and certainly as her spiritual mentor. Both of them wondered how to make sense out of the loss of a beau ideal, and how to think about legacy and the afterlife of one who is lost—evidently, without the specific confirmation of the sanctifying grace necessary for eternal life in the presence of the Father.

Their father Lyman Beecher added drastically to the grief of his daughter by informing her that Fisher was most certainly damned for eternity due to his lack of profession of a saving faith in Jesus Christ. Beecher was a stern taskmaster with his children and insisted on working to show that each of them had fully committed to the teachings of Christ in such a way that their salvation was secure and obvious to all. This search for the clear signs of salvation was for Beecher almost an obsession, and in many ways his approach was a common feature of early nineteenth-century Calvinistic religion in general. Catherine took these edgy pronouncements about the eternal fate of Fisher very hard, and often debated the subject with her father: debates witnessed by Harriet and Henry Ward.

Lyman Beecher's cold and dogmatic arguments explaining damnation had a drastic effect on all of his children, but most immediately on Catherine. Catherine succeeded in founding a successful academy for young girls, the Hartford Female Academy, and taught there for many years. But she never married, and somehow the loss of Fisher radically altered the "carefree, sensible Cate" the younger Harriet had come to know and admire.[31] Catherine's book, *Common Sense Applied to Religion* (1857) advanced her belief that there must be areas of belief and modes of knowledge beyond the merely rational: "theological theories that seemed at war with both the common sense and the moral sense of mankind" can often blunt or even annihilate "the great end for which the human mind was created."[32] It also documented her powerful sense that Calvinism's answers were not always satisfactory: "There must be a dreadful mistake somewhere."[33] Catherine appealed to "intuitive truths" and the heart of the believer throughout her career. As they matured, her younger siblings Harriet and Henry Ward would recall the heartache over the death of Catherine's fiancé as a spiritual turning point in their own critiques of Calvinism—especially Lyman's harsh treatment of his daughter in her grief.

Years later, the cholera epidemic of Cincinnati was similarly vexing for Hatty in terms of her emerging theology: she simply never became accustomed to a traditionally Calvinist view of judgment as her father Lyman represented. On Independence Day 1849, she lamented the scale of the epidemic: "One hundred and twenty burials from cholera alone yesterday, yet to-day we see parties bent on pleasure or senseless carousing, while to-morrow and next day will witness a fresh harvest of death from them. How we can become accustomed to anything!"[34] But at that point she had no idea how close to home the "harvest" might come. On July 10 she wrote to Calvin: "yesterday Little Charlie was taken ill, not seriously, and any other season I should not be alarmed. Now, however, a slight illness seems like a death sentence." Again, to the out-of-town Calvin on July 23: "At last, my dear, the hand of the Lord hath touched us. We have been watching all day by the dying bed of little Charley, who is gradually sinking. . . . Do not return. All will be over before you could possibly get here, and the epidemic is now said by the physicians to prove fatal to every new case. Bear up. Let us not faint when we are rebuked of Him. I dare not trust myself to say more but shall write again soon."[35] Here we see the biblical language of God's rebuke: she understood Charley's illness and her trials to be the instruments of the Lord's discipline. And when Charley died on July 26 she wrote again to Calvin: "At last it is over. . . . He has been my pride and joy . . . I have just seen him in his death agony, looked on his imploring face when I could not help nor soothe nor do one thing, not one, to mitigate his sufferings, do nothing but pray in my anguish that he might die soon."[36]

These are haunting words, a mother praying that her infant son might die, to alleviate the horrible suffering of the disease. The term "anguish" became a favorite word of Harriet's, a trope attempting to capture the sheer horror of her own suffering. She wrote to Sarah, her brother George's widow: "You see my dear sister through what a scene of anxiety peril & anguish I have passed. . . . I am too much worn out & exhausted to write much but your sympathy would be a comfort to me."[37] Elsewhere Stowe wrote of her profound acquaintance with such pain: "all the strange ways in which this anguish will reveal itself,—the prick, the thrust, the stab, the wearing pain, the poison that is mingled with every bright remembrance of the past."[38] Besides the death itself, Charley's final days saw him wracked with intense pain, and the agonies of her dying son were overwhelming: "Poor Charlie's dying cries and sufferings rent my heart," she wrote to Delia Bacon on July 29.[39] To Sarah: "the dying the sinking the fading is worse than the loss—my heart has been weary with poor Charley's dying struggles."[40] And to Charlotte Forten, she confessed that "my poor Charley died for want of medical aid timely rendered" (a circumstance and charge that would be repeated later for Lincoln, Howells, Twain, and Du Bois as well): "There were circumstances about his death of such bitterness, of what seemed almost cruel suffering, that I felt that I could never be consoled of it, unless this crushing of my own heart might enable me to work out some great good to others."[41]

The "unless" is telling. Even in the bitterest moments, Hatty looked for redemption. From the very beginning of her decades-long acquaintance with parental grief, Stowe's religious understanding of what was happening to her rested on a biblical account of how God is able to redeem tragedy for His glory. When she implores Calvin, "Let us not faint when we are rebuked of Him," she alludes to one of the great chapters on hope through suffering in all the New Testament, Hebrews 12: "And ye have forgotten the exhortation which speaketh unto you as unto children, My

Charley Stowe (Samuel Charles Stowe, son of Harriet Beecher Stowe, died 1849). Courtesy of the Schlesinger Library, Radcliffe Institute, Harvard University.

son, despise not thou the chastening of the Lord, nor faint when thou art rebuked of him" (Hebrews 12:5, KJV).[42] We are "rebuked of Him," in other words, for our own good, and so that we might better enter into the suffering of others around us. Stowe felt that Charley's death had provided for her "one more great lesson of humanity which must needs be learned to attain perfection."[43] Perfection as Stowe used it here was rapidly becoming a keyword of American evangelicalism, with its roots in Wesleyan piety and the Holiness movement, and its propagation by the likes of Phoebe Palmer. Stowe envisioned her trials as crucial elements in the lifelong process of becoming nothing less than a minister to the bereaved, with the goal of admonishing survivors onward to the "peaceable fruits" afforded by suffering, as promised in the Letter to the Hebrews (12:11). This process of sanctification after loss was called "improving the affliction," and it called for any spiritual disciplines that could aid in producing the fruit of righteousness and thus help us "realize" our loss and reap the rewards of God's promise. In 1832 she wrote to a friend,

Elizabeth Bates, urging her to "improve this affliction": "[a tragedy that is] at first so grievous . . . [might in the future be found to have] wrought out for you the peaceable fruits of righteousness."[44]

For Stowe, one's response to tragic circumstances would be a barometer of one's spiritual maturity and fruitfulness. She might even learn, through spiritual maturity, to receive pain with a humble, even a thankful heart. Several times she wrote of the need to "kiss the rod"—meaning, not only to accept the Lord's discipline but also to embrace it and even cherish it. The "rod" is a common metaphor in the Bible for authority and discipline, often in a kindly and caring manner, as in Psalm 23: "thy rod and thy staff, they comfort me." Matthew Henry, in his widely read *Bible Commentary on Proverbs* (1706), wrote: "we all need to be corrected by our heavenly Father (Hebrews 12:6, 7), and under the correction we must stroke down folly and kiss the rod."[45] To Calvin, Stowe wrote: "Bear up [. . .] when Sarah Pierrepont Edwards learned the death of her husband, she passed over the scientific aspects and made the traditional response: 'A holy and good God has covered us with a dark cloud. O that we may kiss the rod and lay our hands on our mouths! The lord has done it.'" Charles Foster writes of this passage, "As a Puritan she regarded every event as somehow a part of the divine plan, [. . .] she felt the obligation insisted upon in her faith that man must convert even his losses into the furthering of the kingdom."[46]

At times Stowe clearly perceives the fruit that might eventually supplant the suffering: "There were circumstances about his death of such peculiar bitterness, of what seemed almost cruel suffering that I felt I could never be consoled for it unless this crushing of my own heart might enable me to work out some great good to others."[47] Later, Stowe recognized in hindsight that the long period of grief over Charley did result in powerfully redemptive effects in her life and career: "I allude to this here because I have often felt that much that is in [*Uncle Tom's Cabin*] had its root in the awful scenes and bitter sorrow of that summer. It has left now, I trust, no trace on my mind except a deep compassion for the sorrowful, especially for mothers who are separated from their children."[48] For many grieving mothers of this period, "mourning was regarded as the most sacred of social feelings because the heart softened by affliction turned with greater love not only to the departed loved one, but to all living members of the family, and finally to all mankind."[49] Although she was quite overwhelmed by the loss of her favorite child, perhaps traumatized, by Stowe's own account Charley's death became a crucial motivating factor in her decision to write *Uncle Tom's Cabin*. After the publication of the novel, she wrote about this aspect in a letter to a friend: "I have been the mother of seven children, the most beautiful and most loved of whom lies buried near my Cincinnati residence. It was at his dying bed and at his grave that I learned what a poor slave mother may feel when her child is torn away from her. In those depths of sorrow which seemed to me immeasurable, it was my only prayer to God that *such anguish might not be suffered in vain*"[50] (emphasis mine).

Stowe's letter illustrates a version of spiritual grieving that was characteristic of American romanticism and sentimentalism: the belief that can potentially turn one of life's darkest moments of pain and suffering into something redemptive and constructive for society. It is a belief that continues to have vast cultural power today. Psychologist Dan P. McAdams has studied the "transformation of bad life scenes into good outcomes," referring to this narrative feature as a "redemption sequence": "The discourse of generativity . . . is full of stories about people suffering and making sacrifices in order that the future will be good. . . . [They] are variations on a more general theme of transforming bad into good—the essence of redemption."[51] The records of nineteenth-century American authorship are filled with such redemption sequences, though it did become attenuated over the course of the century. But Stowe's experience with Charley, followed by her constructive memories of that time and grieving, are an exemplary tale of these phenomena and represent the continuing bonds with the dead and the redemptive elements of suffering as well as any story in our history.

Most importantly, Stowe consciously depicted herself as a lead character in a redemption sequence: a grieving mother who found hope and solace in the idea of maintaining bonds with her dead son Charley, bonds that would be redemptive for social good. While today's researchers recognize the importance of calling for the continuing bonds with the deceased, particularly in the case of parental loss of children, Stowe understood this intuitively over 150 years ago, and her achievements testify to her belief. Stowe's masterwork *Uncle Tom's Cabin* was a major consequence of the loss of her son Charley, a product of the insistent generativity of a bereaved mother. She came to view her novel in just these terms: as an example of the "peaceable fruits of righteousness" promised in scripture. "My heart was bursting with the anguish excited by the cruelty and injustice our nation was showing to the slave, and praying God to let me do a little and to cause my cry for them to be heard," she wrote in a letter.[52] In fact, history suggests that she did manage to do "a little," and that Charley did not "die in vain"—not if Harriet's great achievements had anything to do with it. Hatty's grief bore the "peaceable fruits of righteousness"—and changed history as well.

Charley's death pressed Hatty deeper into the things of God and religion: though her devoted faith in God was certainly lifelong, Charley's death culminated a decade-long process of spiritual maturity that ultimately led to her great achievements as a writer. Joan Hedrick has claimed that the death of Charley "marked an epoch in her consciousness" after which things could never be the same for Stowe. This sort of crisis and then maturation is not unusual: much current research indicates that the loss of a child commences a time of aggravated spiritual crisis in the life of a surviving parent.[53] Even so, says Hedrick, "her real spiritual Reformation began early in the 1840s. It was a crucial time of spiritual transformation. . . . She found herself yearning for something deeper and richer, a baptism of the Spirit."[54]

Hedrick's language echoes the emerging Wesleyan and Holiness concepts like "entire sanctification" and "second blessing," goals that were becoming for many believers a lifelong quest: "Entire sanctification or Christian perfection is neither more nor less than pure love; love expelling sin, and governing both the heart and life of a child of God. The Refiner's fire purges out all that is contrary to love."[55] Harriet was a widely read theological thinker, and her friends and family were a veritable who's who of nineteenth-century liberal theology, emerging spiritualities, and feminist thought. Her husband, Calvin, was one of the most prominent biblical scholars in the nation and had profound familiarity with the German forms of Romantic thought (especially his fascination with the works of Friedrich Schleiermacher, who championed "feelings" over arguments) and other sources of religious liberalism. They had frequent, deep discussions about such theological matters, often in bed, suggesting an intimacy and agreement about these important matters, as Calvin once wrote to her: "On matters of religion and taste our opinions and feelings, though quite independent and different from the rest of the world, are very much alike; and I believe there are very few husbands and wives in the world, who have so many real good talks together on such matters as we have. If old Richard Baxter [Puritan divine] and his wife used to lie in bed and sing psalms together for their mutual edification, I am sure some of our *discourses in sheets* have been not less agreeable and edifying. I wish we could have another this very night."[56] Calvin and Harriet yearned for a more significant experience of God and the spirit.

The spiritual journey of Calvin and Hatty Stowe was common among intellectuals in America during these years. Simultaneously, American religious culture was undergoing rapid, even paradigm-shifting changes. One historian has gone so far as to call this the period of the "American invention of spirituality," largely premised on "a search for a religious world larger than the British Protestant inheritance."[57] These developments gave rise to the so-called seeker spirituality popularized in the present day, but even the term *seeker* became common before the Civil War, as did the concept of the "New Age."[58] The 1840s were not just a time of spiritual crisis and transformation for Stowe; the years of "inventing spirituality" were some of the most significant and chaotic years for American religion's encounter with a variety of newly influential "isms": liberalism, transcendentalism, supernaturalism, romanticism, and spiritualism, among others. American Christianity began seeing radical changes early in the nineteenth century. A first major shift was toward a "democratization," meaning the opening up of leadership and preaching duties to the lay person, a shift that revalued the priesthood of the common individual in the pew.[59] The upshot of democratization in Christianity was an elevation of subjective response to Scripture and the birth pangs of what has lately been called by one scholar America's "pervasive interpretive pluralism."[60] As a result, democratized Christianity developed a "liberal" branch that was fuelled by a growing interest in "mysticism" and, perhaps surprisingly to readers today, the first common usage of the terms *spiritual* and *spirituality*.

Liberal Christianity is a wide-ranging term that is used to denote many phenomena of the past two centuries in the American church, but in discussing Stowe, several features should be mentioned. By the end of the 1840s, religious liberalism included a growing contempt for dogma and creed; a grand and romantic sense of freedom and liberation; a privileging of inner, mystical experience; a yearning for direct communication with the Divine; and the potential for diversifying spirituality beyond the merely sectarian. Later, the religious historian Horatio Dresser would dub the nineteenth century in America "the epoch of religious liberalism . . . to be liberal is to be of the new age."[61] Disciplined seeking among religious liberals led to all kinds of heterodox activities; for instance, direct conversations with spirits, or angels, as in the testimony of one of the period's chief intellectual forces, Emanuel Swedenborg, who spoke soberly of his ability to "converse with angels and spirits in the same manner as I speak to men." As Robert Alfred Vaughan wrote in his influential study *Hours with the Mystics* (1856): "[mysticism] is a state of thinking and feeling, to which minds of a certain temperament are liable at any time or place. . . . Mysticism is the romance of religion." And for Vaughan, the American exemplar of such mysticism was none other than Ralph Waldo Emerson, a "God-intoxicated man . . . he is the chief singer at the high court of Mysticism." Even President Lincoln would invoke mysticism (and angels): in his first inaugural address of 1861, he famously hopes that America's "mystic chords" will be "touched" by "the better angels of our nature" as a solution to the nation's impending crisis.[62] Lincoln's construct is rightfully considered one of the most celebrated endings in American rhetoric, yet its spiritual implications are often overlooked.

Liberalism also promoted the growing influence in the Protestant church of women and feminist thought. One of Emerson's chief protégés, Margaret Fuller, believed that mystical experience was necessary for the full emergence of women: "Mysticism, which may be defined as the brooding soul of the world, cannot fail of its oracular promise as to Woman."[63] Sometimes liberalism embraced religious thought from alternate traditions, including Roman Catholicism, which Stowe found intriguing enough to influence her choice of art while in Europe. Prominently displaying paintings of the Virgin Mary in her home may seem trivial today, but at the height of Stowe's fame, it signaled both a liberal and protofeminist sensibility that ultimately proved controversial.[64] The image of the divine mother, important in Catholic iconography, was of particular value to women like Stowe. Indeed, many women of the period believed that women were specially endowed with supernatural gifts that far exceeded men in certain areas, including conversing with the spiritual realm.

For Stowe, the Methodist lay leader Phoebe Palmer was the most influential of the deeply religious, protofeminist women. Palmer's volume *Promise of the Father* (1859) can be understood largely as a direct appeal to the church to allow women to speak more openly, allowing their greater spiritual giftings to bless the entire body. Palmer argued that it was wrong that the church "imposed" silence on women (based largely on verses such as I Corinthians 14:34). She preached instead that women often had greater gifts than men with regard to hearing the voice of the Holy Spirit: "when in union with the heart of Infinite Love, how melting and subduing are the tones of her voice in its influences as it falls upon the ear of hardy men!"[65] Stowe was deeply inspired by the Methodist emphasis on perfection and holiness and became friendly with the key figure of the movement, Phoebe Palmer. Both she and her sister Catherine had read Palmer's book *The Way of Holiness* by 1845, and had been influenced by Palmer's teachings about a more rigorous relationship with God: "but I do believe, and my thoughts have turned much to it this week, in a baptism of the Spirit, —a second conversion that is to the Christian as real in advance, as his first regeneration. . . . The deep immortal longing."[66]

Palmer was also well acquainted with parental grief, having lost three of her first four children in the 1830s. As with Stowe, Palmer's losses triggered a search for a deeper encounter with God and the spirit. Palmer advocated individual freedom as opposed to the deterministic view of the self that was typically associated with old school Calvinism. By 1840, perfectionism "was becoming one of the central themes of American social, intellectual, and political life."[67] Prior to Palmer, it was most associated with preachers like Charles Grandison Finney, the young nation's most famous evangelist during Harriet's Cincinnati years and the founder of Oberlin College in Ohio. When abolitionism caused a stir at Lane Seminary during Harriet's time there, the firebrand Theodore Weld left to go work with Finney and his cohorts at Oberlin to the north. Finney's evangelical approach focused on the freedom of will that individuals have in determining their relationships with God: he demanded that people "make up their minds then and there to give themselves to God. Their destiny lay in their own hands, no matter what the Calvinists told them." Finney's daring claim that "the will is free and . . . sin and holiness are voluntary acts of the mind" directly opposed the older versions of Calvinism. In effect, Finney and then Palmer represented orthodox Christianity's version of the heretic Ralph Waldo Emerson's more famous "American Scholar" address of 1837, hailed at the time as America's "cultural declaration of Independence."[68]

Harriet knew Finney's teachings well, writing passionately about the Holiness movement's influence at Oberlin in a letter of 1844: "there is a great and real change which Christ is now working in the hearts of his church . . . to this sentiment, this longing is to be ascribed the success of the Oberlin paper and doctrine."[69] Stowe adhered to aspects of the doctrine of Christian perfection and holiness. She defended them, for example, in two reviews of books written by her friend Thomas Upham, both of which appeared in 1845 in the *New York Evangelist.* Stowe considered the Uphams to be a model of holy family life: "This family is delightful, there is such a perfect sweetness and quietude in all its movements. . . . It is a beautiful pattern of Christian family, a beautiful exemplification of religion."[70] Phoebe Palmer had facilitated Upham's conversion. In one of her reviews, Stowe asserted tacit consent to the Holiness concept of the "second blessing": "Christians . . . appear to themselves and others to have experienced a kind of second regeneration, and the change in their own eyes and in that of others, is almost as great as the first conversion."[71] The year before, she had had extensive contact with another of Palmer's converts, William Boardman, a student at Lane Seminary, who along with his wife lived for a time with the Stowes in 1844. In his book *The Higher Christian Life* (1858), Boardman describes the Holiness conversion of "a lady of distinction . . . well known both in Europe and America, both by the brilliance of her genius, and the liberality of her gifts, but as she is still living her name is withheld." The details Boardman supplies, according to one historian, "leave little doubt that this mystery celebrity must have been Stowe." While living with the Stowe family, Boardman observed Hatty's spiritual struggles firsthand. He describes well her experience of the "second blessing": "The hand of the Lord . . . at last placed upon her pillow—for she was ill at the time—Upham's 'Interior Life.' . . . Coming to the chapter on 'Consecration,' she . . . said to herself, '*This* I have not done. I have tried to trust in Jesus, but I have never yet in all these attempts, made an entire surrender of myself to him, to *do his will*, but only to receive his salvation.'"[72] So long before Charley's death, Harriet's deepening religious journey was well underway, and her spiritual adventuring had begun.

Moreover, religious liberalism fostered feminist thought and practice. Women became more secure in their spiritual abilities as speakers and listeners, and this affected spiritual practice and adventure, often encouraging controversy. Recently, David Reynolds has emphasized Stowe's profound "debt to the visionary mode," which he sketches as "an anti-Calvinist device." Jonathan Edwards had condemned "the pretended immediate converse, with God in Christ, and saints and angels of heaven." But for the remainder of her life, Stowe would embrace and believe in the reality of those ongoing conversations, especially with Jesus and with the beloved dead saints: "She yearned for contact with the spiritual world. And visionary devices were soon integrated into her fiction including visions of otherworldly beings who uttered consoling truths or gave a little ring [of] information about the afterlife."[73] Stowe became curious about the charismatic elements of the various African American autobiographies with which she became familiar, as the following passage from *The Key to "Uncle Tom's Cabin"* (1853) demonstrates: "We are not surprised to find almost constantly, in the narrations of their religious histories, accounts of visions, of heavenly voices, of mysterious sympathies and transmissions of knowledge from heart to heart without the intervention of the senses, or what Quakers call being 'baptized into the spirit' of those who are distant."[74]

Closer to home, unusual claims about spiritual phenomena were a regular part of the Stowe household. Her husband, Calvin, often had visions of celestial forms passing through walls or floating in the air around him. An early biographer of Harriet who knew Calvin Stowe personally reports that he took his spiritual struggles with satanic forces very seriously and realistically; in one instance, discussing his encounters with Satan: "I was ready for him last night. I had fortified myself with passages of Scripture. I found some things in Ephesians which were just what I wanted, and when he came last night, I *hurled* them at him. I tell you, it made him bark like a dog, and he took himself off. He won't trouble me again."[75] As early as 1834 he wrote and spoke about the various spirits who visited him on a regular basis: beautiful women, fairies, Native American spirits, and crowds of doubles facing the abyss of hell. As Reynolds writes, "Oddly, he did not consider these visions to be abnormal in any way, and evidently Harriet agreed with him on this. Calvin's experiences with the paranormal had an impact on Harriet's thinking about visionary experience and they certainly contributed to her use of spiritual adventuring in her fiction, including *Uncle Tom's Cabin*."[76]

Besides Calvin's strange visions, Hatty had her own paranormal experiences throughout her life. Calvin, though one of New England's most respected biblical scholars, encouraged her spiritual dabbling. He asked in a letter, "Is it absurd to suppose that some peculiarity in the nervous system . . . may bring some [people] more than others, into an almost abnormal contact with the spirit-World?"[77] Hatty evidently believed herself to be peculiarly gifted in that regard: she experimented with the "planchette," an early form of what we call today the Ouija board, with which spirits of the dead might move an object around a board to spell out words of a message. One acquaintance noted that her experiments "evoked surprising manifestations."[78] Stowe was intrigued by spiritualism and wrote serious essays about it. She also became known for her public performances and her thwarting of certain gender expectations. She was a forerunner of those in favor of a view that women possessed a more refined sensibility in the private realms of the spirit than was available to men. Stowe found such views not only plausible but also convincing at a time when liberal Christianity of the 1840s drastically reevaluated the discernment of the common church member, especially women. Perhaps women could hear the spirit better than men, she opined.

Mystical voices, spirits, and angels; Perfectionism and Transcendentalism; Catholic aesthetics and Wesleyan piety; but also the lingering influence of the New England Calvinists: altogether, this period produced a perfect storm of religious and spiritual influences for the liberalization of American Christianity, and Stowe very often found herself at the center of these doctrinal debates. She lived in the perfect context for religious and mystical experimentation, and some of her practices and opinions represented unorthodox positions verging at times on heresy (as in spiritualism). And so, although Stowe is often remembered today as a religious conservative (which in many ways, she surely was), during her lifetime she was considered a maverick in a number of ways, dedicated to what Reynolds has called "spiritual adventuring." As such she was a product of her age. And thus, in many ways, Stowe's "revolutionary" spiritual insights, manifested brilliantly in her masterpiece, were in keeping with the trending theological and spiritual developments of her time.

But one other area of theological debate marked the spiritual crisis of her formative era, a set of questions that would have a crucial bearing on Stowe's literary works and those that would come later. It signaled a crisis in American theology that affected each of the other figures discussed in this study. As with so many other bereaved parents, Stowe's grief forced her into the deep waters of the problem of evil, also called the problem of pain, which would become a growth industry in theological circles. The debates over the problem of evil would be greatly exacerbated by the disaster of the Civil War the following decade, when nearly every town and even family suffered the loss of young men and boys. The problem of evil emphasizes the fallenness of the world, the injustices of a depraved system dominated by evil and suffering, with no evident meaning or redemption for those suffering the most. In theological terms, recognizing and wrestling with these broken circumstances forces one of the most difficult challenges for belief: If God is a good God, and has unlimited power, then why is there so much pain and suffering in the world?

The answer to this question is called a theodicy: a defense of God in the face of radical evil. In effect, grieving mothers like Stowe found answering such questions to be crucial to their self-understanding as believers. At the heart of Stowe's message for the bereaved and her desire to provide solace are her remarkable attempts to rethink traditional Christian theodicies. Her reformulations were undertaken in light of the rapidly changing Protestant church of midcentury, which would soon be faced with the crisis of a brutal civil war. Often, religious parents who lose children find it to be the commencement of a long-term "spiritual crisis" that calls into question central tenets about their own faith. Grieving parents are sometimes unable to come up with a satisfactory answer to the problem of pain and evil. In many cases, counterintuitively, such traumas might actually reinforce previously held religious beliefs: sometimes a person of faith emerges stronger than ever from grief, despite much wrestling with doubts; and sometimes tragedy forces the believer into a "new ignorance" that generates fresh insight and revelation. As theologian Shelly Rambo explains: "Witnessing the suffering that remains involves encountering the ways in which death pervades life. . . . The phenomenon of trauma brings theology to a new ignorance, unsettling familiar categories and placing the discourse of theology in a more tenuous place. But the shifting ground underfoot also unearths a discourse of remaining."[79]

Stowe, ardent professor of faith in God's goodness and providence, like many intellectuals during that same period, was forced through her own personal suffering to develop a satisfactory theodicy—a "discourse of remaining." Hers was not a glib appeal to blind faith, but instead emerged from genuine spiritual strivings after which her faith became stronger than ever. Specifically, Stowe drew upon Christian understandings of the nature of suffering bodies, focusing on the counterintuitive nature of that suffering—for Paul, the "scandal" of Jesus's crushing pain. Stowe believed that Christian revelation allows one to see pain from a heavenly perspective. But such revelation never came easy; it required painstaking mystical connection with the Spirit of God and concerted effort on the part of the seeker. Such striving might produce a genuine mystical breakthrough that the world would reject and even mock, as it did at the crucifixion of the Lord. Theologian David Jasper has emphasized the shocking end to the life of Jesus as significant for the suffering we all face every day: "the enactment of what Paul calls the 'scandal,' the paradox that in the depths of human defeat is found the victory in death of God."[80] As Paul writes in I Corinthians 15: "O death where is thy sting? . . . be ye stedfast, unmoveable, always abounding in the work of the Lord, forasmuch as ye know that your labour is not in vain in the Lord" (vv. 55, 58). Stowe took comfort from such verses; as scandalous as was the death of her Charley, or the murder of innocent slaves, it was still possible to find some consolation in the promise of ultimate victory.

Such a scandalous death achieving final victory—and in fact mocking death in so doing—would find the century's greatest literary expression not once but twice in Stowe's masterpiece, with the twinned demises of Little Eva and Uncle Tom. Stowe's cosmic vision in *Uncle Tom's Cabin*, echoing the New Testament, is founded on a promise of happy reunion and the immortal souls of her "beloved ones" in God's presence, actively learning the truths of a "higher sphere." For Stowe, the teleology of Christian belief trumps the pain of everyday life, and the beauty of the presence of God trumps the horrors of the "earthly sphere." Elizabeth Barrett Browning always remembered her final parting from

Hatty in Rome, in 1860: "Her last words to me when we parted, were, 'Those who love the Lord Jesus Christ never see one another for the last time.'"[81] Thus fervent hope is the crucial ingredient in Stowe's theodicy, which is founded on a view of the work of sorrow and suffering. Likewise, *Uncle Tom's Cabin* is arguably America's greatest narrative theodicy, a near perfect "redemption sequence" fully dependent on the continuing bonds with the dead.

In the novel, pain and suffering abound, but hope and meaning are found in our connections to the dead—especially the young. To that end, *Uncle Tom's Cabin* is famously haunted by premature deaths, including any number of named and unnamed children, along with children ripped violently away from mothers. We should even add to that list of premature deaths the title character, Tom. He is certainly an adult father, but his exact age remains a mystery (as it was for many adult slaves). One critic describes the reader's encounter with these atrocities in Stowe's novel a function of "sentimental wounding," with the wounding designed to bring about substantive moral changes.[82] But the novel offers much more than mere "sentimental wounding": it proposes the ongoing assistance of the dead, as lifelong spiritual presences to lead and direct our steps. The prematurely dead, writes Stowe, are "an especial band of Angels, whose office it was to sojourn for a season here, and endear to them the wayward human heart, that they might bear it upward with them in their homeward flight." In Stowe's fictional world, the lost child is often depicted as a spiritual guide for those left behind. Our memories of them are the "buried treasures of yearning hearts" that can lead the "wayward human heart" on its "homeward flight."[83] These angelic beings are to act forever as our spiritual guides, leading us upward to an angelic moral awareness. It was a common sensibility of the time: in 1855, Sarah Hale claimed that "to bring about the true Christian civilization, which only can improve the condition of our sex, the men must become more like women, and the women more like angels."[84] Many assumed that the feminine segment of society, ruled over by women's "hearts," or by what Lincoln called its "better angels," would be the decisive factor in achieving a "true Christian civilization." *Uncle Tom's Cabin* drew upon these ideologies to map out a spirituality of continuing bonds that would help Americans achieve a just and righteous nation.

More simply, the novel can be read as one heroic yet bereaved mother speaking courage to other bereaved mothers, assuring them that the lost child is hovering just beyond their vision. At the center of Stowe's purposes for *Uncle Tom's Cabin* are numerous examples of dead children and the hysterical mothers left behind. The depiction of the depths of hysteria and a crushing desolation are also important elements of her landscape. Stowe could accurately depict these emotions since she was herself rather prone to them at times. And yet at times in the midst of the suffering, the bereaved mother rediscovers certain convictions that allow her to go forward: "this crushing of my own heart might enable me to work out some great good to others." The "crushing" metaphor reminds us of the Suffering Servant of Isaiah: "he was bruised for our iniquities." But the prophet then describes the miraculous fruits of this wounding: "by His stripes we are healed" (Isaiah 53:5). Hatty perceived that, like Jesus (the passage from Isaiah was commonly interpreted as a type of the scourging of Jesus prior to his crucifixion, the "stripes" being the lacerations of the whip upon His back), His followers must undergo their punishment stoically and silently, like a sheep led to slaughter.

Stowe also perceived that such fruit might only proceed for those with the right attitude: the famous "right feelings" that she dissects in the "Concluding Remarks" of the novel. The "right feelings" are crucial: "If the mothers of the free states had all felt as they should," she tells us, the wrongs of slavery would have all disappeared. What can any single person do, she asks? "They can see to it that *they feel right*." The "see to it" slang insinuates that it's up to us: our attitudes are our responsibility, and we must sacrifice and purify them. The book's final scriptural reference is to Malachi 4:1, with its depiction of the purifying fires of God: "for that day shall burn as an oven."[85] Such revelations as she illustrates in the novel, in short, can only take hold in those willing to place their battered hearts upon God's altar, pursue holiness, and begin to "feel right."

Out of profound suffering comes those "right feelings," especially deeper compassion and sympathy for the downtrodden, hence the novel's rarely remembered subtitle: "Life among the Lowly." Stowe claimed later that the long period of grief over Charley "has left now, I trust, no trace on my mind except a deep compassion for the sorrowful, especially for mothers who are separated from their children."[86] This "deep compassion" amounted to a close identification with the slaves (usually mothers) who have lost their children, through either death or theft via a corrupt system of commerce. Numerous incidents urge the reader to recognize the mothering skills of the slaves and to be properly moved by the anguish and sadness of separation from their children. Several times, the grief of white parents is equated with the grief of the slaves, a strategy for building the sympathies of her white readers. To accomplish this, Stowe often turns to the second-person voice to speak directly to the reader, emphasizing that the slave mothers are just like them, just as human in their grief. When Tom begins sobbing heavily, saying goodbye to his children after learning he has been sold away, Stowe points the finger at us: Tom was shedding "just such tears. Sir, as you dropped into your coffin where lay your first-born son; such tears, woman, as you shed when you heard the cries of your dying babe." Such lines are eerily realistic, given that Hatty's own son died wailing in her arms just a couple years earlier. In the chapter with the archetypical title "The Mother's Struggle," she asks the reader, "If it were your Harry, mother, or your Willie, that were going to be torn from you by a brutal trader, to-morrow morning . . . how fast could you walk?" At the home of Senator and Mrs. Bird, whose child has died and who are now moved to help the fleeing Eliza keep her child from being torn away, the narrator asks, "And oh! Mother that reads this, has there never been in your house a drawer, or a closet, the openings of which has been to you like the opening again of a little grave?"[87] Again, the passage has autobiographical intensity: Stowe stored some of the clothing her son Charley had worn the last time he was healthy in a drawer, occasionally opening it, for many years, to look at the contents as a "tiny memorial."[88] The emotional value in the personal effects of the deceased is common, and they are called "linking objects" in the literature on grief. Almost all of Stowe's readers probably kept numerous "linking objects" in close proximity—powerful reminders of the dead.

The first mention of parental loss comes only a few pages into the novel, with Haley the slave trader telling the story of a woman who "went ravin' mad, and died in a week" after her baby was carried off. Even the depraved Haley recognizes this to be "inhumane," a recognition for which Stowe dubs him ironically a "second Wilberforce" (her irony runs thickest in recording the idiotic arguments of slaveholders). Soon enough, Eliza's boy is "torn away" and sold off. The verbs Stowe used to illustrate this atrocity of separation are generally active and violent: "ripped," "torn away," "it cried itself to death"—all merely "little incidents of lawful trade."[89] In a letter written to her son years later, Stowe indicates a first-hand knowledge of this violation—her experience of the violent separation from Charley through infant mortality: "I remember many a night weeping over you as you lay sleeping beside me, and I thought of the slave mothers whose babes were torn from them."[90]

Other tragedies take center stage throughout the narrative, briefly yet poignantly: we hear of an unnamed cook whose "young 'un . . . got drowned in a wash-tub." We hear of Lucy, a sold slave with child being transported "down the river," whose baby is snatched away silently by Haley and given to "a stranger." Lucy discovers this and, in hysterics, jumps overboard to drown herself in despair: "the poor bleeding heart was still at last."[91] One of the most horrific incidents is the tale of Prue, a "breeder" who suffered the theft of her offspring any number of times (so many that the number is not revealed). With her "peculiar scowling expression" and "sullen, grumbling voice," Prue is the dehumanized product of a vicious system of commerce who has turned to alcohol for comfort. On the very first page of volume 2, we learn that Prue has been found suddenly dead in the cellar. It's a scene, the cook Dinah exclaims, to which the young Eva should not be exposed: "it isn't for sweet, delicate young ladies, like you."[92]

Up to the midpoint of the novel, Prue's tale may be the low point of maternal grief, but it's surpassed later by the horrors Cassie endures. After birthing a child from a white master and becoming fearful of her baby being sold away, Cassie determines that she must take matters into her own hands to keep her son away from the depraved system. "Something in my head snapped," she explains in telling her tale to Tom, and she gives her baby, only two weeks old, a fatal dose of laudanum, "and held him close to my bosom, while he slept to death. How I mourned and cried over it!" The motif of murdering a child to keep it out of the slave system had several historical precedents and would become a harrowing feature of later slave literature as well.[93] Death, it was thought by some, might be preferable to being subjected to slavery, and the dilemma of considering the murder of one's child represents the darkest of maternal options. Stowe suggests that even entertaining such a thought may be the dreaded "unpardonable sin" against the Holy Spirit, marking one as reprobate, as Cassie confesses: "Now, I'm a lost soul, pursued by devils that torment me day and night."[94] Despite the worst fears, in Stowe's spiritual economy, ultimately even one like Cassie can find redemption and salvation, as she does just a few chapters later.

These premature deaths and the numerous, immoral thefts of children set the scene for the deaths at the heart of the story. Poignant as each episode may be, none can surpass the circumstances surrounding the novel's twins of redemptive death: Eva and Tom, girl and man, white and black, rich and poor. Eva's death was widely considered the most famous literary scene of the entire century in American culture. Importantly, Stowe contrasts the "felt" response of Eva's thoroughly corrupt mother Marie with the more reliable feelings of the stoic and pragmatic New England stalwart Miss Ophelia. Marie did feel the loss of Eva, at least "as deeply as she could feel anything," but the effect of Eva's death for her is an intensifying of her "tyrannical and selfish exactions." Ophelia, meanwhile, had a "good and honest heart." For Ophelia, Eva's loss "bore fruit unto everlasting life," yet another reference to Hebrews 12. Ophelia's heart is "softened" by the traumatic loss; she became "more gentle," and the lessons of the death were taught "not in vain." Miss Ophelia is transformed, becoming more loving toward Topsy, the "wild" slave girl given to her as a civilizing project, and Ophelia learns how to view Topsy "through the softened medium" of Eva's presence. Finally the fruit is fully borne in Topsy's life as well: "the life and death of Eva did work a marked change in her. The callous indifference was gone; there was now sensibility, hope, desire, and the striving for good."[95] There was now, in other words, evidence of the "peaceable fruits of righteousness" (Hebrews 12) that are the proper outworkings of suffering. These fruits can only emerge, this long passage suggests, in those like Ophelia, who have a "good and honest heart."[96]

Consequently, Tom seems at times to hear Eva's voice after her death, as in a dream. By the time she wrote the novel, Stowe was confirmed in her conviction of the reality of supernatural elements to faith, including the "dreams and visions" mentioned in the book of Joel and later repeated in the gospels and the book of Acts as being available to both sexes: "I will pour out my spirit upon all flesh; and your sons and your daughters shall prophesy, your old men shall dream dreams, your young men shall see visions" (Joel 2:28, cf. Acts 2:17). In this prophetic context Stowe asks her reader about the true nature of Tom's spiritual experience: "Was it a dream? Let it pass for one. But who shall say that that sweet young spirit, which in life so you earned to come and console the distressed, was forbidden of God to assume this ministry after death?"[97]

Although the question rhetorically seems to leave the issue unsettled, prior to *Uncle Tom's Cabin*, Stowe had written numerous essays and stories revealing her convictions about the spirits of the dead. She wrote, for instance, in 1849 that the most logical identities of those hovering about us are our own dead friends and relatives. "May we look among the band of ministering spirits for our own departed ones? Whom would God be more likely to send us?" Her argument in support of her views is biblically based, a position that would be shunned in today's evangelical world. In fact, she posits, perhaps God allows some young people to die because their ministrations as spirits might even surpass what they could achieve on the earth: "It may be possible that a friend is sometimes taken because the divine One sees that his ministry can act upon us more powerfully from the unseen world than amid the infirmities of mortal intercourse."[98]

By the early 1850s these views had become rather common in the culture. Evidence of this is extensive, but one of the strongest cases comes from the rapidity with which readers embraced the supernatural elements of *Uncle Tom's Cabin*. The ending of the passage describing Tom's perception of Eva's ongoing presence features a quatrain that became something of a cultural marker afterward, and certainly one of the most often quoted passages of the story. The brief poem goes like this:

> It is a beautiful belief,
> That ever round our head
> Are hovering, on angel wings,
> The spirits of the dead.[99]

This passage became well known to readers of the novel, and its popularity harks back to the spiritual adventuring of her western years in Ohio. The poem as it appears in the novel was altered by Stowe from a popular poem, and later a hymn, both composed by James H. Perkins. Perkins was a well-known Congregationalist writer in Cincinnati during the 1830s, where Stowe had known him intimately as a regular member of her literary salon, the Semi-Colon Club. She likely knew his poetry very well and admired his mystical sensibilities. His memoir is peppered with dozens of uses of the words "spiritual" and "spirituality."[100] Stowe wrote to her brother Henry about Perkins in 1835: "He had a very pretty piece of poetry too some line of which touched my heroic feelings. . . . I do love him."[101] As Hedrick suggests, there may have even been a brief period after her arrival in Cincinnati during which Stowe considered Perkins a good match and a potential soul mate.[102]

The "very pretty piece of poetry" she heard from Perkins and reported to Henry may well have been the source for some of the novel's most famous lines. Perkins's original poem "Spiritual Presence" was published first in 1833 and later in different versions. The 1833 version reads:

> It is a beautiful belief,
> When ended our career,
> That it will be our ministry
> To watch o'er others here[103]

Perkins's poem was augmented and revised as a hymn, and published in 1849 in *A Book of Hymns for Public and Private Devotion*, a few years before Stowe's novel appeared. Stowe would have found very attractive his sentiment that after death our "ministry" to those remaining would continue. In many ways, Perkins's poem summarized a key aspect of her argument in *Uncle Tom's Cabin*. And so Stowe combined lines from the poem and the hymn to create one of the most memorable and often-quoted passages of the novel.

The image of spirits hovering around us again alludes to the "clouds of witnesses" motif of the Book of Hebrews (12:4). Stowe clarifies the dead to be "angels," an increasingly common construction at that time that recalls the mystical writings of Swedenborg. One historian of the period explains that according to a sentimental view, "death was not powerful enough to sever the bonds of domestic love. The departed loved one acted as a guardian angel who shed continued influence over the heart of the mourner."[104] The "hovering" motif was also a prominent feature of much writing on the dead during this period. As one popular mourning manual put it, combining the two images, "The memory of the sainted dead hovers, a blessed and purifying influence, over the hearts of men. At the grave of the good, so far from losing heart, the spiritually minded find new strength. They weep, but as they weep they look down into the sepulcher, and behold angels sitting, and the dead come nearer, and are united to them by a fellowship more intimate than that of blood."[105]

Stowe's lengthy tract on this topic, titled "On the Ministration of Departed Spirits in the World" and published in 1849, also highlights the notion of our ministry to survivors continuing after entering our eternal reward. In this tract, she claims her views as having biblical endorsement: "First, then, the Bible distinctly says that there is a class of invisible spirits who minister to the children of men. 'Are they not all ministering spirits, sent forth to minister to those who shall be heirs of salvation?'"[106] Her text is Hebrews 1:14. Stowe published the essay in the *New York Evangelist*, and it is there that we see for the first time the redacted stanza based on Perkins's lines. Tellingly, the quatrain functions as the epilogue for the article. Thus it is clear that by the late 1840s, Stowe had fully embraced a religious theory of continuing bonds with the dead—including the idea that perhaps we are all destined to join the league of "hovering spirits" and to continue ministering to our surviving friends and families.

The quatrain next appears, most famously of all, at the end of chapter 32 of *Uncle Tom's Cabin*. The chapter, titled "Dark Places," is a gothic depiction of the plantation of Simon Legree that is one of the most frightening sections of the book. In this context, the hovering spirits of the dead are symbolized by Eva's presence, whose "gentle voice" inspires the desolate Tom, filling his heart with "rays of warmth and comfort." The poem as it appears in the novel developed a reputation well beyond the popularity of Perkins's hymn. The four lines are quoted in full in numerous, widely divergent literary contexts, often without attribution (suggesting that the reader need not be told that it was a quote from *Uncle Tom's Cabin*). It appeared almost immediately, for example, in a letter of condolence from Elizabeth Dickerman to a friend whose son Eddie had recently died. Dickerman does not mention Stowe's name, even though the letter was written in 1852 and so very shortly after the chapter's publication as an installment. "How precious, too, the assurance that we have a friend in heaven who can sympathize with us in all our sorrows," writes Dickerman after the poem.[107] The "friendliness" of the hovering spirits, a "beautiful belief," symbolizes by extension the friendliness of God—contrasting with the more frightening versions of the so-called Calvinist God. Thus the tone of the poem exemplifies what one critic has called a "sentimental incarnationalism," which "emerged in the 1840s as an effort to make God more emotional and expressive . . . the basic difference between neoclassical and sentimental characterization turned . . . on the depiction of love . . . sentimental sympathy was a fusion of pity with love."[108]

Stowe's poem quickly became a commonly repeated cultural shorthand of the "continuing bonds" belief: that spirits of the dead were indeed ministering to us, and that our bonds with the dead continued to inspire and instruct. This little poem and its curious staying power symbolize how readers embraced *Uncle Tom's Cabin* as an affirming depiction of a redemptive view of the loss. And Stowe's insistence on continuing bonds helps unlock the novel's benediction, delivered at the end of chapter 44, "The Liberator," as a eulogy for the martyred Tom by the young George Shelby. The final lines of the story proper read: "Think of your freedom, every time you see UNCLE TOM'S CABIN; and let it be a memorial to put you all in mind to follow in his steps, and be as honest and faithful and Christian as he was."[109] The upshot of this directive, signaled especially by the capitalization, is the metamorphosis of Tom's modest shack into a temple to the saintly Tom. This sacred memorial temple is on the one hand symbolic of Tom's physical body, which has become glorified as a temple of the Holy Spirit. But it is also a temple of the Republic, as suggested by one detail from the novel's first passage describing the cabin: the "wall over the fireplace was adorned with some very brilliant scriptural prints, and a portrait of General Washington, drawn and colored in a manner which would certainly have astonished that hero, if ever he had happened to meet with its like."[110]

America was in the process of building its first grand, national memorial when Stowe wrote and published her novel. The Washington Monument had been excavated and its construction commenced on July 4, 1848, and by the time of the publication of *Uncle Tom's Cabin* the obelisk stood roughly a third of its final height, when funding ran out. Washington, as reigning spirit of America's War for Independence, is nothing less than "colored" in the picture adorning Tom's "memorial": made to represent more closely the African heritage of the home. The presence of a blackface General Washington has its peculiarities and difficulties: it speaks of the irony of the early republic's claims about "freedom," given Washington's history as a slaveholder.[111] However, one critical point is clear: Washington has taken his rightful place in the homes of those seeking revolutionary independence. The colored Washington's elevation alongside of Scripture in the memorialized home of Uncle Tom exemplifies the joining of the social, the racial, and the sacred for future generations to exemplify. The appeal to the past is the classic mark of the jeremiad mode in American history; the coloring of that past appeals to our sense of its incompletion and its spiritual weakness (as it might have reminded readers at the time of the uncompleted memorial in Washington, DC). Stowe may have been blinded to her own bondage to romantic racialism, but she truly believed that General Washington had much to learn from the spiritual sensibilities of Uncle Tom.[112]

As George Shelby laments, Tom's home should remain "a memorial to put you all in mind to follow in his steps." George's appeal is to a continuing bond with the dead saint Tom, that we might "follow in his steps." This appeal mirrors the discipleship of Christians, called to follow Jesus even unto death. It's no coincidence that the motif would end up becoming the title of the quintessential social gospel narrative of the century: Charles Sheldon's *In His Steps*, published in 1897 with sales that even surpassed *Uncle Tom's Cabin*. Likewise, this key motif of memorialization is at the heart of the far more famous memorials on the National Mall. All invoke the continuing bonds with the dead, and although we build memorials for a variety of reasons, perhaps the yearning for redemptive action as a legacy for the dead is one of the most obvious—though also, perhaps, the least verbalized.[113]

If *Uncle Tom's Cabin* is a memorial to Charley, then a new memorial would soon be required. Despite her admirable strength and her nearly obsessive desire to memorialize her dead son and to help grieving parents, Stowe suffered a great deal in the years after her great success. Her own grief was severe, long lasting, extremely complicated, and indeed lifelong. And sadly, more wounding would soon visit the battered heart of

Harriet Beecher Stowe, and the genesis of Stowe's minor masterpiece, *The Minister's Wooing* (1859), also occurred in the midst of the anguish of parental grief: the tragic death by drowning of Henry, her oldest son and a college student at Dartmouth, in 1857. Like *Uncle Tom's Cabin*, it also resounds with Hatty's appeals to the continuing bonds with the dead.

Henry was also very close to his mother, having traveled to Europe with her in 1853, after her great triumph. But he was sporting in a river on a hot summer day when he was taken under by a strong current and found himself unable to recover. Although Henry was an affectionate son and a virtuous and intelligent student with success within his reach, there were good reasons for his mother and her family to doubt his conversion to a true faith in Christ. With Henry's salvation at the time of his death in doubt, an additional hardship became part of the grief experience for his mother Harriet. At this time she became somewhat obsessed with contacting her dead son. While in Rome with Elizabeth Barrett Browning, Stowe "received some surprising evidences of things occult and strange."[114] Browning, a renowned poet and intellectual herself, would write about Stowe's numerous encounters with the dead: "[Stowe] had heard, she said, for the fifth time from her boy (the one who was drowned in that awful manner) . . . She gave me a minute account of a late manifestation, not seeming to have a doubt in respect to the verity and identity of the spirit. In fact, secret things were told, reference to private papers made, the evidence was considered most satisfying."[115] This kind of activity is illustrated in her novels, where typically it is spiritual women who are most sensitive to the faint voices of the spiritual realm. She writes in *The Minister's Wooing*, "In our own days, most uncommon manifestations of divine grace have been given to holy women. It was my privilege to be in the family of President Edwards at a time when Northampton was specially visited, and his wife seemed and spoke more like a glorified spirit than a mortal woman,—and multitudes flocked to the house to hear the wonderful words."[116]

Eerily enough, the circumstances of Henry's death also mirrored in certain strange ways the sad tale of her older sister Catherine's loss, thirty-five years earlier. At that time, Lyman's children had been shocked by their father's unemotional and harsh treatment of their oldest sister. By way of contrast, in *The Minister's Wooing*, Stowe developed a revisionist reading of early American Calvinists, emphasizing the emergence of sympathetic ministry and romantic intuitions. Stowe presents an accommodating view of Calvinism, treating its spokesmen with respect and gentle humor, and taking seriously many of Reformed theology's central doctrines. She depicts Jonathan Edwards, the kingpin of American theology in the time period of the setting of *The Minister's Wooing,* as being overcome with an "'inward and sweet sense,' which came to him once when walking alone in the fields," a description sounding more like Emerson than his forebears. Even the great Edwards, writes Stowe, was an early recipient of "Divine interposition, which carried the soul far above the region of the intellect, into that of direct spiritual intuition."[117] Certainly the rejection of dogmatic judgments about the dead and the appeal to "intuitive truths" and "direct spiritual intuition" were featured in *Uncle Tom's Cabin* (where it is possible to envision the deeply divided and almost pagan Augustine St. Clare as having died in faith). But in the shadow of Henry's death, they became crucial themes in *The Minister's Wooing.* Nevertheless, *The Minister's Wooing,* as in *Uncle Tom's Cabin,* represents a respectable revision of Calvinism more than a total rejection of it. And clearly that accommodation is in light of her struggles as a grieving mother trying to make sense of her son's untimely death.

In the novel, James's mother, Mrs. Marvyn, is depicted as suffering extreme religious doubt and melancholy, and the institutional forms of Christianity seen in the novel are unable to bring any relief. Again, an inspiring way of understanding *The Minister's Wooing* is to read it as Stowe's heartfelt advice to grieving parents about how one can navigate the choppy waters of the death of children. James bears a striking resemblance to Henry, both in age and in religious sensibilities. Sadly, intellectual forms of Calvinism were unable to help grieving parents come to terms with their loss, especially mothers, and this is one of the novel's central preoccupations. Calvinist clergymen are chastised for their coldly logical treatment of mothers in particular: "where theorists and philosophers tread with sublime assurance, woman often follows with bleeding footsteps;—women are always turning from the abstract to the individual, and feeling where the philosopher only thinks."[118] Traumatized mothers are urged to embrace God's will and accept with humility that their dead child, if indeed unregenerate, has been assigned to hell: such hard and fast mandates ring of oppression, "the effect of a slow poison, producing life-habits of morbid action."[119] The Reverend Hopkins, the town's divine and former disciple of Edwards, illustrates the basic premise of much Calvinist thinking on the destiny of the deceased; he "recognizes the fact, that the greater part of the human race, up to this time, had been eternally lost." God reveals his power by strengthening the bodies of the damned to withstand "torments which otherwise would be intolerable." Calvinist preaching on God's judgment often amounts to a "refined poetry of torture," and as she wrote later in life, it presents God as a "severe and unsympathetic being."[120] But it is a highly unsatisfactory poetry that forces the motherly heart to one particular question: "is God not a God of mercy?"[121] By way of contrast, in *The Minister's Wooing*, Stowe substitutes warmhearted human feelings for academic theology, suggesting how a "feminized" approach to ministry for the bereaved is far superior to the cold and drafty logic of the patriarchs. This emphasis is similar to what some critics have called a "judicious sympathy," by which they refer to a style of moral reasoning during the antebellum period that jointly considers feelings and facts through rational means.[122]

To illustrate this emerging style, Stowe offers the wisdom of Candace—a slave at the story's inception who is freed during the course of the narrative. Candace was based on an actual slave who ministered to Stowe at the time of Henry's death in 1857. Candace speaks mercifully to Mrs. Marvyn of the love of Jesus and consoles the suffering mothers of the world with sympathy and gentle reminders of God's promises. "Why, de Lord a'n't like what ye tink,—He loves ye honey! Why, jes' feel how I loves ye,—poor ole black Candace. . . . He *died* for Mass'r Jim,—loved him and died for him,—jes' give up his sweet, precious body and soul for him on de cross! Laws, jes' *leave* him in Jesus's hands! . . . *Look right at Jesus.* Tell ye, honey, ye can't live no other way now. Don't ye 'member how He looked on His mother, when she stood faintin' an' tremblin' under de cross, jes' like you? He knows all about mothers' hearts."[123] Candace invokes the traumatized Mary, the quintessential bereaved mother. Jesus, even as he died, "looked on" Mary with a sublime and loving compassion, as He does with all grieving mothers, says Candace. Understandably, the female characters of the novel often turn to Candace for her pietistic sympathy and her cracker-barrel wisdom, which often flies in the face of the male ministers who ostensibly preside over the town. Finally, Candace is very funny at times. When told that a preacher considers the bringing of the slaves to America to be part of God's plan for the "fullness of the Gentiles," she snorts, "Fulness of the fiddlesticks! . . . Go look at one o' dem ships."[124] Humor is often subversive, as with Candace's use of it, acting as a sort of spiritual dynamite uncovering the cant and hypocrisies of the faithful.[125] The humor is typical of Stowe, and perhaps is one of her most charming and underrated abilities. Her public lectures were notable for the laughter they provoked; she notes in letters home, "How they do laugh! We get into regular gales."[126] As in *Uncle Tom's Cabin*, Stowe provided much humorous relief from the trials of life. By way of contrast, in *The Minister's Wooing*, the white male patriarchs of Newport are almost universally humorless—a detriment to their ministerial duty to console and encourage. For these reasons, Candace is one of the most interesting black characters in all of Stowe's fiction—and her role is essentially to minister to the grieving mothers struggling to come to grips with the pain of their loss and to rethink their views of a benevolent God.

Joan Hedrick sums up the novel's ambition this way: "In her advice to troubled and grieving women, Stowe's efforts were repeatedly focused on removing from their shoulders the added burden of feeling that they should not feel the way they did, a burden that was largely the result of Calvinist preaching by male ministers. . . . Women turned to Stowe for relief from a particular kind of religious scruple that they would not have been able to express to their ministers."[127] As such, Stowe's compulsive and yet theologically rich examinations of parental grief, especially in *Uncle Tom's Cabin* and *The Minister's Wooing*, set the stage for the oncoming rush of writing that considered these same themes and theological issues, a rush that was greatly motivated by the widespread loss of young men during the war. Not only did she fully embrace the idea that her dead sons continued to hover around her, just beyond her physical abilities to perceive them, but also she actually envisioned her sons as continuing to exert positive energy and inspiration in her everyday life. Stowe's stories perfectly capture how social good can indeed come from suffering. Further, in her own personal trials, she models the heroic ability that survivors like her often share: a remarkable ability "to make sense of their own lives through an idealized story script that emphasizes, among other themes, the power of human redemption. In the most general sense, redemption is *a deliverance from suffering to a better world*."[128] By that definition, for roughly four million black slaves, the Civil War must be understood as redemptive, and no one memorialized it better in that regard than the martyred president, Lincoln. For African Americans, the deliverance was real, and yet the fulfillment of a better world still lay far in the future.

Sadly, even after Henry's drowning, Hatty's sorrows were not yet ended: she would suffer further grief after her legendary meeting with Lincoln and the Union victory of the war. In a poignant twist, another vague connection with Lincoln and his great speech in the Pennsylvania cemetery would come. As it turned out, her son Frederick was one of the thousands of casualties at the Battle of Gettysburg. Afterward, Fred never recovered: he struggled with alcoholism and shell shock, despite the best attempts at therapy arranged and funded by his loving mother. In 1871, he had shipped to San Francisco in hopes that a long trip might help in his recovery; he evidently arrived safely, hoping to board another vessel for a longer sea voyage over the Pacific.

But Fred was never heard from again. Possibly a suicide like his uncle George (he had once alluded to committing suicide in a letter to his mother); possibly a victim of crime or dissolution through binge drinking. His sad parents never discovered what happened. Hatty sent detectives all the way to California, hoping to pick up his trail.

She certainly hoped, as Lincoln put it in his speech, that Fred's sacrifice at Gettysburg "would not be in vain." But she also struggled to "realize" his death, which is always a challenge for those who never confront the body of the deceased. Once the aging Hatty embraced a total stranger on a street in Hartford, believing him to be Fred finally returned. And until her dying days (often muddied by a growing dementia), she kept checking the mail in hopes of finding a missive from her long lost son Fred. Nothing ever turned up, unfortunately, and so it was another blow in her lengthy battle with parental grief, now her third son lost.

Stowe's greatest novels *Uncle Tom's Cabin* and *The Minister's Wooing* had much in common, including an appeal to the continuing bonds with the dead. But *Uncle Tom's Cabin* became the story most directly connected in the public imagination with conflict, premature and unjust death, and civil war. Although emancipation has never been attributed to the death of a young boy in Cincinnati and the fitful response of his bereaved mother, a linkage of Lincoln's greatest achievements with the death from cholera of Charley Stowe is certainly compelling. Stowe insisted in her famous letter that the death of her son "shall not be in vain"—and, in retrospect, and due mainly to her own brave perseverance, it wasn't.

Important as it might have been, the death of Charley would not be the only premature death to influence Lincoln's courageous call for emancipation in 1863. And Tom's cabin would not be the only "memorial to put you all in mind" to follow in a specific person's footsteps. Another young boy's untimely death, and another far greater memorial, were yet to come.

2

Lincoln's Grief

Willie, Antietam, and the "Meditation on the Divine Will"

It seems fitting and proper that Mrs. Stowe met the president in 1862. Already by then, Stowe's novel was widely considered to be among the most important precursors of the war. A legend developed that President Lincoln's first words to her, upon their first meeting in 1862, attributed the war to her novel: "Is this the little woman who made this great war?" Whether President Lincoln uttered these specific words, or even whether he made this sort of observation in general, is left up to the anecdotal memory, mostly from many years afterward, of Harriet's siblings and descendants. But it has become a standard myth of the American experience, and the genial statement is in keeping with what we know of Lincoln's homey personality.[1]

Not long after her meeting with Lincoln, Stowe wrote about the sitting president. Her portrait is flattering, and it reveals some of the matters upon which they might have agreed most strongly. But she also noted the marks of trial and endurance featured on the president's well-worn face. She characterized Lincoln in these words: "In times of our trouble Abraham Lincoln has had his turn of being the best abused man of our nation. Like Moses leading his Israel through the wilderness, he has seen the day when every man seemed ready to stone him, and yet, with simple, wiry, steady perseverance, he has held on, conscious of honest intentions, and looking to God for help. All the nation have felt, in the increasing solemnity of his proclamations and papers, how deep an education was being wrought in his mind by this simple faith in God, the ruler of nations, and this humble willingness to learn the awful lessons of his providence."[2]

Harriet knew from experience the nature of those "awful lessons," which she believed could yield the "peaceable fruits of righteousness," as Scripture assured her. Now, halfway through the nightmare of the war, Stowe recognized Lincoln as a fellow traveler along the pathway of cultural trauma mixed with parental grief (his son had died just a few months before their meeting): "we see evidence that in passing through this dreadful national crisis he has been forced by the very anguish of the struggle to look upward, where any rational creature must look for support. No man in this agony has suffered more and deeper, albeit with a dry, weary, patient pain, that seemed to some like insensibility. 'Whichever way it ends,' he said to the writer [i.e., to Stowe], 'I have the impression that *I* sha'n't last long after it's over.' After the dreadful repulse of Fredericksburg, his heavy eyes and worn and weary air told how our reverses wore upon him, and yet there was a never-failing fund, of patience at bottom that sometimes rose to the surface in some droll, quaint saying, or story, that forced a laugh even from himself."[3]

Lincoln's comments about not lasting long after the war, a comment Stowe recalled and recorded long before his death, are haunting. Lincoln had premonitions of his untimely demise, which he seems to have considered somehow prophetic and which he repeated to more than one listener. A few months before the war's conclusion, he told his friend Owen Lovejoy that he might die even before peace came: "This war is eating my life out; I have a strong impression that I shall not live to see the end."[4] Harriet's discernment of the president wrestling to make sense out of "the awful lessons of [God's] providence," published a full year before his elaboration of that toil in the second inaugural address of 1865, is impressive. And like her own memory of the struggles with the memories of her dead children, she noted the same sort of "anguish" about him, a weariness that his contemporary observers would note again and again of the martyred president.

It's fair to say that Stowe and Lincoln shared a bit more than most historians and critics have so far observed. Although they have rarely been described this way, Lincoln's most famous speeches have much in common with Stowe's great novels: mainly, as profound, therapeutic attempts to help parents deal constructively with the loss of their children, and as articulations of a redemptive hope through the suffering in this world. And upon investigation, it's humbling to note (as with Stowe) that Lincoln's fullest genius might have remained unrealized, hidden beyond the veil of public life, had it not been for the loss of his beloved son William Wallace Lincoln. Better known as Willie, he was the third of four sons, an intelligent, kindhearted, and artistically inclined boy who struck the elder Lincoln as the son most like himself, the favored prince of the household. The Reverend Phineas Gurley, close friend and pastor of the New York Avenue Presbyterian Church, where the Lincolns attended services, remembered that Willie was "always interested in the war and used to go down to the White House stables and read the battle news to the employees and talk over the outcome. These men all loved him and thought, for one of his years, he was most unusual."[5] Willie was the son most like his father, so it must be counted as even more tragic that Willie was the one who died upstairs in the White House. As William Herndon put it: "[Lincoln] worshiped his children and what they worshiped; he loved what they loved and hated what they hated."[6]

On February 20, 1862, around five in the evening and during the course of a long-winded and rather dreary dinner party hosted by his parents in the public rooms below, young Willie passed away at the age of eleven. Having contracted typhoid from the contaminated drinking water of the District of Columbia, Willie had come down with a raging fever. Phineas Gurley visited the death chamber during the course of the evening and later recalled this story about the dying boy: "When he was dying he said to me, 'Doctor Gurley, I have six one dollar gold pieces in my bank over there on the mantel. Please send them to the missionaries for me.' After his death those six one dollar pieces were shown to my Sunday school and the scholars were informed of Willie's request. He died in what was always called the 'Prince of Wales Room,' as the prince occupied it when visiting President Buchanan."[7]

The death of Willie was very hard on the Lincolns. Mary was convulsed with grief for years to come, and opinions about her recovery vary widely. As numerous intimates recorded, Mary's grief was "inconsolable." According to Elizabeth Keckley, Mary "was an altered woman . . . she never crossed the threshold of the Guest's Room in which [Willie] died, or the Green Room in which he was embalmed. There was something supernatural in her dread of these things, and something that she could not explain "[8] After the funeral, Mary wore black for a year and by almost all accounts never really recovered. Later, she was at the side of her husband when he was shot in the head, so the wildly critical attacks on Mary over the years should probably be tempered by the sheer horror of her traumatic White House years. Mary suffered all of these traumatic episodes after having lost her own mother at the early age of six and then, in 1850, losing her first son Eddie as well.

Still, as Michael Burlingame's recent biography shows, Mary was a deeply troubled wife, whatever the causes. She had a sharp tongue, was

Willie Lincoln (William Wallace Lincoln), third son of President Abraham Lincoln, shortly before his death. Died February 20, 1862, at the age of eleven. Photograph by Matthew Brady. Courtesy of the Library of Congress, Prints and Photographs Division.

involved in taking bribes and other forms of financial fraud, and probably suffered from extreme PMS. Orville Browning, a close family friend, recounted often hearing from the president stories of his constant domestic disagreements with Mary and his fears of public embarrassment because of her eccentricities. Lincoln even hinted that she was losing her mind; as Keckley recalled, he once "gently led her to the window. With a stately, solemn gesture, he pointed to the lunatic asylum. 'Mother, do you see that large white building on the hill yonder? Try and control your grief, or it will drive you mad, and we may have to send you there.'"[9] She attempted numerous séances within the White House during the year after Willie's death, one of which Lincoln might have attended. However, Lincoln was no spiritualist, just a grieving father desperately seeking connection with his dead son. As the Reverend Gurley reported, "After his son's death, Mr. Lincoln was greatly annoyed by the report that he was interested in spiritualism. He told me he thought the report originated from the fact that a medium had chanced to call on Mrs. Lincoln. 'A simple faith in God is good enough for me, and beyond that I don't concern myself very much,' he added."[10]

Most surprisingly, perhaps, Burlingame's claim that Mary was often physically abusive to her husband, even while they lived in the White House, is plausible. Dr. Robert K. Stone, the Lincoln family physician in Washington, denounced her as a "devil," while Benjamin Brown French called her a "hyena." Lincoln's secretaries and later biographers, John

Nicolay and John Hay, referred to her as "her Satanic majesty," and Hay likened her to a "Hellcat," then topped it by saying she was becoming "more hellcattical by the day."[11] Burlingame is generous enough to note that Mary is more to be pitied than to be castigated, as she clearly is in these very unkind contemporary remarks of people who knew her well. However, by all accounts, the Lincolns never enjoyed much of a blissful partnership. And the death of Willie made their lives together even more sad and woeful. All of which compounded the president's stressful worries.

As for father Abraham: he took Willie's death very hard as well, but of course he had an important job to do, and so was forced to trudge onward. Several witnesses described a despairing father who often shut himself into a room to sit, read the Bible, weep, and pray to a silent God. At night he often had dreams about his deceased son, happy dreams from which he would awaken to a joyless home without Willie. Clergymen came to assure him that Willie lived, a message that Lincoln tried to take to heart, with some minor success. The best eyewitness accounts paint a dire scene of the president reacting to Willie's passing, as here by Elizabeth Keckley: "Great sobs choked his utterance. He buried his head in his hands, and his tall frame was convulsed with emotion. I stood at the foot of the bed, my eyes full of tears, looking at the man in silent, awe-stricken wonder. His grief unnerved him, and made him a weak, passive child. I did not dream that his rugged nature could be so moved. I shall never forget those solemn moments—genius and greatness weeping over love's idol lost. There is a grandeur as well as a simplicity about the picture that will never fade. With me it is immortal—I really believe that I shall carry it with me across the dark, mysterious river of death."[12] Keckley, an intimate of the Lincolns and dressmaker for Mary, notes a certain "grandeur" in Lincoln's traumatic bereavements, and her account is filled with words bespeaking a sort of spiritual mystery and awe regarding the extent of the great leader's humble despair in the face of death. And after the bedroom scene, Lincoln famously walked down the hall to the office of his secretary, John Nicolay, who was tired and possibly dozing. Lincoln startled him with the abrupt news: "Well, Nicolay, my boy is gone—he is actually gone!"[13] Nicolay later remembered poignantly the sight of the president bursting into tears. As such, Nicolay's anecdote captures perfectly the posthumous memory of the stricken president, whose parental grief somehow exemplified the far greater loss of sons brought about by the great Civil War. Father Abraham wept for us all, it seemed to many firsthand witnesses in retrospect as they likened his misery to that of Jesus: "He saw the city, and wept over it" (Luke 19:41).

Long before Willie died, Lincoln had often been associated with melancholy and grief. These symptoms were then greatly compounded by the brutal events of 1862: Willie's death in February, along with the subsequent horrors of major battles including Shiloh (April), Antietam (September), and Fredericksburg (December). The battles of 1862 were unprecedented in terms of size and sheer violence, and they shocked the president as they did the Union at large. Lincoln's melancholy increased dramatically during this year of great loss, and evidence suggests that the trauma of Willie's death plunged him to new emotional depths. As a result, he was almost certainly afflicted by what we would call today a mood disorder (possibly clinical depression). He also may have suffered at various times, including the spring and summer of 1862, from post-traumatic stress disorder.[14]

Any thorough diagnosis of mental illness would certainly need to consider the two alleged "breakdowns" earlier in life—the first in 1835, then again in 1840–41—events that are largely accepted by today's historians as evidence of long-term psychological affliction. The debate regarding the reasons for these breakdowns continues, as does the extent to which Lincoln may have been, on at least one occasion, suicidal.[15] But Lincoln's deep melancholy and mournful appearance were a common feature of many firsthand accounts throughout his presidency, as in these comments by British writer Edward Dicey in 1862: "[I was struck by the] look of depression . . . I am told by those who see him daily, was habitual to him, even before the then recent death of his child, whose loss he felt acutely. You cannot look upon his worn, bilious, anxious countenance, and believe it to be that of a happy man."[16] And yet the writer Grace Greenwood could fondly recall that "my eyes have gazed full into those sad, prophetic eyes, whose tired lids were pressed down at last by the long-prayed-for Angel of Peace."[17] There seemed to be something angelic even in Lincoln's melancholy.

Perhaps counterintuitively, Lincoln's generative, "habitual" grief served many useful ends throughout his career: biographer Joshua Wolf Shenk goes so far as to provide an extensive account of the many "benefits" of Lincoln's melancholy, including the fostering of such attributes as resolve, perseverance, vision, and even an ultimate sense of purpose: the survival of the Union. In this regard, perhaps none of the benefits of Lincoln's sadness and grief were so majestically illustrated, as in the sentiments expressed at Gettysburg in November 1863, a speech that is saturated with grief and the invocation of the unending bonds with the dead. Lincoln's uncanny notion of continuing bonds with the dead is eerily reminiscent of Lincoln's figure of the "mystic chords of memory"; after 1862 he seemed to become almost obsessed with the ways the survivors must continue to be motivated by the better angels of the deceased. As he put it in the Gettysburg Address, "It is for us the living, rather, to be dedicated here to the unfinished work which they who fought here have thus far so nobly advanced."[18] Lincoln's calling for the presence of the dead heroes alludes to biblical passages such as the Letter to the Hebrews 12:1–3, where we are asked to be mindful of the fact that we are forever "surrounded by a cloud of witnesses." Thus the habitual sadness associated with Lincoln is another way of noting the continuing presence of the dead. This "cloud of witnesses" is a phenomenon that is not merely negative but also generative and highly motivating: as stated in Hebrews, these spirits remind us to "run the race with endurance," and to "throw off" whatever tries to hinder us (Hebrews 12:1)—including incapacitating grief. We must "not grow weary," and press ever onward—because we are surrounded by those departed.

The hope and consolation Lincoln derived from such biblical concepts were decisive in his struggle to adapt to the loss of Willie. In fact, hope and generativity permeate the greatest writings of Lincoln's final three years, during which he wrestled with his own doubts and spiritual crisis. The blatant horror of the wartime casualties foregrounded a primary cause of spiritual crisis: the problem of evil, the hell of war. To take one example: on December 13, 1862, thousands of Union troops were ordered to cross a temporary bridge over the Rappahannock River and into the town of Fredericksburg, Virginia, a move many observers considered a suicide mission. Disasters like the great battles at Antietam or Fredericksburg, undertaken in the name of God and country, caused Lincoln to question his deeply held convictions about the nature of the conflict. Both sides were motivated by the certainties of a deeply felt civil religion informing their causes; both sought the blessing of a benevolent God in their sacred effort. Or, as Abraham Lincoln stated simply and directly in his second inaugural: "Both [sides] read the same Bible and pray to the same God, and each invokes His aid against the other."[19] In so few words, Lincoln captured a crucial irony of the religious petitions of millions of Americans; in effect, these believers sought God's wrath to be poured out upon their adversaries. Much of Lincoln's greatness as a leader and visionary was his uncanny ability to speak solemnly about the nature of

God, the purposes of prayer, and the meaning of the Civil War. And yet it is a bit surprising that Lincoln's contributions as a theological thinker and writer have been so commonly overlooked. But those who lived through the crisis with him certainly understood him in religious terms. His status as a spiritual figure and ultimately as Christian martyr became iconic within weeks of his death and culminated decades later in the construction of the grandest "spiritual" shrine in our nation's history: the Lincoln Memorial.[20]

As bad as 1862 appeared, the worst was yet to come: mind-numbing butchery at Chancellorsville, Gettysburg, and Chickamauga in 1863, followed by Spotsylvania and the Wilderness in 1864. By the war's weary end, Christian prayers in support of either side had begun to resemble pagan acts of moral degeneracy, a resemblance that would be famously captured decades later by Mark Twain in the feud chapters of *Adventures of Huckleberry Finn* (1884) and, even later, in Twain's wickedly accurate satire "The War Prayer" (unpublished in his lifetime). As Edward Blum notes, Twain understood the "ghastliness" of such prayer; that "in their supplications for protection of their sons, [the congregants] were asking God for the deaths of others. The silent prayers approached God as a murderer and a nationalist."[21] The Civil War's spiritual foundations, including a clear-eyed moral certainty with both sides praying for the destruction of other Americans, became threadbare after four grueling years and thus contributed to an emerging national crisis of belief. Lincoln's greatness rests in large part in his successful search for a solution to this national crisis.

The war's ramifications for religion and belief have been overlooked ever since. Many contemporary Americans are embarrassed to admit their nation's sad record of violence in the name of religious fanaticism, an admission that seems decidedly antimodern, even anti-American. But the Civil War was very much a clash of religious worldviews; it was effectively a religious war deriving from a theological crisis.[22] Much recent historical work counters this omission by analyzing "how, in fundamental respects, religion stood at the center of the American Civil War experience."[23] At times, the religious fanatics of both sides have been charged by some historians with leading America into an unnecessary deadly conflict, brother against brother.[24] But besides the motivations of those who fought, another crucial outcome of this crisis was its impact on American theology, and much of that was a response to the lingering grief and trauma over the massive loss of sons and brothers, husbands and fathers, which spawned widespread doubt about God, providence, and the

American mission. The result was a spiritual crisis that violently shook the faith of many American evangelicals—a crisis that was mirrored in the memory of the nation's melancholy president immediately after his tragic death.

The debates about Lincoln's faith—or lack thereof—began early on in his political career, but they were jump-started with vigor at his death, and they continue right down to this day. Some writers wanted to emphasize Lincoln's doubts and irreligion. The chief figure in this regard was William Herndon, who obsessively worked for decades, insisting on an agnostic and freethinking Lincoln who abandoned orthodox Christianity early in life and never went back. Herndon was Lincoln's law partner beginning in 1844, and later he became one of the key biographers and collectors of Lincoln materials for the remainder of his life. Versions of Lincoln as a pious, Christian gentleman, as typified by Josiah G. Holland's characterization in the first major biography, *The Life of Abraham Lincoln* (1866), enraged Herndon, and he spent much of the remainder of his life angrily disputing them. Herndon's vast work set the terms for all further discussion of Lincoln's religious belief. He is best known today for the materials he gathered from friends, family members, and coworkers in the years after the president's death. Herndon's collaboration with Jesse Weik, known as *Herndon's Lincoln* and containing extensive primary materials, was published in 1889.[25] As stated in a plethora of essays regarding Lincoln's religious beliefs, Herndon seemed convinced that it was his duty and vocation to set the record straight: Holland's account, he sniffed, was "*romantic* . . . all mere bosh, a lie."[26] Herndon's depiction of Lincoln was copied and popularized by Robert G. Ingersoll, the man known as "America's infidel," who went even further than the controversial Herndon. Ingersoll described Lincoln as a liberator of intelligent men from the bondage of superstition: "Nothing is grander than to break chains from the bodies of men—nothing nobler than to destroy the phantoms of the soul."[27] In the eager hands of Ingersoll and Herndon, Lincoln was remembered (and caricatured) as a largely antireligious thinker, and was impressive mostly for his destruction of all hypocrisy, mystical cant, and superstition.[28]

But Herndon's view seems strangely deaf to the spiritual strains of Lincoln's best works—not to mention a huge amount of eyewitness testimony from reliable witnesses who knew the president well. (Ironically, some of the best witnesses produced their accounts for Herndon, and we would not even have these memories if it were not for Herndon.) And it is telling that depictions of an antireligious Lincoln by the likes of Herndon, Ingersoll, and others were widely scorned in their day. In the decades after the war, most Americans resented "heretical" claims that Lincoln was not an orthodox Christian, or worse, that Lincoln was a scoffer at religion. The scorn multiplied as the Lincoln myth of the profound, Job-like Christian prophet was simultaneously being etched deeper into stone. Herndon was attacked by Lincoln's intimate friends from the White House years, as in the following remarks of Noah Brooks in 1872: "Mr. Lincoln was at heart a Christian man, believed in the Savior, and was seriously considering the step which would formally connect him with the visible church on earth. Certainly, any suggestion as to Mr. Lincoln's skepticism or Infidelity, to me who knew him intimately from 1862 till the time of his death, is a monstrous fiction—a shocking perversion."[29] Other Lincoln intimates made similar claims: John T. Stuart wrote, "Mr. Lincoln had changed his opinion, and become a believer in the truth of the Christian religion," and Gurley said that "after the death of his son Willie and his visit to the battlefield of Gettysburg, he said, with tears in his eyes, that he had lost confidence in everything but God, and that he now believed his heart was changed, and that he loved the Saviour."[30] Perhaps the strongest rebuttal of Herndon's dismissal of Lincoln's faith came from the Reverend James Smith, a Presbyterian pastor in Springfield who knew the Lincolns intimately. Smith's famous account is among the more effusive: "while I was Pastor of the 1st Presbyterian Church of Springfield, Mr. Lincoln did avow his belief in the Divine Authority and Inspiration of the Scriptures . . . To use [Lincoln's] own language 'he examined the Arguments as a lawyer who is anxious to reach the truth investigates testimony.' The result was the announcement by himself that the argument in favor of the Divine Authority and inspiration of the Scripture was unanswerable."[31]

Taking this proreligious position to its most extreme, there are also a large number of even more radical accounts of Lincoln's faith and orthodoxy. In particular we might consider a story told by Colonel James Rusling, in which he recalled meeting Lincoln not long after Gettysburg. Rusling was surprised to hear Lincoln say he was not at all worried about the recent great battle at Gettysburg. The president explained his assurance (as remembered by Rusling):

> I went into my room one morning and locked the door, and got down on my knees, and prayed Almighty God for victory at Gettysburg. . . . I made a solemn vow with my Maker, that if He would stand by you boys at Gettysburg, I would stand by Him! I prayed,

> "Oh God, have mercy upon me and my afflicted people! Our burdens and sorrows are greater than we can bear! Come now and help us, or we must all likewise perish! And Thou canst not afford to have us perish! We are Thy chosen people, the last best hope of the human race!" And so I wrestled with Him, as Abraham or Moses in ancient days.

And after so 'wrestling' with God, sincerely and devoutly, in solemn prayer, for a considerable time, I don't know how it was and I can't explain it (I'm not a 'Meeting man,' you know), but some how or other a sweet comfort crept into my soul, that God Almighty had taken the whole business up there into His own hands, and things would come out all right at Gettysburg. And He did stand by you boys there, and now I will stand by Him!" Although historians have questioned this tale, it was corroborated on many occasions by Gen. Dan Sickles, the other person in the room during the episode and one of the key commanders at Gettysburg and elsewhere. Rusling famously told the story publicly on perhaps hundreds of occasions over many years, and also claimed that "I wrote home about it the same day, and now give it here as the very truth of history."[32]

Among the voluminous accounts of Lincoln's religion in the decades after his death, many were like Rusling's; sincere and even boastful, they present a view of the president ready to "witness" in a manner that seems influenced by the evangelical zeal of the observer. We may simply demur from such enthusiasms, of course; still, it is telling that the vast majority of the first generation memoirs and anecdotes depict a deeply religious president, and many of these were based on eyewitness testimony. For instance, Elizabeth Keckley recalled, "I discovered that Mr. Lincoln was reading that divine comforter, Job. He read with Christian eagerness, and the courage and hope that he derived from the inspired pages made him a new man. I almost imagined that I could hear the Lord speaking to him from out the whirlwind of battle: 'Gird up thy loins now like a man: I will demand of thee, and declare thou unto me.' What a sublime picture was this! A ruler of a mighty nation going to the pages of the Bible with simple Christian earnestness for comfort and courage, and finding both in the darkest hours of a nation's calamity. Ponder it, O ye scoffers at God's Holy Word, and then hang your heads for very shame!"[33] Keckley's view places Lincoln totally at odds with "scoffers" such as Herndon and Ingersoll: "A simple faith in God is good enough for me, and beyond that I don't concern myself very much," Lincoln told his pastor-friend the Reverend Gurley after Willie died.[34] Similarly, F. B. Carpenter stated, "I believe him to have been a sincere Christian. . . . I believe no man had a more abiding sense of his dependence upon God, or faith in the Divine government, and in the power and ultimate triumph of Truth and Right in the world."[35]

This question of the president's renewed quest for the things of God is not beside the point; rather, I argue that Lincoln became caught up in a sort of spiritual seeking as one clear outcome of his grief over his dead son Willie. Attaching this rebirth of interest in the things of God to the death of his son was a very common observation made about the president by his friends. The terms these respondents might use to describe this mood were often different, but the collective sense of Lincoln's genuine and growing religious sentiments among scores of eyewitnesses is the key point of agreement.[36] Often the most ingenious accounts of Lincoln's religion found creative ways to combine the feminine elements of his faith (the romantic and mystical "heart") with those considered more masculine (the pragmatic and scientific "head"). Harriet Beecher Stowe wrote of Lincoln, "We do not mean to give the impression that Lincoln is a religious man in the sense in which that term is popularly applied. We believe he has never made any such profession, but we see evidence that in passing through this dreadful national crisis he has been forced by the very anguish of the struggle to look upward, where any rational creature must look for support." All particular doctrines aside, Stowe celebrated "[Lincoln's] simple faith in God, the ruler of nations, and [his] humble willingness to learn the awful lessons of his providence."[37]

Like Stowe herself, Lincoln's belief tended toward the romantic, or as Mary Lincoln memorably put it, the president had "a Kind of Poetry in his Nature."[38] Mary's sentiments are echoed in James Russell Lowell's essay, where he found it difficult to state the precise nature of this aspect of the president's genius: "That penetrating fire ran in and roused those primary instincts that make their lair in the dens and caverns of the mind. What is called the great popular heart was awakened, that indefinable something which may be, according to circumstances, the highest reason or the most brutish unreason."[39] Whatever it was ("that indefinable something"), it tapped into the "great popular heart"—or, as Lincoln memorably described it, those "mystic chords of memory." Similarly, Phillips Brooks stated: "it is that glorified childlikeness, that high and reverend simplicity, which shames and baffles the most accomplished astuteness and is chosen by God to fill his purposes when he needs a ruler for his people, of faithful and true heart, such as he had who was our President."[40] Many other sentimental observers focused on

Lincoln's heart, especially the great sympathies they believed had been strengthened by the grief and trauma he faced. This strength was inward and somehow spiritually attained, they proposed, not merely an aspect of intelligence or mind.

Among modern historians, it has "become a commonplace to say that the religion of Abraham Lincoln will forever be a mystery," as two prominent historians have stated. And yet despite the fact that "important ambiguities remain," it's clear that "elements of Lincoln's faith are beyond doubt." A listing of these elements should include the fact that "the mature Lincoln believed in a personal, sovereign God."[41] This assertion by the historians Samuel Calhoun and Lucas Morel is now becoming a mainstream opinion for many Lincoln scholars, though it is certainly not yet a consensus. Calhoun and Morel are also correct to dismiss the common rejoinder that Lincoln was simply giving his political audience what they wanted to hear. This charge was often debunked by those who knew him best, such as by Noah Brooks in 1872: "There is no possible reason to suppose that Mr. Lincoln would ever deceive me as to his religious sentiments. . . . Certainly, any suggestion as to Mr. Lincoln's skepticism or infidelity, to me who knew him intimately from 1862 till the time of his death, is a monstrous fiction—a shocking perversion."[42] Indeed, the charge goes against our essential idea about "honest" Abe. And yet oddly, many historians have perpetrated this view, rather than taking Lincoln at his word.

My argument draws on and augments the convincing and thorough analysis of the biographical and critical materials by Calhoun and Morel. But I go beyond that analysis to suggest that Willie's death and the sustained shock of the war turned Lincoln back to the roots of the religion he learned on the frontier and at the deathbed of his beloved mother. Traumatic circumstances forced him to consider a more intimate and meaningful belief, as numerous friends and acquaintances testified. As a theologian has put it recently, "The phenomenon of trauma brings theology to a new ignorance, unsettling familiar categories and placing the discourse of theology in a more tenuous place."[43] If true, evidence of this "new ignorance, unsettling" the president should be expected both in his major writings after 1862 and in Lincoln's everyday behavior in the White House. And this is precisely what we do see: theistic belief informed his major writings in new and profounder ways, with particular attention to his developing understanding of Providence—and, as we can now discern, as influenced with his deep encounter with grief and trauma.[44] In fact, as Calhoun and Morel suggest, it is a belief in a personal

God, one whom Lincoln seems to be approaching more and more as a real presence, and with whom he tries to create a relationship of some significance. This God in which Lincoln believed after Willie's death was no longer "a mere abstract force," but was "divine agency, a being with an independent will and the power to implement it."[45]

As I will argue, this return to a personal vision of God was influenced to some large extent by the death of Willie; Lincoln's ultimate embrace of such a God was the outworking of his own encounters with the fires of parental grief. Clearly, much primary evidence has witnesses describing a significant change in Lincoln's faith after Willie's death. Often the change is associated with Lincoln's many meetings with clergymen. Gurley gives many examples of the president's obsession with life after death: "We have been talking of the state of the soul after death. That is a subject of which Mr. Lincoln never tires. I have had a great many conversations with him on the subject. This morning, however, I was a listener, as Mr. Lincoln did all the talking."[47] One visit from the Reverend Francis Vinton, just weeks after Willie's death, was crucial. Lincoln was deeply moved by Vinton's confidence that Willie was yet "alive, since God is not the God of the dead but the living" (Luke 20:38).[48] Vinton exhorted the saddened president: "Your son is alive, in Paradise." Lincoln asked for Vinton's sermon on the topic, and often read and reread it. "Mr. Lincoln's views in relation to spiritual things seemed changed from that hour."[49] His prayer life changed dramatically as well, according to numerous witnesses. Lincoln often walked alone to the prayer meetings held at the New York Avenue church. It became widely known that Lincoln often attended these meetings, so much so that other people came simply to have access to the president. This became a nuisance for the Reverend Gurley, and so he allowed Lincoln to enjoy the service from the privacy of his own office, which was nearby, with the door ajar. Later Lincoln told the Reverend Gurley that "he had received great comfort from the meetings."[50]

Lincoln spoke of his spiritual struggles with Willie's death to many listeners: he asked Salmon Chase, "Do you ever find yourself talking with the dead? I do. Ever since Willie's death I catch myself involuntarily talking to him as if he were with me—and I feel that he is!"[51] Lincoln was especially moved by the funeral sermon prepared by the Reverend Gurley, especially the final paragraph. The main theme of this section is the worship of God, which as we've seen was the prominent theme of Christian funerals for most of the century: "In His light shall we see light; by His grace our sorrows will be sanctified—they will be made a blessing to our souls—and by and by we shall have occasion to say, with blended gratitude and rejoicing, 'It is good for us that we have been afflicted.'"[52] Lincoln requested a copy of Gurley's sermon, read it over and over in the coming months, often with his wife Mary, and even sent further copies on to their grief-stricken friends.

One other powerful episode illustrates how Willie's death stayed with the president, and how it lingered in his imagination as well. Shakespeare's *King John*, featuring lengthy passages about the death of a son, became a particular favorite. Lincoln was known to have memorized certain sections of the play, or to read them aloud with great pathos. G. B. Cannon, chief of staff for Major General John Ellis Wool at Fort Monroe, Virginia, recalled a visit from the president during the war, at which time Licoln requested "either a Bible [or] a copy of Shakespeare." For much of the day the president sat alone in an office reading from the volume. The next day, the officer was invited into the room to listen to the president read: first from *Macbeth*, then *King Lear*. Finally Lincoln recited from *King John*, where Constance laments the death of her son:

> And, father Cardinal, I have heard you say
> That we shall see and know our friends in heaven.
> If that be true, I shall see my boy again; . . .
> Grief fills the room up of my absent child:
> Lies in his bed, walks up and down with me,
> Puts on his pretty looks, repeats his words,
> Remembers me of all his gracious parts,
> Stuffs out his vacant garments with his form.
> Then have I reason to be fond of grief? . . .
> Oh Lord! My boy, my Arthur, my fair son!
> My life, my joy, my food, my all the world!
> My widow-comfort, and my sorrows' cure![53]

After reading aloud from *King John*, according to Cannon, the president's "voice trembled and he was deeply moved. Laying the book on the table, he said: 'Did you ever dream of a lost friend and feel that you were having a direct communion with that friend, and yet a consciousness that it was not a reality?' . . . I dream of my dead boy, Willie, again and again.' The officer concludes with this response: "I shall never forget the sign nor the look of sorrow that accompanied his expression. He was utterly overcome; his great frame shook, and, bowing down on the table he wept as only such a man in the breaking down of great sorrow could weep. It is needless to say that I wept in sympathy, and quietly left the room that he might recover without restraint."[54]

Some critics have made the connection between Willie's death and the rapid change in Lincoln's faith, as I am doing, though in less pointed ways. Early on, the connection was much more carefully noted, suggesting that a more sentimental embrace of grieving and death was at work among the writers. Biographer Nathaniel Stephenson regarded Lincoln's encounter with grief over Willie's death to be a mystical experience: "Lincoln's final emergence was a deeper thing than merely the consolidation of a character. . . .Those elements of mysticism which were in him from the first, which had gleamed daily through such deep overshadowing, were at last established in their permanent form. . . . Out of this strange period of intolerable confusion, a gigantic figure had at last emerged."[55] In addition, the astute journalist Ida Tarbell concluded: "There is ample evidence that in this crushing grief the President sought earnestly to find what consolation the Christian religion might have for him. . . . From this time on he was seen often with a Bible in his hand, and he is known to have prayed frequently."[56]

But later writers have also made the connection, even in a more modern and perhaps secular environment. Lincoln quickly associated the death with the countless losses of other sons in the war; even Burlingame admits, Lincoln "reflected more intently on the ways of God after [his son] Willie's death" in 1862.[57] And as David Donald says, "he came to identify the loss of Willie with that of so many other young Americans . . . his private grief became the source for an even greater resolution to preserve the Union."[58] Donald does acknowledge that Lincoln as president more "frequently asked for God's aid" than he had before, and that following Willie's death "he increasingly turned to religion for solace." But Donald rejects the notion of a personal God: he "did not experience a religious conversion . . . nor did he abandon his fundamental fatalism." Calhoun and Morel's conclusions reject this odd dissonance; given Lincoln's own words and actions, it appears that he certainly did abandon an impersonal fatalism in favor of a more personal and dynamic view of God's Providence. These and other testimonies suggest how Lincoln's grief allowed the president to approach some version of a more personal God in the months and years after Willie died.

In short, it is now becoming a commonplace observation of Lincoln biographers to suggest that Lincoln's religious views did in fact change drastically in the period surrounding the death in the White House of his son Willie (February 1862) and later, the great battles of the Civil War throughout 1862–63. Today there is a growing scholarly consensus that Lincoln, in a manner similar to numerous other noteworthy Victorian intellectuals, underwent not a crisis of faith but the opposite: a "crisis of doubt" that led him back to his earlier convictions about Providence.[59] Although profound levels of grief and trauma plagued the president, especially after 1862, the struggle triggered a sort of spiritual reawakening for him. It led to a generative outcome similar to Stowe's, and was beneficial for America, as was hers. In Lincoln's case, a return to religious disciplines such as prayer and Bible reading (as illustrated in the accounts above by Keckley and Rusling), along with more regular conversations with clergymen such as the Reverend Gurley, marked this reawakening and triggered a return to a more personal view of God. Other intellectual trends can be identified in Lincoln's rapidly developing religious philosophy after Willie's demise: his growing reliance on fundamental biblical concepts and allusions in his later speeches, his refusal to equate America with the Kingdom of God, and his decided embrace of the continuing and everlasting bonds with the dead.[60] And there were long-lasting effects upon Lincoln's political theology, especially his growing reliance on a mysterious yet somehow ever-present Providence. This dependence, importantly, includes the "burden" of submissive discipleship, including a willful acceptance of decisive action on the part of the follower. As historian Stephen Webb explains: "Providence is a burden . . . [and] has provided a strong check against any superficial American triumphalism. Probably no American leader felt the burden of providence more strongly than Abraham Lincoln."[61] This burden was exacerbated by the devastating battles of 1862–63, but arguably most of all, the burden was heightened by the president's ongoing spiritual crisis over the loss of Willie.

Genuine faith in a personal and yet admittedly a largely unknowable Providence became increasingly a cornerstone of Lincoln's belief in the stressful middle years of the war, as the president wrestled with parental grief. One historian notes, "[Lincoln] said throughout his life that he believed in providence, that is, the ordination of all earthly events by a higher power, which he frequently called God . . . even though Lincoln always subscribed to the same technical definition of providence, the role that this concept played in his rhetoric underwent a gradual but dramatic change during his presidency." Earlier in his career, Lincoln's view of such matters was a much more freethinking type of theism. But the war came, and changed all that—intensified by the death of Willie: "His statements on religion took on a different cast. The notion of God that appeared in his language gravitated ever closer to that of Calvinism: an activist, independent, and judgmental God whose designs informed every single earthly event but whose purposes often seemed inscrutable to human eyes. Linked to this notion was a Calvinist-like view of humanity as utterly sinful, deserving of retribution, and entirely dependent on God in all aspects of life. Lincoln's deep commitment to republicanism never lost its motive power, but by the end of the war, his new Calvinist tendencies acquired strength equal to that of his never-changing democratic beliefs."[62] Considering the sheer mountain of material available, however, it's easy to forget that Lincoln's account of his spiritual crisis, composed in the privacy of his own solitude, is fascinating. His spare meditations provide much useful wisdom and at times are brilliant and revealing. In the second inaugural address, Lincoln composed one of the most theologically astute interpretations of the Civil War, before or since, as numerous historians have claimed. On the centennial of the Gettysburg Address in 1963, theologian Reinhold Niebuhr claimed that "Lincoln's religious convictions were superior in depth and purity to those, not only of the political leaders of his day, but of the religious leaders" as well.[63] Another prominent historian has more recently judged, "none of America's great religious leaders . . . mustered the theological power so economically expressed in Lincoln's second inaugural . . . [which was] a theological statement of rare insight."[64]

The second inaugural address is certainly a masterpiece. But in recovering Lincoln's experiences of the divine in solitude, one of the most remarkable extant texts is the "Meditation on the Divine Will" (1862) composed nearly two years earlier. Although it is little more than a scrap of paper, its direct relation to the stunning second inaugural—and its many parallels with that much more famous text, for which it is a sort of first draft—have helped it become one of the most highly regarded documents of Lincoln studies. John Hay, one of Lincoln's closest confidants, expressed well its value and its stunning admission of Lincoln's renewed faith: "Perplexed and afflicted beyond the power of human help, by the disasters of war, the wrangling of parties, and the inexorable and constraining logic of his own mind, he shut out the world one day, and tried to put into form his double sense of responsibility to human duty and Divine Power."[65] Hay correctly states the meditation's worth; he also rightly points out it was not written to be seen, meaning it reveals Lincoln's deepest beliefs. And so it is worthy of a full quotation here:

> The will of God prevails. In great contests each party claims to act in accordance with the will of God. Both may be, and one must be wrong. God can not be for, and against the same thing at the same time. In the present civil war it is quite possible that God's purpose

> is something different from the purpose of either party—and yet the human instrumentalities, working just as they do, are of the best adaptation to effect His purpose. I am almost ready to say this is probably true—that God wills this contest, and wills that it shall not end yet. By his mere quiet power, on the minds of the now contestants, He could have either saved or destroyed the Union without a human contest. Yet the contest began. And having begun He could give the final victory to either side any day. Yet the contest proceeds.[66]

According to the most authoritative accounts, the fragment was written "in September, 1862, while his mind was burdened with the weightiest question of his life. . . . It was not written to be seen of men."[67] While the precise dating remains a mystery, the fact is that those closest to the president associate it with the "weightiest question of his life," which certainly must refer to the question of emancipating the slaves of the Confederate south. This scrawled meditation probably came after the Second Battle of Bull Run, which plunged the president into one of the deepest depressions of the war—and which came only six months after the death of Willie. As such, scholar Roy Basler dates the brief contemplation around September 2, 1862.[68] If that dating is correct (or at least close), then the "Meditation on the Divine Will" was produced at a decisive moment of truth for Lincoln and for the nation. In it we detect the contours of the second inaugural address, today often considered Lincoln's greatest speech due to its fullness as a theological statement about the Civil War. Hay called the second inaugural "a new chapter of Hebrew prophecy" that has provided a telling account of the fragmentary meditation's composition and meaning: "Mr. Lincoln admits us into the most secret recesses of his soul. . . . It shows . . . the awful sincerity of a perfectly honest soul, trying to bring itself into closer communion with its Maker."[69] The "Meditation" certainly predated the massive Battle of Antietam, which commenced with the pursuit into Maryland of Gen. Lee's army by Gen. McClellan's forces in early September 1862. A decisive battle was obviously looming on the horizon, a battle that might become the crucial scene of success or failure for the war up until that moment. McClellan caught up with Lee's army on September 17, and the victory there (with unprecedented casualties) led directly to Lincoln's call for emancipation, a decision that needed to be made at a time of evident military superiority, as various historians have pointed out.[70]

But Antietam was more than a pragmatic political opportunity. Lincoln evidently considered the victory over Lee at Antietam to be a direct answer to what evangelical believers sometimes call a "fleece." The concept of "putting out a fleece" or "making a fleece" before the Lord takes its name from the book of Judges chapter 6. In a time of invasion by the Midianites, Gideon wished to know God's will more specifically before fully committing himself and his troops. And so Gideon laid a woolen fleece upon the ground and asked that God have it become heavy with dew the first morning, but remain dry the second morning. Gideon believed that the lack of dew would provide a clear sign of victory (see Judges 6:36–40). Gideon said to God, "if thou wilt save Israel by mine hand, as thou hast said, Behold, I will put a fleece of wool in the floor; if the dew be on the fleece only, and dry upon all the earth, then shall I know that thou wilt save Israel by mine hand, as thou hast said" (vv. 36–37, KJV). Thus the putting out of a fleece suggests Lincoln's more personal approach toward God: it was one way of testing God's specific intentions, through faith. When a person of faith puts a "fleece" before the Lord, it signifies that they are asking for a direct answer, in this case, a miraculous sign of His Providence in the Union's favor as instrument of God.

It appears that Lincoln pursued a Gideon-like search for providential direction at almost precisely the moment he inscribed his fragmentary vision of God's Will in September 1862. As biographer John Stauffer puts it, for Lincoln, God was "inscrutable rather than indwelling. The most one could hope for on earth was to discover signs of God's presence and to establish a covenant (or sacred agreement) with Him. . . . God would reciprocate this trust by guiding the faithful toward righteousness"[71] Another scholar, Stewart Winger, notes the president's admission of being "superstitious": Lincoln believed in the significance of dreams and premonitions, a fascination that also later became a regular feature of the Lincoln legend, bolstered by his premonitions of his own untimely demise, which he seems to have considered somehow prophetic. For instance, a few month's before the war's conclusion, he told his friend Owen Lovejoy that he might die even before peace came: "This war is eating my life out; I have a strong impression that I shall not live to see the end." He made a similar prediction to Harriet Beecher Stowe: "Whichever way it [the war] ends, I have the impression that I sha'n't last long after it's over." And long before the war ended, he told another friend, "I may not live to see it. I feel a presentiment that I shall not outlast the rebellion. When it is over, my work will be done."[72]

The most interesting evidence that Lincoln viewed Antietam's outcome as a decisive, mystical moment of God providing a sign of His Will comes from the diary of Gideon Welles, then secretary of the navy, after a cabinet meeting on September 22 at which the battle was discussed in some detail. Welles convincingly recalls there that Lincoln defined the great battle of Antietam in religious terminology: "[Lincoln] remarked that he had made a vow, a covenant, that if God gave us the victory in the approaching battle, he would consider it an indication of Divine will, and that it was his duty to move forward in the cause of emancipation. It might be thought strange, he said, that he had in this way submitted the disposal of matters when the way was not clear to his mind what he should do. God had decided this question in favor of the slaves. He was satisfied it was right, was confirmed and strengthened in his action by the vow and the results"[73] Welles's memory is essentially confirmed by at least one other key player: Salmon Chase, who also attended the meeting, and later wrote it down and then told the story to F. B. Carpenter, who became an intimate of both Chase and Lincoln at this time. In his diary, Chase wrote his account of Lincoln's wording at the meeting: "When the rebel army was at Frederick, I determined, as soon as it should be driven out of Maryland, to issue a Proclamation of Emancipation such as I thought most likely to be useful. I said nothing to anyone; but I made a promise to myself, and (hesitating a little)—to my Maker." And in his account given to Carpenter, Chase recalled that Lincoln had told him: "I made a solemn vow before God, that if General Lee was driven back from Pennsylvania, I would crown the result by the declaration of freedom to the slaves."[74]

Chase's version focuses on Lincoln's promise to his Maker, a "solemn vow before God," and so although Welles and Chase never mention the exact term of a fleece, the gist of the challenge is well described: a covenantal agreement made through a vow, the strangeness of such a method, the submission of a weighty matter to God's answer through a specific sign, and most crucially a deep yearning for the clear indication of God's will. Welles even admits that some might think it "strange" that the president would "submit" such weighty matters "in this way"—meaning, as a fleece. There is even the added irony that a man named Gideon recorded the incident—reminiscent of the Hebrew judge and military leader. As Allen Guelzo has remarked, it reveals the striking nature of the president's changing religious sensibility: Lincoln offered "as his reason for the most radical gesture in American history a private vow fulfilled in blood and smoke by the hand of God."[75] Finally, the seemingly providential elements of the battle itself (before which Union soldiers discovered Gen.

Lee's battle plans, which had been wrapped tidily around some cigars and then carelessly dropped in a field) punctuated the seemingly miraculous nature of the events at Antietam.[76] Guelzo argues that it is rather astonishing to consider the possibility that the president committed America to full emancipation "on the strength of a sign he had asked from God, as though it were the Emperor Constantine or Oliver Cromwell rather than Abraham Lincoln sitting at the head of the cabinet table."[77] Or, as he even more pointedly says, "like Gideon of old."[78] William Barton correctly concluded: this episode "settles forever the essentially religious character of Abraham Lincoln."[79]

Coupled with Lincoln's reliance on Providence was a growing sense of humility toward this Providence—another common response for many bereaved parents. While most commentators in the north spoke confidently about the ways of God during and after the war, Lincoln injected a strong note of modern uncertainty into his speeches and letters. In effect, Lincoln presented what some readers today might understand to be a new sort of American modesty toward this great and awesome God. In fact, Lincoln's humility was not so new at all: contrition before God's sovereignty and our ignorance before Him was very much a hallmark of Calvinism. For Lincoln, this mysterious God was very difficult for mankind to comprehend fully.[80] One critic has gone so far as to characterize the second inaugural as primarily "a call to humility."[81] As such, Lincoln's analysis anticipated major shifts in American thinking after the war. He articulated what some observers have described as a progressively modern view of the providence of God as mysterious and obscure, best illustrated by the irony of his final, and possibly greatest, speech: the second inaugural.[82] But again, Lincoln's embrace of a mystical Providence is more traditional and even old-fashioned, when compared with the romantic leanings of the period, than it is progressive. Moreover, as the fleece episode illustrates, He was still a personal God, interested in the lives and prayers of His individual children, and actively engaged in those lives—ideas more in tune with an earlier generation. And so, throughout the second inaugural, Lincoln emphasized to his listeners his firm belief that the will of God is not easily discerned, and it is often affected by contingencies and human stupidity. Certainly, the episodes surrounding Antietam indicate a profound, heartfelt desire to know for certain God's providential plan. And yet his head told him otherwise, that God was inscrutable to human understanding. As one historian has well stated, "This combination of convictions—confidence in Providence along with humble agnosticism about its purposes—transformed the central section of the second inaugural into a theological statement of rare insight," an insight that pushed Lincoln "into post-Protestant, even post-Christian theism."[83]

In many ways, key elements of the second inaugural echo sentiments from the "Meditation on the Divine Will" from just before Antietam, a moment of crisis for the president that ultimately shaped what many are now calling "Lincoln's Greatest Speech."[84] The "Meditation" of 1862 is very much a seed of the second inaugural, and humility toward this personal yet mysterious God is the key factor in both. In the second inaugural, Lincoln states the primary irony of his crisis: "Both read the same Bible, and pray to the same God; and each invokes His aid against the other. It may seem strange that any men should dare to ask a just God's assistance in wringing their bread from the sweat of other men's faces; but let us judge not that we be not judged. The prayers of both could not be answered; that of neither has been answered fully. The Almighty has His own purposes."[85] In the "Meditation" one and a half years earlier, he had written, "In great contests each party claims to act in accordance with the will of God. Both may be, and one must be wrong. God can not be for, and against the same thing at the same time." Each statement focuses on the similarities of both sides, and the certainty that both feel about interpreting God's will. The "Meditation" states, "Yet the contest began." The second inaugural states: "And the war came." The "Meditation" claims, "God wills this contest, and wills that it shall not end yet"; the second inaugural claims: "He gives to both North and South, this terrible war. . . . God wills that it continue, until all the wealth piled by the bond-man's two hundred and fifty years of unrequited toil shall be sunk." The "Meditation" began with a simple line: "The will of God prevails." Similarly, the second inaugural repeats several times Lincoln's appeal to God's will: "The Almighty has His own purposes," he claims, and later directs our attention to those purposes, but with some disclaimers ("as God gives us to see the right"). Lincoln expands this crucial concept through his uses of Scripture, which all emphasize a humble and teachable deference to the all-encompassing will of God, including Psalm 19:9: "the judgments of the Lord, are true and righteous altogether." As such, the "Meditation on the Divine Will" was essentially a first draft of the major theological concepts underlying Lincoln's final, great speech.

When James Russell Lowell noted in 1864, "in our opinion, there is no more unsafe politician than a conscientiously rigid *doctrinaire*. . . . Mr. Lincoln's perilous task has been a rather shaky raft through the rapids, making fast the unrulier logs as he could snatch opportunity," he was reminding his readers of Lincoln's frontier experience on a flatboat.[86] In retrospect, Lowell's figure might remind today's readers of the abused fourteen-year-old orphan Huck Finn with the runaway slave Jim, caught up in a monstrous river that was quite literally a geographical border, set directly between north and south, freedom and slavery, or metaphorically set between doubt and certainty, head and heart. Lincoln perceptively evinced a sort of protomodern religion that navigated expertly the fashionable intellectual ways of the freethinkers as well as the conservative old-school theologians, taking the best from both heritages. He seemed to understand intuitively that "the Civil War proved to be the climax, but also the exhaustion, of the synthesis of common sense, republicanism, and evangelical Christianity" in America. Lincoln recognized that a new path for belief would need to be forged into the modernizing world: a path more humble and circumspect, and less certain that we are always "on God's side."

Similarly, our memorial to Lincoln on the mall in Washington signals "the climax, but also the exhaustion" of our national *embrace* of a providential past. As Lincoln was one of the first to realize, America's talk of its providential past has been steeped in an arrogant certainty. It is Lincoln's profound questioning of that certainty that many visitors to the memorial fail to recognize. Instead, Lincoln offers us a humble view of a mysterious God, a view that had been deeply formed by the tragedies of the war and of the loss of his beloved son. He spoke with humility that came out of the deepest despair a father can ever experience. And he coupled his reliance on God with a powerful affection for the bonds with the dead, those "clouds of witnesses" that he saw hovering around him on all sides. His memorial also signifies the profound vision of continuing bonds that characterized his generation.

The Lincoln Memorial is almost undoubtedly the greatest monument ever built in honor of any single American, and will probably never be surpassed in that regard. There, Lincoln sits underneath the inscription, "In this temple, as in the hearts of the people for whom he saved the Union, the memory of Abraham Lincoln is enshrined forever."[87] Given this concrete expression of our understanding of his metaphysical legacy, "enshrined forever" in the unsurpassed "temple" of American civil religion, it is ironic that Lincoln was also a key prophet of the demise of the old-fashioned arrogance of American civil religion that the memorial represents. And yet it is that prideful certainty that Lincoln's greatest speech evaluates, and ultimately rejects. In fact, his was one of the very few clarion voices who recognized how the war had called into question

America's brazen confidence in a "clear-eyed moral certainty about God and His will."[88] We should be "firm in the right," says Lincoln in the second inaugural. But then he slyly reminds us: "as God gives us to see the right." Certainty leads to violence, he came to see.

And so the grand memorial should symbolize the hard-earned humility of our great, grief-stricken president as well. One might be struck by the way that Lincoln's untimely death seemed to punctuate his symbolic transformation, which led to the erecting of such a sublime monument. Abraham Lincoln and his most cherished words have now become forever the direct link between the religious and the political realms of the Union. His life, and perhaps most importantly his death, sealed his fate in public memory as the absolute embodiment of America's mythic ideals about itself. In many ways, Lincoln symbolizes more than any American the continuing bonds with the dead: what he called those "mystic chords of memory."

It is impressive and humbling to recall that Lincoln's greatest accomplishments as a politician and orator emerged from the shadows of parental grief. Those shadows included not just the "honored dead" whose graves Lincoln memorialized at Gettysburg. They included, most of all, the bonds with the spirit of his beloved son Willie. And so the residual power of Lincoln's sacred memory, based on his greatest achievements as a statesman, deserves to be forever linked to the tragic death in 1862, in the middle of a great war, of his eleven-year-old son from contaminated water. Although Willie is nowhere named at the memorial, his memory hovered over his slain father during the darkest moments of his presidency.

3

Howells's Grief

Winny and the Fur-Lined Overcoat

Young W. D. Howells, a largely unknown yet promising writer from Ohio, managed to secure an important Lincoln connection that changed his life, though it is mostly forgotten today. Follett and Fowler, the publisher of his first thin volume called *Poems of Two Friends* (1859), contacted Howells in 1860 to request that he prepare as quickly as possible a campaign biography for the presumed Republican Party nominee for president, Abraham Lincoln. Titled *Lives and Speeches of Abraham Lincoln,* Howells dashed through the composition process and somehow had a manuscript within a week. It was published in May 1860, and excerpts from it suggest similarities between the frontier youths of Lincoln and his biographer Howells. These similarities made Howells an excellent observer of Lincoln's voracious appetite for both everyday hard work and the enchantments of the printed page:

> At New Salem, [Lincoln] now found the leisure and the opportunity to initiate a system of self-education. At last, he had struggled to a point, where he could not only take [a] breath, but could stoop and drink form those springs of knowledge, which a hopeless poverty, incessant toil, and his roving, uncertain life, had, till then, forbidden to his lips.
>
> There seems never to have been any doubt of his ability among Lincoln's acquaintances, any more than there was doubt of his honesty, his generosity, and gentle-heartedness. When, therefore, he began to make rapid progress in his intellectual pursuits, it surprised none of them— . . . This young backwoodsman had the stubborn notion that because the Lincolns had always been people of excel-

> lent sense, he, a Lincoln, might become a person of distinction. He had talked, he said, with men who were regarded as great, and he did not see where they differed so much from others. He reasoned, probably, that the secret of their success lay in the fact of original capacity, and untiring industry.[1]

What Howells wrote about the candidate Lincoln could just as easily have been said about the author himself. Howells, who between 1860 and 1921 published thirty-six novels, twelve books of travel, ten volumes of short stories and sketches, and many other collections of literary criticism, poetry, and drama, even as he edited the most important literary journals of his day, proved to be as untiring as the martyr president. After his election in November and his inauguration in March 1861, Lincoln rewarded Howells for his campaign contribution by naming him US consul in Venice, Italy. The man who would much later reign supreme as America's "dean" of letters, first as editor of *The Atlantic* and then as contributing editor at *Harper's*, had agreed to do some quick political hack work in hopes of receiving favor from a new administration, and the trick paid off (although he originally wished to go to Germany).

Besides the romantic new overseas posting for the young man from Ohio, another romance was on the horizon. By the time of his sailing for Italy in 1861, love was already beginning to bloom in Howells's heart. He had met Elinor Mead just a few months earlier, and once abroad his love for her grew deeper. "She's not violently intellectual, by any means. She has artistic genius, and a great deal of taste, and she admires my poetry immensely. I think she's good looking, and rather suppose she was picked out for me from the beginning of the world. . . . I love her very much, which may remotely account for my intending to marry her," he wrote his father in May of 1862.[2] They were married in Paris on Christmas Eve 1862, and just a few months later conceived their first child in Venice. Named Winifred, she was born on December 17, 1862, almost exactly one year after their wedding, and in one of the most enchanting cities of the world. As such, being the firstborn love child of a true romance, and being raised on the banks of the Grand Canal in Europe's most exotic locale, Winifred became for her famous father an emblem of those enchanting days of Italy, the tangible evidence of that youthful romance, an enduring embodiment of Venetian enchantment. He believed "that the city of her birth characterized her with sensibility to all that was beautiful; and what is true is that she began as a child, a very little child, to utter this sensibility in verse."[3] This Italian mystique remained a preoccupation of Howells's prolific writing for decades to come: he wrote at least five volumes on Italy alone.[4]

Winifred, called within the family "Winny" (or sometimes spelled "Winnie"), was a precocious and bright young girl who early on desired to become a writer, like her increasingly famous father. In this regard they had a special relationship, and Howells encouraged her in her authorial pursuits. She also had some talent, as is evidenced in the many poems she wrote over the years, including several published in a variety of venues. She was raised "in the love and nurture of poetry. . . . She had exquisite ideals."[5] Her poems tended toward the darkly romantic, including a fascination with doubt and suffering mixed in with a strong veneration for the innocence and playfulness of childhood. A number of her poems were published in her lifetime, some at an early age and a few in prestigious magazines, marking her as a bit of a poetic prodigy. Later, famous poets anthologized some of Winifred's best, as in Edmund Clarence Stedman's *American Anthology*. Howells remembered his daughter as characterized by a tragic, mystical Romanticism: "her life was deeply interior; it sank more and more beyond our site; and it is only the records of it which teaches how intensely poetical it was."[6] His younger daughter Mildred also desired to become a writer, but Howells would always measure her accomplishments against the high standard Winifred set, which he esteemed much more.

Winny's best poems display a personality of childlike joyfulness mixed with what seems like a prescient doom, as in the poem titled "Past," which appeared in *Century Magazine* in 1886:

> And looking up, she saw upon the shelf
>   In dusty rank her favorite poets stand,
>   All uncaressed by her fond eye or hand;
>   And her heart smote her, thinking how herself
> Had loved them once and found in them all good
>   As well as beauty, filling every need;
>   But now they could not fill the emptiness
> Of heart she felt ev'n in her gayest mood.[7]

Winifred's quickly shifting moods are often depicted in her poems' personae: sometimes a buoyant joy comes suddenly but disappears just as rapidly, as in "A Mood":

Winifred Howells, daughter of W. D. Howells, as a child (left) and in her early twenties (below, died 1889). Courtesy of the Howells/Frechette Collection at Alfred University; used with permission of the William Dean Howells family.

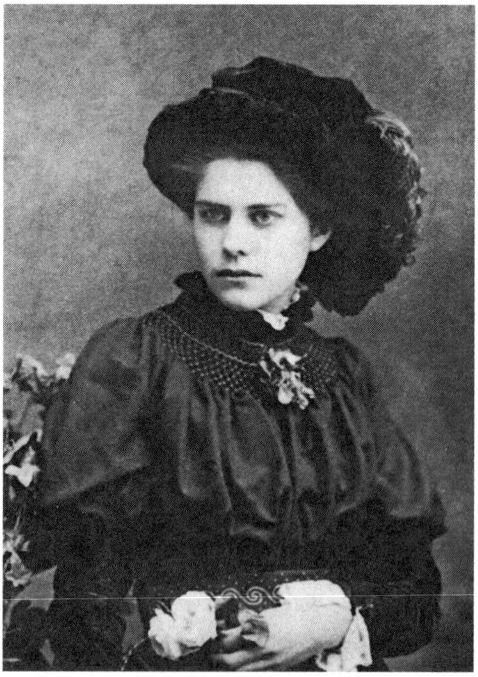

THE WIND exultant swept
Through the new leaves overhead,
Till at once my pulses leapt
With a life I thought long dead,
And I woke, as one who has slept,
To my childhood,—that had not fled,
On the wind my spirit flew;
Its freedom was mine as well.
For a moment the world was new;
What came there to break the spell?
The wind still freshly blew;
My spirit it was that fell.[8]

Although we need not interpret these poems as merely autobiographical, it's difficult to read them and not discern a strong element of self-doubt and blame, if not even self-loathing, that must have rung true for the poet herself.

Perhaps the most telling of her poems is titled "A Wasted Sympathy," in which the young narrator describes a fatalistic futility for any attempts to help her, or to provide sympathy. As John Crowley perceptively notes, it is the only poem in which Winny spoke of herself as a woman, and not as a child. "A Wasted Sympathy" features a "leaden heart" that might remind some readers of certain images Emily Dickinson produced in some of her strongest work on grief. The ending of "A Wasted Sympathy" might seem to be the final declaration of a person who has given up and lost the will to go forward:

DO not waste your pity, friend,
When you see me weep as now;
Keep it to some better end.
When dry-eyed I went about
With a leaden heart locked in
By a silent tongue, ah! Then
Had you brought it, it had been
Sweet indeed to me; but now
When the depths of my despair
Are upheaved and through the portals
Of my heart come free as air,
It is useless.[9]

These poems document a level of psychological horror that cannot be appeased. Winny's descriptions resemble symptoms of the depression and self-doubt that Howells also suffered from as a young person. By the time this poem was composed, Winny had already lived a troubled life, including severe illness that would make her a confirmed invalid for the last several years of her life. At the age of twenty-one, in the fall of 1885, she suffered a relapse of what was called nervous prostration. At that time, her parents began searching for a proper way to treat her condition. Howells wrote in one letter that he and Elinor were now constantly "wandering about in the health search."[10] Finally, in the summer of 1887, they confined Winny to an expensive and elaborate sanatorium in Danville, New York, in order to receive treatment from Dr. S. Weir Mitchell, the famous inventor of the rest cure. Howells and his wife lived in nearby Buffalo. For a while it seemed that Winny would recover. She began to gain weight and to take regular exercise. Her countenance was lifted, and she even began writing again. Dr. Mitchell reported early in 1889 that Winifred was in a very improved condition physically. However, he also mentioned that she "still continues rebellious and won't admit that she's at all better, though she has gained fifteen pounds, and is able to do anything she likes."[11]

The eccentric Dr. Mitchell was a commanding figure whose charisma was nearly irresistible in this period: his biographer notes, "he was impossible to ignore. With perfect assurance, it was his way to size up and immediately take command of a situation."[12] He was also, however, profoundly wrong in his assessment of Winny's physical condition: in just weeks she would be dead. In his elegiac memoir of Winny, written in the year after her death, Howells's emotions found full release: he confessed that he had made many errors concerning his daughter, and that remembering those mistakes brought a burning bitterness that he doubted would ever be healed.[13] Howells felt his gifted daughter possessed a powerful poetic sensibility, but one marked by a debilitating disorder that remained beyond her control, as illustrated in her verse: "My spirit it was that fell"; as the narrator says in "Past," her favorite books are powerless to "fill the emptiness / Of heart," which is present "ev'n in her gayest moods." For the Howellses, and for years after Winny expired, no solace seemed possible: "We were denied the sad consolation of bidding her good bye. She had been dead five hours when we heard, and while we still thought her on the way to recovery. It is hard to bear."[14] Henry James wrote to his bereaved friend with these consoling words: "[Winny's sufferings] were untalkable—& I know they were for you a perpetual fountain of pain. When a man loses a loved child everything that is most tender in him must be infinitely lacerated."[15] Four years later Howells was still feeling tortured by guilt and despair, as Mark Twain suggests in writing to a mutual acquaintance: "Oh, I know! I know! But there is no help; nothing will ever cheer Howells up again; his heart is buried in Winnie's grave."[16] Howells even invoked the anguish of his experience, a favorite word of the antebellum sentimentalists, including Harriet Beecher Stowe: "It is anguish, anguish that rends the heart and brain; but you can understand how inevitable it is. It must go on, I suppose, till the futile impulse wears itself out."[17] Six years later he still felt it: in a May 1895 letter to another family member he writes, "I went out to Cambridge . . . but it was terribly painful to me, with all the ghostly past rising up at every step. . . . Of course I went to the cemetery, but I could not realize Winny there, while in a hundred other places, she was still a little girl, holding my hand. I drove up by our house on Concord Avenue, and it was anguish everywhere. I believe I could be happier in Jefferson, where I should have nothing of my ambitious past to torment me, or where it would be so old, that I could forgive it."[18]

Among the writings after her death, perhaps the most telling and the most poignant regarding Howells's view of his daughter, and the role she played in his life going forward, are those recorded in *Winifred Howells*, which Howells published privately one year afterward. In fact, as Mark Twain would later memorialize his own daughter Susy on the anniversary of her death, Howells remembered Winny a year later as an enlightened, near–mystical prophetess, one with an unusual insight into the sad and unjust aspects of life. It was almost as if Winnie (and Susy, in Twain's mind) had attained an uncanny ability to see into the depths of horror in the emerging American scene. Howells writes in the memoir: "it puzzled, it hurt, it stupefied her to find what men and women were; and a strain of a maze, which of course took literary excess in her poetry, appears again and again in her work. . . . Life did pain and bewilder her. She often spoke to me of its anomalies, —such as the cruelty and hardness of certain girls who were beautiful, and who wounded her expectation by their vulgarity of heart." The ending of his memoir rises to even greater heights when she is described in the celestial terms that were a common feature of the Victorian sensibility: "she was, if I may so express it, an unconscious conscience; every impulse in her was wise and good; she seemed no more to think or to feel evil than to do evil. . . . She could not comprehend unkindness, it puzzled and dismayed her. She had an angelic dignity that never failed her in any squalor of sickness; she was on the earth, but she went through the world aloof in spirit, with a kind of surprise. She was of so divine a truthfulness that in her presence I felt the shame of insincerity as in no other."[19]

In these descriptions we should perceive similarities with aspects of Howells's emerging theory of realism. His account of his dead daughter's prophetic gift also prescribes a way of looking at the urban landscape of the late nineteenth century. This description of his daughter suggests a growing awareness of trouble brewing in America, one filling the observer with puzzlement and dismay. And a solution is offered: an appeal to the "unconscious conscience," and the conviction developed directly from her presence, where Howells "felt the shame of insincerity as in no other." And in these comments we should perceive Howells's recognition of the potential power of his continuing bonds with Winny.

Howells would need all the help he could get. At the same time that Howells and his wife were struggling through the endgame and ultimately the demise of their talented daughter, America was facing steep decline. In October 1888, just months before Winny would perish, Howells had written a letter to his friend Henry James, saying that he was "not in a very good humor with America, which now seemed the most grotesquely illogical thing under the sun. After 50 years of optimistic content with civilization and its ability to come out all right in the end, I now abhor it, and feel that it is coming out all wrong in the end, unless it bases itself a new on a real equality. Meantime I wear a fur-lined overcoat, and live in all the luxury my money can buy."[20] Furs, a prominent commodity associated with the exploitation of the American West, were also strongly associated with another New York resident, the robber baron John Jacob Astor. One historian speaking in 1916 went so far as to claim, "the history of American expansion might almost be written in terms of the fur trade. . . .The fur trader has blazed the way across the continent." And as Eric Jay Dolin has recently stated, "the fur trade determined the course of empire. It spurred the colonization of eastern North America."[21]

Howells's small aside resonates by signifying another darkened chapter of American wealth and power. The letter mentioning his "fur-lined overcoat" has often been regarded as a confession of sorts; it seems symbolic of a turning point in the career of the man considered at the time America's most influential literary voice. Often overlooked in reading this somewhat comical remark, however, is how Howells's souring mood on American expansion and empire was being exacerbated by the decline of Winny. As time went on, he connected the death of a child with

American decline even more explicitly, as in one of his most famous stories: "Editha," produced during a period of intellectual engagement on the topic of empire that he undertook with another grieving friend, Mark Twain. The story of their "anti-imperialist friendship" as connected to the memory of their daughters will be told in the next chapter.

In the eyes of Howells, as his daughter descended into madness and death, so did America. One result of his terrifying experience was the commencement in earnest of a spiritual quest that marked the rest of his career as a writer and as the editor of many of America's great younger writers. It is not uncommon to detect a striking corroboration between the decline of his daughter and the growth of his political consciousness and the erosion of his confidence in America. Just as Howells was growing tired of America's failed promise, his daughter Winifred was in the final months of an excruciating existence. His wife Elinor had also sunk into a long-term chronic mental illness beginning around March of 1888, putting Howells into the role of caregiver for the balance of his earthly life. Despite Elinor's afflictions, she and Howells together searched to discover a means of saving their daughter. During this same period of trial, while Howells was busy inventing American literary realism, he was simultaneously undergoing these drastic changes in his family life. And yet rarely has a sustained connection been made between these two concurrent processes.

Thus we should reconsider how the illness of Winny and then her death on March 2, 1889, followed by the obsessive grief experiences of her forlorn parents in the years thereafter, influenced the shape of Howells's career—and the shape of American literature going forward. The invocation of the "fur-lined overcoat" in his letter to James speaks to Howells's growing awareness of his own bourgeois tastes, his own growing sense of cognitive dissonance between a Christian socialism and the ease and wealth of America's increasingly genteel society. But the death of Winny took whatever transformation had begun to another level, and it commenced a searching reexamination of the implications of death and dying on our moral lives as Americans by the famous, now forlorn father of American realism. Later he wrote to Twain in response to a token he had received in remembrance of his good friend's late daughter: "Two days ago came the beautiful picture of your Susy with her heavenly face and her eyes of Angel innocence. They affect me as the eyes of Winny sometimes did: with the error and the wrong that every man's life seems to include. I am afraid to look in them, and think of what I am."[22] The memory of Winny's eyes haunted Howells for the remainder of his life—

and also inspired him to a greater moral urgency and spiritual awakening than he had previously felt.

This chapter will attend to these phenomena with more focus and detail than previous critical appraisals have, suggesting that Winny's death radically changed Howells. I argue that Winny's decline and death did not sever their relationship, but rather fostered in Howells a powerful need to maintain the bonds with his dead child. Howells's grief commenced a yearning to be changed dramatically by the grief experience and the continuing bonds, even as his more rationalistic response mitigated this impulse. A divided, despairing dialogue between the doubting self and the hopeful believer is notable in many of the fictions he wrote in the years after Winny died. This search for resolution is especially important in his greatest novel, *A Hazard of New Fortunes* (1890), much of which was composed as Winny was dying. But perhaps the division and the struggle are captured most poignantly in what Howells considered his best volume of poems, *Stops of Various Quills* (1895), a surprisingly powerful and underrated achievement that deserves much wider appeal than it has gained over the years. As depicted in *Stops of Various Quills*, Howells's multifarious responses typify the Victorian age's divided and ambivalent responses to an earlier, romantic appeal to the bonds with the dead and Christian consolation. With Howells's work after 1889, we witness a strong move away from a sentimental grieving of an earlier period and toward a more naturalistic, modern attitude toward death. But he could never shake the convictions of that earlier age.

A consideration of Howells's quest for peace represents some of the shifts in patterns of grief in American culture after the Civil War. Howells goes beyond Lincoln's fatalistic ruminations (with which he was very familiar, as author of the earliest Lincoln biography and stalwart admirer of Lincoln for the rest of his life). He also anticipates the anger and vitriol of Mark Twain's later rejection of God's grace and Christian consolation (even as they entered into a deeper relation as kindred spirits after Twain lost his own gifted daughter). But Howells certainly also demonstrates a powerful desire to maintain bonds with the dead child as well, despite his more modern temperament. In fact, he believed that recognizing such bonds was at the heart of the American project. And as I will argue, his fiction presents a critique of the "death of dying" trends during the era of his greatest literary influence. As late as 1915, he still placed hope in "the unbroken embrace of the love that links together a life here and hereafter."[23] Thus in my account of *Continuing Bonds*, W. D. Howells is a key transitional figure for documenting in literary history the emerging, modern American way of death, and the critique thereof. And Howells will conclude that it is only by fully encountering death that our truest humanity can overcome.

There is a striking corroboration between the decline of the daughter, the growth of the father's political and spiritual consciousness, and the erosion of his confidence in America. Biographer John Crowley writes that it was "as if the problems of his own family sharpened his sensitivity to the unsmiling aspects of the world at large."[24] Crowley is silently echoing a famous phrase of Howells, who wrote that the realists should consider in the end the "smiling aspects of life," which he deemed essentially American in spirit. Ever since, this comment has become a notorious strike against its writer, garnering for Howells unusual amounts of scorn and ridicule from later authors, perhaps most famously by Sinclair Lewis in his Nobel acceptance speech in 1930. Howells did not seem to get it, suggested Lewis, and life was not always "smiling." Similarly, Theodore Dreiser had stated that Howells's work was an "influence for good," but that he did not understand "misery."[25] Such errors did a real disservice to the memory of Howells and his achievement—for he knew misery intimately. So here Crowley is making a very intriguing comment: that Howells, after Winny's illness and death, knew those unsmiling aspects as well as anyone.

In fact, the unsmiling aspects lingered on for the rest of his life, and he struggled mightily to find a means of dealing with them. During the period of Winny's decline, certain social and cultural phenomena had a very significant impact on him as well: Howells became preoccupied with the legal defense of the Haymarket anarchists, almost simultaneous to his deepening encounter with the social ethics of the Russian novelist Leo Tolstoy, both occurring just as his daughter entered the final phase of her long, painful demise. Her death accelerated the effects of these religious and moral convictions, and altogether these phenomena enhanced his desire to sympathize with the poor and the laboring classes, a sympathy that would later be undertaken even more earnestly in the memory of his dead daughter. But Howells's spiritual transformation had already begun by then, with an immersion into the social teachings of Tolstoy, whom he began reading seriously in the mid-1880s. The experience rocked Howells to his very foundation; as he described it, it was "for me somewhat comparable to the old-fashioned religious experience of people converted at revivals."[26] Howells is certainly being ironic in calling it a conversion; however, in effect this period would result in his discovery of just such a "new meaning and a new motive" for his writing career. But Tolstoy was a key influence in turning Howells's thinking toward social justice, a radical change for one of America's elite literary stars. He described the great Russian's effect on him: "you feel instantly that the man is mighty, and mighty through his conscience; that he is not trying to surprise or dazzle you with his art, but that he is trying to make you think clearly and feel rightly about vital things with which art has often dealt with diabolical indifference or diabolical malevolence."[27] The phrase about "feeling right" harks back to the ending of *Uncle Tom's Cabin,* where Stowe appeals to the mothers of America to correct their dullness of emotion in the face of social injustice and suffering. The mention of "vital things" might also remind of us of Howell's later judgment that his *Hazard of New Fortunes* was in fact the "most vital of my fictions," by which he referred to the novel's connection with the "real," living and breathing and sweating population of the metropolis.[28]

As his biographers have put it, after his reading of Tolstoy, "he began to hope—or at least speak—for a society without servants and underclasses used by those who happen to have more money, and he no longer glossed over the implications of class difference to himself or to American society. Never a Marxist, he tended to look at issues of social justice from a personal or moral perspective but with an increasing awareness of larger, historic forces."[29] The radical, deeply religious challenge of Tolstoy is indicated in a November 1887 letter to two of his other children, Annie and Will: "[we] both no longer care for the world's life, and would like to be settled somewhere very humbly and simply, where we could be socially identified with the principles of progress and sympathy for the struggling mass."[30] As Winny lingered near death in early 1889, the author Edward Everett Hale met Howells and recalled him talking with enthusiasm about "Tolstoi's theories and the Saviour's wishes": "Howells is a loyal Christian, and hates to have anybody say that Jesus made plans or demanded things that are impossible."[31]

It is in the context of his "conversion" to Tolstoy-style pietistic Christianity that Howells wrote to James about his bourgeois and effete tastes in the midst of such a troubled world: "Meantime I wear a fur-lined overcoat, and live in all the luxury my money can buy."[32] Given this muted confession, it is intriguing to see that some of his readers picked up on the religious foundations of his newfound beliefs. After reading Howells's working-class novel *Annie Kilburn* (1888), for instance, in which the title character returns after many years to find her hometown now a bustling factory center complete with electric lighting and department stores, former president Rutherford B. Hayes, who was Howells's cousin by marriage, wrote the following: "it opens the Democratic side of the coming questions. I do not find a ready word for the doctrine of true equality of rights. Its foes call it nihilism, communism, socialism, and the like. Howells would perhaps call it justice. It was the doctrine of the Declaration of Independence, and of the Sermon on the Mount. But what is a proper and *favorable* word or phrase to designate it?"[33] Hayes is noting a blending of American republicanism with the social ethics of Jesus. He is unable to find the correct word for it. But he does recognize the radical shift that Howells has undergone in his thinking. As Howells himself wrote, the unsettling feelings Tolstoy caused resulted in a revelatory experience: "Things that were dark or dim before were shone upon by a light so clear and strong that I needed no longer grope my way to. Being and doing had a new meaning and a new motive."[34]

Then came one of the great political disasters of Howells's lifetime, a key symbolic moment in America's struggle to come to terms with its democratic claims and its identity as a state of social justice. The Haymarket riot is misnamed since there was in fact no riot, but it occurred In Haymarket Square, Chicago, on May 4, 1886. The event began with the announcement of a May 1 strike, which was called in support of an eight-hour workday by the Federation of Organized Trades and labor unions. A group of anarchists came together to call a meeting at the Haymarket site, a large setting that could host thousands of spectators. The mayor of Chicago anticipated trouble and ordered police to stand nearby during the event. The crowd was not large, and soon it began to rain, at which point many in attendance began to leave. Police began encouraging others to also depart, at which time somebody threw a bomb into the crowd and near the police. The policemen opened fire on the crowd, killing some of their own along with four civilians; hundreds were wounded, by the bomb as well as the gunfire, and it was never determined who threw the bomb, or even why. The Haymarket debacle resulted in the indictment of nine men and became illustrative of the emerging labor unrest in America, as well as one of the most famous early instances of domestic terror.[35] The events, media coverage, and trial all affected Howells deeply, and haunted his thoughts for years. Some critics have even suggested that Haymarket changed Howells "more than any other event."[36] But beyond Haymarket loomed another, even greater catastrophe that was in fact the crucial event in the process of his transformation. His prized daughter was dying, and her tortured parents could not save her. And it was Winny's struggle and then death, after all, that changed him the most.

The investigation of various spiritual phenomena became a notable feature of Howells's novels after Winny's death. For example, in his novel *The Shadow of a Dream* (1890) there are ghostly visitations; John Crowley argues that *Shadow of a Dream* anticipates Freud's work on dreams and the unconscious just a few years later: "the dream of mastery dissolves into its own shadow." In *Shadow of a Dream,* we can surmise the author's shattered hopes as manifested by the death of Winny, all fleshed out in the psychological horror that recognizes the self as truly unknowable and mysterious: the "whole region of experience—half the map of our life—that they tell us must always remain a wilderness, with all its extraordinary phenomena irredeemably savage and senseless." As Crowley notes, "they" refers to the recent discoverers of the human unconscious, soon to emerge as "the empire of psychoanalysis."[37] Similarly ghostly is *The Quality of Mercy* (1892), in which "the guilt-ridden protagonist is haunted by the memories of an elder daughter whose death and symptoms of acute anorexia nervosa there are an almost terrible resemblance" to Winny's symptoms in the final years of her life.[38] During this period Howells and his wife became curious about spiritualism and contact with the dead, and even attended at least two séances in 1890–91. Howells's remorse was revealed in numerous dreams he began having not long after Winny's death. "I was about to be hanged for something . . . but I reflected, 'No, I am tired of living; and it's only a momentary wrench, and then I shall be with *her*.'"[39] One dream had her standing before him in a gray dressing gown she commonly wore, and his wife Elinor spoke: "'Here's Winny.' Howells then took her in his arms and held her warmly. After letting go of her, Winny asks, 'Then you do love me?' Howells then responds, choking up: 'O, love you!'" The dream reveals the deep feeling of guilt and remorse he felt for the lost beloved, who wonders if she is truly loved. In another, Howells imagined taking her cheeks between his hands and crying over her, saying in the dream, "Have you come back to poor Papa?"[40]

The suggestive title *Shadow of a Dream,* his novel of 1890, also echoes Howells's ongoing critique of the American Dream, now darkened by shadows like the Haymarket incident. It deepened the critique already well underway in his earlier classics like *The Rise of Silas Lapham* (1884). In these and other fictions produced before and then after Winny's death, Howells wrestled with the competing claims on his sense of vocation and his view of America. But it is especially in the novel *A Hazard of New Fortunes* (1890), and particularly through the characters Basil March, the protagonist, and Dryfoos, whose son Conrad is killed in a public demonstration not unlike the Haymarket incident in the novel's climactic scenes, where Howells seems intent on finding reasons for the terrible loss of an adult child, full of literary ambition. As Robert Ferguson has written, "in the death of his son and the wallowing in sorrow and guilt, Dryfoos resembles no one more than William Dean Howells himself, who grieved in similar terms over the death of his daughter."[41] The profound changes in the perceptions of the novel's protagonist, Basil March, also resemble how Howells was altered by the death of Winny and his subsequent move to New York. It is telling that his elegiac memoir of his dead daughter, *Winifred Howells,* was written just as he was completing this, his most important novel.

In *A Hazard of New Fortunes,* Howells wrestled with the competing spiritual impulses that surrounded Winny's death and were illustrated in his emotional memoir. If his work after 1889 elaborates a philosophy of a collective social ethics that, as one critic has written, "can be best summed up with one word: complicity," then *Hazard* is the culminating statement of that ethic.[42] Another critic notes that Howellsian complicity is "not merely sociological but theological in its overtones."[43] The novel appraises the various secularizing means by which America was quickly being transformed by its rejection of complicity, and its concomitant effects on social cohesion and sympathy. Perhaps surprisingly, Howells's great novel proposes that one of the most sinister, and yet almost imperceptible examples of these means was the growth of "life insurance," a product that was becoming synonymous with the good life for bourgeois, urban Americans. As argued in this volume's introduction, the rise of the life insurance industry was symptomatic of what some historians refer to as the "death of dying" in America: the shift in cultural views of the dead, the removal of death from public contact, and the denial of death's power over the living. Altogether, and along with the embalming of bodies and the rise of the funeral industry, the insurance industry's meteoric growth in the years after the Civil War reflected and fostered these phenomena, especially insofar as life insurance allowed middle-class survivors to worry far less about the aging process and impending death of a spouse—usually the breadwinning husband. Life insurance was an ingenious product that reflected and encouraged the widespread "death of dying" in American culture. Insurance worked to circumvent fear and to domesticate death, and it comforted survivors by diverting them from mundane worries about expenses. Meanwhile, life insurance fueled the growing funeral industry by providing grieving families large amounts of capital for presenting ever more elaborate funerals. Curiously, the twin rise of life insurance and funeral homes fed off each other, but also, ideologically, both together propounded the death of dying. As Burton Bledstein writes, "What strikes the historian is the totality of the Mid-Victorian impulse to contain the life experiences of the individual from birth to death by isolating them as science."[44] Americans were learning to forget about death by "isolating" it and "containing" it, and they were allowing the "professionals" to manage this most unpleasant experience, the loss of a loved one. Importantly, these practices fostered a forgetting of "complicity," the ethical concept that each person has a duty to become his/her brother's keeper, instead of relying on an anonymous insurance claims agent in Hartford or a funeral director whose business it is to present the dead for the distanced gaze of the consumer. Howells was prophetic in realizing how the urban landscape was greatly accelerating such attitudes about death.

First of all, the novel's protagonist, Basil March, must be recognized as a character torn between the promotion of the insurance industry and the belletristic life of a writer and artist. He moves to New York to undertake what is a promotion in the industry, and the novel opens confirming that he is involved in the public "promotion" of insurance. Basil himself owns life insurance (perhaps a benefit of being employed in the industry), and even slyly jokes with his wife Isabel that he assumes one day that she will reap the "enjoyment" of his death benefit.[45] Basil's move to New York to begin his new duties is described as his "destiny," placing the industry into a position of sovereignty formerly supervised by God. Basil is offered "the editorship of the monthly paper published in the interest of the company . . . the authorship of circulars and leaflets in behalf of life-insurance." But this destiny, says Howells, is "tragical," and the "promotion" is only "in the guise of a promotion," thus signaling the author's barely concealed contempt for the industry.[46] It may seem strange to contemporary readers that an insurance company would have such publications at this rather early date, but as Jason Puskar notes, "the industry had dozens, possibly hundreds, of them." Puskar is also the first critic to identify the centrality of life insurance to the context of the novel: "Almost alone among American writers, William Dean Howells noticed the growing cultural importance of insurance and its increasingly intimate relationship with literature, particularly during his political phase during the late 1880s. . . . By 1890, even the word 'hazard' was a recognizable insurance term, used more often in that context than any other." It is intriguing to recognize that the title of the novel suggests the insurance industry, but Puskar also posits how "the white-collar work of underwriting served as a complex shadow of realism's own labors in the literary marketplace. . . . In the late nineteenth century, middle-class urban and suburban life was unthinkable without insurance. Just as insurance cultivates the threat of accident in order to enroll policyholders in its 'mutual society,' Howellsian realism promoted the ungovernable obtrusions of 'the world of chance' in an attempt to forge the mature kind of social interdependence that Howells so desired. No real solution to the serious social and economic problems that *Hazard* diagnoses, Howells's proposed link between insurance and realism held out hope that the dangerous instability of urban modernity might be put to good use, if configured as a radically alien threat against which communities might unite."[47] One critic has claimed that *A Hazard of New Fortunes* was an "unmooring of Howells's convictions, including his literary ones." As Amy Kaplan explains: *A Hazard of New Fortunes* "exposes the drive toward moral unity in realism as a dream of mastery to compensate for the lack of control."[48] But the dying of death is also a "dream of mastery"—one destined to fail, however. What was needed, still, was a "radically alien threat against which communities might unite." Such threats were all around Howells as he walked the streets of New York in 1889—just after the death of his own daughter.

We should consider the beginning of *A Hazard of New Fortunes* in these contexts. Howells's novel represents nothing less than the author's profound encounter with death, occurring in the midst of a cultural context that is rapidly accelerating its own "march" toward denying death. In terms of plotting, the novel depicts Basil and Isabel March and their sustained encounter with death in the big city: an encounter that begins with a lengthy "march" around the city in search of a suitable apartment. Their "march" might suggest an Augustinian depiction of the restless human heart searching for home, and as such the spiritual themes that became crucial for the bereaved Howells. As opposed to distancing and managing death by paid professionals, Howells insists that affluent Americans gaze directly into the face of death, into the open grave, and that we embrace it for all that it's worth for us, metaphysically, morally, and ethically. Howells concludes that it is by denying the denial of death that we will finally discover life. In this way, his overall moral message resonates with certain sayings of Jesus Christ, who often told his disciples that in order to live they must die: "whosoever shall lose his life for my sake and the gospel's, the same shall save it" (Mark 8:35). Howells seems to be suggesting something similar: that unless one encounters death, unless one is willing to deny the denial of death, one will not be able to live. The embodiment of this ethic is Conrad Dryfoos, who like Jesus must die a martyr for his cause. Conrad, says his saintly mother, disregards the treasures of this world: "he says money ain't the thing—or not the only thing you got to give them poor folks. You got to give your time, and your knowledge, and your love—I don't know what all—you got to give yourself, if you expect to help 'em."[49] As such, Howells's great masterpiece is a story about resurrection through one's profound embrace of all that death, decay, and destruction might throw our way in a large, messy, urban world such as New York City in 1890. Howells came to conceive that the truest "life insurance" is an utter emptying of self in the humble service of others less fortunate, a giving away of one's life to save it. And as Conrad remarks in the novel, "I think the city itself is preaching the best sermon all the time."[50]

As already mentioned, the theological ground for such a dramatic change had been well plowed in Howells's life for these developments, first by reading Tolstoy, but also with his frequent contact with liberal clergy, such as the Reverend Joseph Twichell, known in his lifetime as "Mark Twain's pastor." Twichell was a disciple of Horace Bushnell, one of the leaders of the emerging social gospel as preached and practiced in its mecca, Hartford, Connecticut.[51] Howells, like his close companion Mark Twain, had always been friendly with and often intrigued by preachers and priests: an aspect of Conrad's personality in *A Hazard of New Fortunes*. Twichell recalled Howells as having a kindhearted and gentle spirit: in 1875 he wrote in his journal, "Mark Twain and WDH walked home from church with me, and subsequently I went to Mark's and dined with them. . . . When leaving Howells followed me to the door and we had on the threshold quite a talk on religious subjects and I was sorry that we couldn't have more. He seemed very humble and earnest, vastly loveable."[52] But even more important was Howells's deepening acquaintance in the 1880s with a group of Episcopal priests, including most importantly William Dwight Porter Bliss, and progressive laypersons such as Richard T. Ely, all of whom took seriously Jesus Christ's charge to bring God's kingdom "on earth as in heaven" (Matthew 5:14). Howells considered joining Bliss's radical congregation in Boston, called the Church of the Carpenter, after being moved powerfully by Bliss's preaching on economic justice. He reviewed Ely's book *The Social Aspects of Christianity* in *Harper's* in 1890, praising its basic message to the church that "its work is primarily to make justice and peace and love at home upon the earth, and secondarily to save souls for heaven thereby."[53] Ely's book begins by quoting Matthew 22, where Jesus states that His teaching rests on only two commands: to love God and to love your neighbor. Ely claims for this verse that "this is a most remarkable, and at the same time the whole duty of man." And Ely, like Howells, had also been influenced by Tolstoy: he writes, "we must come into real, living contact, into a sort of oneness with people before we can give them and received from them needed help."[54] In this regard, Howells put it simply: "Tolstoi tells us simply to live as Christ bade us, socially and politically, severally and collectively."[55]

And so, like many writers of this era, Howells was deeply influenced by the "Social Christianity" with which he came in contact; in fact, this burgeoning movement was all around him. Passages in *Hazard* sound strikingly similar to passages in memoirs and other writings by the social gospel leaders—which oddly enough often sound like the notes of fearfulness touted by leaders in the insurance industry (and both movements were centered in Hartford). For example, in his memoir *Recollections* (1909), one of the social gospel movement's leaders, Washington Gladden, recalls the power of the urban nightmare he entered first in 1860: "The city from the first day, was a thing stupendous and overpowering, a mighty monster, with portentous energies; the sense of its power to absorb human personalities and to shape human destinies was often vivid and painful . . . the contact with the strenuous life of the great city was a revelation. One was standing in the center of a galvanic field, with lines of force crossing each other in every direction. Everything was alive, yet there was a vivid sense of the impersonality and brutality of the whole movement, of the lack of coordinating intelligence."[56]

Gladden sounds almost like a practitioner of literary naturalism, and the passage's tone is echoed in the rhetoric of the life insurance industry, whose task was obviously to sell their commodities, their social safety net. In a lecture to the National Convention of Insurance Commissioners in 1916, Rufus Potts describes a similar milieu at the heart of the life insurance industry's mission: "the vast impersonal forces of the universe in their irresistible courses crush many, while those not thus destroyed are disabled or become diseased, so that their bodies are filled with pain and misery in their souls with despair. The ways in which humanity is injured or destroyed are innumerable."[57] Potts's address is symptomatic of the rise of the rhetoric of "accident" in America, which is itself symptomatic of the diminishing belief in God's Providence and the increasing denial of death, insofar as the pooling of resources to cover accidents diminishes the pragmatic power of death over the lives of survivors, randomly suffering from "the vast impersonal forces of the universe."[58] The solutions Gladden offered through the social gospel, and that Potts offered through the insurance industry, may be competing opposites, but their accounts of a naturalistic inner-city nightmare are strikingly similar.

We might compare these brief sketches of urban America with some of the many passages in *Hazard*, in which we listen to Isabel and Basil March repeatedly express serious alarm regarding "the frantic panorama" of New York. The terror of the urban nightmare is represented early in the novel by Isabel March: "New York terrifies me . . . it disheartens and distracts me; I can't find myself in it; I shouldn't know how to shop. . . . I could never have any inner quiet in New York; I couldn't live in the spirit there."[59] In his elegant passages of extended terror Howells rises to his most impressive elaborations of naturalistic thought and style: "Accident and then exigency seem the forces at work to this extraordinary effect; the play of energies as free and planless as those that force the forest from the soil to the sky; and then the fierce struggle for survival, with a stronger life persisting over the deformity, the mutilation, the destruction, the decay, of the weaker. The whole at moments seemed to him lawless, Godless; the absence of intelligent, comprehensive purpose in the huge disorder and the violent struggle to subordinate the result to the greater good penetrated with its dumb appeal the consciousness of a man who had always been too self-enwrapt to perceive the chaos to which the individual selfishness must always lead."[60] Riding on the elevated trains "gave you such glimpses of material aspects in the city as some violent invasion of others lives might afford in human nature."[61] March waxes poetic as he marches about the city: he states, "a sense of the striving and the suffering deeply possessed him, and this grew the more intense as he gained some knowledge of the forces at work—forces of pity, of distraction, of perdition, of salvation."[62] March does seek some solace from the oppression of these "forces" by visiting various churches: "as the spirit moved him, [he] listened to those who dealt with Christianity as a system of economics as well as a religion." His return to a sense of complicity with the suffering of the city is not a new life, he says; "it was death in life."[63] The change occurs for Basil as he is able to deny the denial of death; he embraces the death all around him and through that experience he finds a new spiritual lens through which to see, and feel, the city.

When we recognize that Howells wrote the opening chapters of the novel during the last months of Winny's life, it is a little disquieting to know that Howells gives Basil and Isabel March the exact same address in New York where he himself wrote much of the story. The first installment of the novel actually appeared in print the day after Winny expired. Significantly, the novel's first long section, comprising almost a quarter of the text, is a search for home. This search motif characterizes Howells's life during this period. Concurrent with his move from Boston to New York in the autumn of 1888, Howells was deeply involved with several other "searches." Like the Marches, he and his wife had spent much time wandering the streets of Manhattan in search of a proper residence. But he was also searching for a politics that might makes sense to him, after that failure of justice in the Haymarket incident just a year earlier. He was searching for a way to maintain an eroding confidence in America and all the hopefulness about the American project that once was such a source of vision and comfort in his writing. And as Thomas Wortham has recently argued, Howells was also searching for a spiritual reality that might help him make sense out of the social and political failures he saw all around him.[64]

But of all these simultaneous searches, the most deeply personal involved his ailing daughter Winny, as he and his wife frantically sought a possible solution to her lingering health issues. And so there is a maze-like tone to the first quarter of the massive novel that Howells began at this crucial period of seeking, a tone that is symptomatic of the searching going on his life at the same time. Although he wrote these lengthy chapters of the somewhat overwhelmed couple inspecting dozens of potential flats prior to the death of Winny, it is clear that the emotional devastation of years of caretaking and worry about her future had already taken a deep toll. It's hard to read these chapters without thinking of the sheer horror to come for Howells, a horror that was somewhat subsided by the continuation of the story that begins with the long, seemingly futile search for a proper resting place where parents and children can live together in comfort and fellowship. The novel's title is a reference to those masked forces, some sinister, and some perhaps fortunate, by which our lives are fated. The phrase comes from Shakespeare's *King John*, a play that focuses on the violence of politics and the uncertainties of rapid change—and, as mentioned earlier, containing one of Shakespeare's most powerful laments for a dead child. Howells, good student of Lincoln that he was, certainly knew of Lincoln's fondness for this passage. The "Hazard" of the title might even seem at first auspicious, bringing as it does "fortunes," but it is potentially also perilous, possibly even deadly. And hazard was also becoming a common term in the insurance field, thus pointing forward to modern managerial systems of dubious helpfulness.

The title of *A Hazard of New Fortunes*, read in the context of Winny's death, reveals both Howells's sense of futility and a yearning to find something redemptive in the tragic, perhaps even to maintain the bonds with the dead child, even as his more rationalistic response mitigated this impulse. *A Hazard of New Fortunes* also typifies the Victorian age's ambivalent response to the earlier, romantic appeals to the bonds with the dead and Christian consolation. This conflicted response is most clearly illustrated in the agonies of Dryfoos and his wife, whose son is killed in the Haymarket-like incident in the novel's climactic scenes. But one often-overlooked detail is that the Dryfooses have previously lost other children as well, children buried back in the family plot in Ohio. In the interests of a further expansion of the business, these unnamed children will be moved now to a cemetery: "It ain't the fashion, any more, to have family buryin' grounds; they're collectin' 'em into the cemeteries, all round," says Dryfoos. But his wife Elizabeth cries to think of this news: "But I always did want to lay just there . . . [do you remember] how we used to go out there and set there, after milkin', and watch the sun go down, and talk about where their angels was, and try to figger it out?"[65]

In this poignant moment, the bereaved mother speaks for a nostalgic attachment to the physical site of her children's graves, and her frequent desire to sit there and "figger" it all out. But they have moved away from that physical site, and it is now to be further removed from the old farmlands—a removal that underscores the loss of proximity to the dead. And by the time Howells wrote these somber lines, Winny was dead and he had himself buried a daughter in a faraway grave in Cambridge. In his struggle with grief, her memory precipitated the radical shift in Howells's thinking that *Hazard* documents, revealed through the shift in the novel's complex social vision, as observed in Basil March. Howells's real life struggle was overwhelming: "the expression of our bereavement escapes me. . . . I wonder we live; it seems monstrous." He wonders especially how to find consolation, doubting in an afterlife reunion: "If I could believe I was to meet her again I should be the lightest hearted man alive."[66] His words sound a lot like Lincoln's reaction to the Reverend Gurley's words of encouragement—and they also might recall the lament of Constance from *King John*: "And father Cardinal, I have heard you say / That we shall see and know our friends in heaven. / If that be true, I shall see my boy again." And in fact, he wrote to Twain about the comfort he discovered in a mystical work on eternal life: "I read something in a strange book . . . that consoled a little, namely: we saw and felt the Power of Deity in such fullness that we ought to infer the infinite Justice and Goodness which we did not see or feel."[67] In particular, much of the consolation he could discover in the coming years would derive from this possibility—even if slight—of "meeting her again," if not literally, then at least figuratively, in the form of his continuing bonds with his dead daughter.

In this way, Winny haunts the pages of *A Hazard of New Fortunes*, and she would continue to haunt the author's writings for many years thereafter. On the one hand, *Hazard* represents the commencement of a search for solutions to the illnesses of urban America. But on a more deeply felt, personal level, *Hazard* documents the search for some manner of Christian consolation in the wake of Winny's death. If this is plausible, then the culminating depiction of this search may be considered the collection of poems called *Stops of Various Quills* (1895). Although many of the poems in this volume appeared in groups in *Harper's* during the early 1890s, the publication of the complete volume presents them in Howell's final sequence and version, including ordering in such a way as to suggest a redemptive outcome to grief.[68] The many fine illustrations, by the noted artist Howard Pyle, are elegant and classical in subject matter. It is a vastly underrated volume, and what is perhaps most remarkable about it is the way it records Howells's spiritual quest in the lengthy aftermath of Winny's death.

In an essay composed near the end of his own life, Howells wrote that in counseling the bereaved, it is best to turn to the tried and true sources of consolation and hope: "In the hour of 'sharpest pathos,' I would say: Seek the help that offers itself to your seeking from those sources of healing which all the generations of Christianity have known. Go to your Bible, which, perhaps from your long estrangement, will have grown newly potent and significant."[69] It is interesting that Howells assumes among his readers an "estrangement" from Scripture; such an estrangement might be partly a function of the age, but it is also perhaps simply a function of aging. Furthermore, this estrangement may very well be a function of grief. As the great twentieth-century pastor William Sloane Coffin said in his funeral sermon for his son, "While the words of the Bible are true, grief renders them unreal. The reality of grief is the absence of God."[70]

But it is also telling that he suggests how the Bible might become "newly potent" after loss. The passage also assumes a close familiarity with the elegies of Tennyson: "Shall sharpest pathos blight us" is posed by the poet in his "Love and Duty," one of the standard grieving texts of the era. Tennyson's response to the memory of the dead possibly "blighting" the survivor: allow the memory of the dead to "point thee forward to a distant light." Tennyson's achievement rested largely on his dependence on continuing bonds with the dead, and as such his popularity as chief poet-mourner of the period helps explain why his volumes were common gifts to those suffering bereavement. But Tennyson is also a key figure due to his own doubts about the afterlife and his vacillation between seeing death and suffering as meaningless, or as somehow redemptive. Tennyson's *In Memoriam* became a crucial Victorian guide for the bereaved, partly due to how disturbingly it portrays evidence against immortality of the dead while simultaneously a yearning for reunion.[71] Howells's essay also advises that when ministering to a mourner's "incidents of peculiar anguish," it is best to "match these from your own experience," by which he means that those most experienced in matters of grief should be of service to those just entering the excruciating journey ahead.[72] *Stops of Various Quills* is an eloquent, often beautifully written testament to that spiritual journey, as Howells experienced it. Just as Tennyson's *In Memoriam* is suffused with doubt and faith, regret and consolation, *Stops of Various Quills* is a haunting, well-wrought minor masterpiece that speaks powerfully to Howells's continuing bonds with his dead daughter—or at least, his urgent longing to believe in those bonds, and to maintain them.

The title is taken from John Milton's "Lycidas," a pastoral elegy written in 1637 about the drowning of the poet's college friend, named Edward King. As one of the most famous British elegies, many of Howells's readers would have been familiar with "Lycidas" and perhaps even would recognize the allusion of the title itself. Milton's poem reads: "Thus sang the uncouth Swain to th' Okes and Annotate rills, / While the still morn went out with Sandals gray, / He touch'd the tender stops of various Quills."[73] The "Quills" are the multiple hollow reeds in a shepherd's pipe, while the "stops" are the finger holes in the reeds. This title suggests that Howells is writing different types of poetry, each striking a different kind of note, or narrated in a different temperament or voice. The upshot of the image of the quills, shown prominently on the cover of the volume, is one of sad lament, giving words to loss through a variety of voices and moods.

Critics have rarely analyzed *Stops of Various Quills*, but when it has been discussed it has been seen as emblematic of the emergence of the modern temperament, a depiction of "radical doubt and anxiety" typical of the literature that would subsequently be produced in the early part of the twentieth century. As such, Howells's book seemed to presage the coming of a darker, more hopeless view of suffering and death; it signified the emergence of "a tortured, divided 'modern sensibility,' whose awareness of life was rooted in radical doubt and anxiety."[74] Valden Madsen describes *Stops of Various Quills* as "the anguished endeavor of a divided mind that seeks after affirmation and tranquility only to find itself lost in that search. The sense of loss is real and pervasive as the poetry inventories the inner life of a man whose sufferings were corrosive, private realities, shielded from public view by the smiling façade of the grandfatherly Dean of American letters."[75] While this account rings true, what Madsen leaves out is the affirmation made in *Stops of Various Quills* of Howells's serious quest for faith and consolation, in light of all the suffering and pain. If we grant that the divided mind is in fact a common phenomenon among grieving parents, what is most easily seen is the despair and hopelessness side of the equation. But the quest for faith always includes questions of doubt and hopelessness. In this volume, and besides this "modern sensibility" riddled with anxiety and radical doubt, Howells also documents his desire to believe, including his yearning for immortality and the continuing bonds with the dead, especially with Winny.

Stops of Various Quills consists of simple forms, in which private suffering is stated plainly and emotionally. It is even plausible that the volume was influenced by Emily Dickinson's similarly plain yet emotional expressions, since Dickinson's poems received strong praise in a review by Howells for *Harper's* in 1891. He was so impressed by her work that he wrote to Mark Twain touting her as well.[76] As with Dickinson's finest documents of grief, Howells's poems strip away the facades of social convention to show the naked human soul underneath: "How must I shrink and cower before them there, / Stripped naked to the soul and beggared bare / Of every rag of seeming!"[77] Clearly the author is haunted by death and its judgment. In "If," he writes, "Yes, death is at the bottom of the cup, / And everyone that lives must drink it up." In "Living," he desires his own death: "how wildly I hurry, for the change I crave, / To hurl myself into the changeless grave!" (XIII, XII). "Question" poses humanity's ultimate destination: "Shall it be after the long misery / Of these loose pillows, and the waste of flesh / In sickness, till some worn and widening mesh / Frays out at last, and lets the soul go free?" Here, the one certainty is simply death, "which all other things / Have taught my being in its inmost springs / To feel the soul impossibility" (XVI). "Twelve P.M." sounds almost like a precursor to T. S. Eliot's "Prufrock": having returned home after a lengthy dinner party, the narrator must "take off one's perfunctory smile, and be / Wholly and solely one's sheer self again." Taking off his clothes at the end of a social event is like "[putting] off the body, and the whole / Illusion of life, and in one's naked soul / [Confronting] the eternal Verity" (VIII). And in "Change," the narrator remembers the lost beloved (certainly reminding us of the daughter Winny): "Suddenly I think of her that died, and know, / Whatever friendly or unfriendly fate / Befall me in my hope or in my pride, / It is all nothing but a mockery, / And nothing can be what it used to be, / When I could bid my happy life abide, / And build on earth for perpetuity, / Then, in the deathless days before she died" (IX). The confession is made that he no longer believes his work can build anything worth building after Winny's death. These and other poems are saturated with the futility of loss.

But besides these looming meditations of death and despair, other poems are suggestive of hope. Without this aspect, there is no real "dividedness." In one titled "Sympathy," solidarity is discovered through mutual suffering:

> I wonder, should I speak and be
> the first
> To own just where in my soul it
> hurt worst,
> And you revealed in yours the spot
> its flames
> Scorched fiercest, if it might not be the same. (XXII)

In "Statistics," the poet sounds almost as if he is describing the work of actuaries at an insurance company, trying to predict how many will die in a given month, how many will suffer from theft and arson, and so forth. "And from these figures science can discern the future in the past," he claims. But despite the statistician's attempt to predict the forces of evil, this tribute to the explanatory powers of insurance ends with an appeal to something beyond: "your facts are facts, yet somewhere there is God" (XXIII).

Throughout the poems, Howells also includes numerous biblical allusions, often finding in these quotes elements of redemption. "Sphinx," a riddle about what happens after death, insists that "losing alone is finding," echoing the words of Jesus in requiring us to lose our lives in order to find them (XXIX; Mark 8:35). In "Judgment Day," when faced with all the guilty before him like a "shoreless sea," God is struck dumb by the desire for mercy, and yet complies: "high above them, in His sovereign place, / He lifted up the pity of His face" (XXXIV). "Parable" is one of the longest poems in the collection; it is a retelling of the parable of the rich young man, who was told by Jesus to sell all that he has and give it to the poor (Matthew 19:16–23). Rather than doing so, the rich man decides to become instead "the humble agency and instrument of good others not intelligent enough to use the gifts of God right," after which he "rose up with a heart at peace" (XXIV). There's one titled "Calvary," where Howells compares his own doubts with those of the Savior on the cross, "in the defeat and loss of seeing all my selfish dreams fulfilled." He even echoes the words of Jesus from the cross: "My God, my God! Why hast thou forsaken me?" (XIX; Matthew 27:46). But this echo is also exasperation and defeat to be followed by victory and resurrection. This confession is immediately followed by "Conscience": "Judge me not as I judge myself, O Lord!" (XX).

Near the end of the volume, several poems gesture strongly toward belief in God and redemptive hope, yet previous critics conveniently leave these out of accounts of the book's message. In "Another Day," the narrator even experiences what can only be described as a romantic spot of time: "that brute joy, / Or that prophetic rapture of the boy whom every morning brings as glad a breath / As if it dawned upon the end of death!" It is a day "that should come to bless me past the scope / And measure of my farthest-reaching hope." Such days are still possible, the poem tells us. And yet this uplifting poem is immediately followed by more misery, in "Some One Else": "Live my life over? I would rather not" (XXXVII). "Temperament" argues that both "love and hate, honor and infamy" are part of our mystical makeup—the "one immutable thing" being the "body of our hope and fear." There is the poem itself titled "Hope." Here we listen to the narrator, sighting land while out sailing in the ocean, imagine another crossing, to another kind of existence, beyond death: "I shall see arise another world out of that waste time lapse, / Like yonder land. Perhaps—perhaps—perhaps!" (XVII). The "perhaps," repeated three times, is telling: he is divided in his response, deeply longing for that other place but uncertain about its reality. Although the poem is titled "Hope," the word "hope" is not mentioned in the poem itself, and it is buried underneath the uncertainties of the three uses of "perhaps." But it is there nevertheless. And as an expression of hope, it can be read in both directions. In this way, it is very much like the final lines of *A Hazard of New Fortunes*, where Basil and Isabel March encounter Margaret, now wearing her "dress of the sisterhood" as a nun. Although Margaret never speaks on this final page of the novel, the Marches "felt that the peace that passeth understanding had looked at them from her eyes."[78]

Basil's comment alludes to Paul's letter to the Philippians (4:7), with the "passeth" signaling the diction of the King James version. The passage speaks of an unearthly, or supernatural sort of peace, and the allusion would also serve the young T. S. Eliot at the end of *The Waste Land*, modernism's influential monument to spiritual despair. This idea of supernatural peace seems real, but the ending of *Hazard* (as with *The Waste Land*) can also go both ways: as Isabel questions her husband about the meaning of Margaret's mysterious smile, all Basil can say is this: "Well, we must trust that look of hers." Given the restrained gesture toward redemption at the end of *Hazard*, we might compare it with the final poem of *Stops of Various Quills*, titled "What Shall It Profit?" Again we have another allusion to the teachings of Jesus, in this case Mark 8:36: "For what shall it profit a man, if he shall gain the whole world, and lose his own soul?" Howells is wrestling with the consequences of giving up his faith in God. He asks, "If I orphan my own soul of One / That seemed a Father, and make void the place / Within me where He dwelt in power and grace, / What do I gain by that I have undone?" (XLIII). The conclusion seems to be like Pascal's wager: the idea that a rational person should at least live as though God does exist, even if there's a chance that he doesn't. The poem tells us that formerly God dwelled in the narrator "in power and grace," as a confession of spiritual experience is given. But now the narrator feels on the verge of becoming an orphan, voluntarily. However, the conclusion to "What Shall It Profit?" and to the volume of poems is that it is just not worth it; there is nothing to gain by denying what the narrator knows, or at least hopes, to be true. It is significant that Howells ended his collection with this poem, since endings reveal so much about our ultimate beliefs. He has decided to trust, even though he confesses to feeling like an orphan, one "[withering] up with doubt."

Although we cannot ever know for certain, it all comes down to trust, says Howells. Thus does the novel end, we might say, regarding that "peace that passeth understanding": "Perhaps—perhaps—perhaps!" As his father once told Howells, "Youth is the time to believe, age is the time to trust." And then Howells remarks, "there are many things that I doubt, but few that I deny; where I cannot believe, there I often trust."[79]

If *Stops of Various Quills* suggests "the divided [modern] mind that seeks after affirmation and tranquility,"[80] then it was a later production that established beyond doubt, and most forcefully, the fact that Howells's bonds with Winny continued for the rest of his life. A remarkable essay that he published in 1910 reveals the wisdom gained from navigating two decades of parental grief, and it does so in a way that very few other writers have been able to achieve. Titled "A Counsel of Consolation" and published in a collection called *In After Days*, this meditation reveals a mind that has been at work on the issues of bereavement, loss, and the afterlife in a deep and penetrating way. It also reveals how Winnie's presence continued to influence him, although she is never named in the essay. The meditation is saturated with faith and doubt, and as such it is a transitional moment in the experience of grief in American culture. It harks back to the sentimental consolation of an earlier era and it presages the coming of an agnosticism that disallows such consolation. Nevertheless, Howells is clearly favoring a continuation of the bonds with the dead. Another very appealing aspect of this essay is the way that Howells qualifies his counsel by stating his own experience of grief, and how he works so hard to say only the things to the bereaved that have been useful to himself. In other words, the essay is not some grand philosophical defense of God, or even much of a theodicy; instead, the essay attempts to present theodicy only in terms that the newly bereaved would be able to accept.

This sort of advice that comes out of real experience is similar to the old concept of *solvitur ambulando* as the proper attitude for grief counseling and approaching questions of theodicy. As contemporary theologian Thomas Long explains, *solvitur ambulando* is "a delightful Latin phrase, often associated with Augustine but older in origin, meaning 'it is solved by walking.' . . . It describes instead a completely different way of knowing, unknowing that comes only to those who are actively engaged in the questions they are asking. . . . But for some questions personal and passionate investment in the outcome is not an impediment but an asset, perhaps even the necessity."[81] Howells's essay, after twenty years of engagement with life's toughest issues, is filled with wisdom and compassion and is a perfect illustration of this concept of *solvitur ambulando*. He begins with a statement of the first principle of *solvitur ambulando*: "nothing you can say from your thinking will avail with the newly bereaved, but anything you say from your knowing and believing and feeling will be precious." Howells advises the grieving "to trust not only to eternity, but also to time, for consolation, and to trust time first, for time is here and now, and eternity is hence and of the future. This counsel does not imply forgetting; to grief, which is of love, that is impossible; but it is well to realize from the universal human experience that the agony of tomorrow will not be the agony of today; the sharpness will have been dulled a little, and a morrow will, when the lacerating edge will be rounded so that you shall not feel it except as a stress that will no longer tear your heart, and then no stress, but a valued consciousness. You shall even wish to feel it; there will be a sweetness in it which you would not forego, but would keep with you for life."[82] Perhaps this passage's most jarring insight is the combination of competing emotions: not only is there the value of a consciousness that will finally come from grief, but also a certain sweetness that might be found in it. As he wrote in a letter of 1909 to Twain, "as the years pass we like to renew our grief for the lost, which is all we have left of them, and like to feel our hearts bleed again. We pretend otherwise, but this is the truth, and it is strange enough."[83] Oddly enough, it is comforting to feel, yet again, the sheer pain.

"A Counsel of Consolation" is the work of a seasoned, thoughtful veteran of grief, and Howells waxes quite spiritual throughout this glowing essay, in surprising and often even charming ways. A lengthy passage from it is informative:

> There are many things that I doubt, but few that I deny; where I cannot believe, there I often trust; and as all faith is mystical, I would have the bereaved trust their mystical experiences for much truth which they cannot affirm. In their darkness it will be strange if there are no gleams of that outer life which wraps our whole ignorance of this life. These will penetrate it sometimes in what seem preternatural experiences of the waking hours, and sometimes in visions of the night, which I would have the sorrower at least passively accept, or not positively refuse. Others can say that such visions, such dreams, are figments of the overwrought brain, but no one whose despair they have brightened will reject them. Whether they are natural or supernatural, they are precious. . . . They are to be cherished and kept in the heart, and not cast out of it as idle and futile. They may be the kaleidoscopic adjustment of our jarred and shattered being; they may be prismal rays of celestial light: who shall say from knowledge? What they often just involve is that reunion with the absent which the whole soul yearns and grieves for.[84]

In these lines we recognize a powerful yearning for reunion, an expression of it as a real possibility, and also the impending modern skepticism. He also admits he cannot tell if the phenomena are "natural or supernatural. But as in his novel *Hazard* and his collections *Stops of Various Quills,* Howells finds some solution in self-emptying and giving to the poor and oppressed. The title of the essay is repeated near the end: "if there is a counsel of consolation which I would offer above all the rest to the mourner it would be to seek out in the very ecstasy of pathos some instance of affliction and minister to it." The expression "ecstasy of pathos" is certainly a striking one, and it speaks directly to the redemptive possibilities of suffering. The conversion of pain into ministry is only possible, says Howells, through the continuing bonds with the dead:

> The time will come when you shall not indeed forget your dead, but when they shall be hopefully, not hurtfully, with you. The passion, the wild, headlong, hopeless passion for reunion with them, will have resolved itself into a patience in which they will always be present, and responsive to your thought, which, whenever it strays from your work or your play, will seem to find them quietly grateful for it. You will not forget. You may no longer see the mystical beauty, the sublimity of the dead face, but out of the farther past the living eyes will look, and now and then, among the myriad faces, infinitely unlike one another, there will chance a face from which an evanescent semblance will flash a radiance into the place where her face, his face, is in your heart and restore it to your vision.[85]

This is among the most moving passages Howells ever wrote on parental grief; there is something supremely consoling about its magisterial peacefulness. But as this chapter has argued, it has been a hard won peace, and we cannot read this passage without thinking about Winny and her "mystical beauty, the sublimity of the dead face." Howells mentions again how "the living eyes will look" for the beloved, reminding him perhaps of Winny's eyes, so powerfully expressive of all that she held dear in her heart. As he wrote to Twain in 1898, "[Susy's] heavenly face and her eyes of Angel innocence . . . affect me as the eyes of Winny sometimes did: with the error and the wrong that every man's life seems to include. I am afraid to look in them, and think of what I am."[86] Now Howells could reach out to console his friend, but in fact Susy's death triggered in Howells another close encounter with bereavement, if not trauma. He wrote to another friend, "I have felt deeply the death of poor sweet little Susy Clemens. My own child seemed to die again in it."[87]

In his friendship with Twain, Howells exploited a "poetics of sentimentality," by which his grief experience might serve to "reattach symbolic connections that have been severed by the contingencies of human existence."[88] This sentimental mode seems to be a final product of his nearly decade-long experience of grief. Such a poetics featured "a kind of mourning for the world that preceded" the post–Civil War era of industrialization and frenzied growth.[89] And yet his literary efforts, as in his letters, are tinged with the chaos and uncontrollable frenzy of the emerging, terrifying modern world, symbolized by New York and as dramatized in *Hazard* and elsewhere. Twain would later dub this dual and divided nature a sort of "systemless system." On the one hand, a passionate yearning to control and reform a dark and fallen world; on the other hand, a deeply cynical inability to believe that such reform is even possible. Hope remains, but it is no longer the grand, imperial hope of the Romantics and transcendentalists. In fact, the dying of such imperial dreams, aided by an enlightenment of the collateral damage and horror caused by American Empire, became a central preoccupation of the Mark Twain–Howells friendship after Twain returned from Europe in the fall of 1900. Described by Twain as "a pair of old derelicts drifting around, now, with some of our passengers gone & the sunniness of the others in (total) eclipse," they turned their joint attention to rescuing America from its prodigal ways, which will be discussed in the next chapter.[90] The sustained attack on empire by these two aging literary superstars should be viewed as a direct consequence of the prolonged grief experiences in the years leading up to that time. We might call it a kind of modern hope: theirs is a hope dogged by the doubts of modern man, one in which the Christian hope of an earlier, more sentimental era has become compromised if not entirely dismissed.

These two "derelicts" were similar in many ways, but it also seems that Howells held on to elements of an earlier Christian hope longer than Mark Twain, and there is evidence for this in the writings he produced in those saddened years after 1889. His novels of this period, particularly *Hazard*, are often analyzed for their deep sense of confusion, darkness, chaos, and things falling apart. However, one can also see in this novel how hard the author is attempting to hold onto some version of an earlier, perhaps even Christian hopefulness. We might connect this urgent desire with what later became known as "Christian realism," a term most often associated with the twentieth-century theologian Reinhold Niebuhr. Niebuhr theorized, in the years during and after World War II and its horrendous atrocities, that it would be unthinkable for the kingdom of God to be established on the earth because of the thoroughly corrupt tendencies of human beings and society as a whole. Niebuhr focused on the utter sinfulness of humankind, including the strong tendency toward evil and injustice when operating in large groups.[91] There is a sense in which the American literary realists anticipated in interesting ways Niebuhr's Christian realism of the 1940s and 1950s, especially insofar as writers like Howells and Mark Twain focused on the fallenness of man and the corruption of human society. But they were also, in turn, challenged themselves by the social gospel leaders of their settings, as well as by the towering accomplishments of Tolstoy before them.

"A Counsel of Consolation" supports my claim that twenty years after Winny's death, Howells still maintained a sense of the mystical bonds with his dead daughter. Those bonds may or may not be supernatural in origin, but they clearly had ethical and moral implications. His conclusions were unlike his close friend, Mark Twain, who ended his life in a state of growing disbelief about their supernatural origins. In his dirge for Susy, written in 1898, Twain states clearly that there is no going back:

> We know them lost to us—
> Forever lost; we cannot have them back;
> We miss them as we miss the dead,
> We mourn them as we mourn the dead.[92]

If Twain rejected supernatural reunion, he at least grew in sympathy for the oppressed peoples of our world, to some large extent motivated by the memory of Susy. Through a sharing of sympathies energized by grief, there emerged what I would like to call the "Anti-Imperialist friendship" of Twain and Howells. This joint enterprise was founded for both participants in a common tragedy: the loss of grown daughters of similar artistic and moral sensibilities, and the clear-eyed recognition that America's imperial adventures would inevitably result in even more widespread occurrences of a futile, irreparable parental grief, of which they were both sufferers.

Conversely to Twain's antisupernaturalism, for Howells, the hope of a supernatural bond and a reunion with the dead "in after days" remained a live hypothesis, as their contemporary William James might put it.[93] Not certain, but not dead either. But by this stage, these two close friends, in the end, did disagree. And thus, with the passing on of the baton from Howells to Mark Twain, do we see the radical shift from nineteenth-century sentimentalism and its vague afterglow, into a modern, hardened temperament for whom reunion with the dead was itself almost certainly a dead hypothesis. It was a position featuring denial of the supernatural, ridicule of belief in an afterlife, and a sense of utter abandonment by the Christian God, and Twain became one of its advocates. If for Howells the wire remained alive (even if suspiciously so), for Mark Twain, the wire eventually went dead, and life in those final years began looking like a "systemless system." But for Howells, his "hopeless passion for reunion with [Winny]" had "resolved itself into a patience in which [Winny] will always be present."

And so Howells ended up, near the end of his own life, endorsing a full embrace of the continuing bonds with the dead: "'Keep before you,' I would conjure them, 'the vision of the face, the form, you shall see no more on earth, and let it pass only of itself, hoping, longing for its return when it fades away. . . . Return in your tenderness, turn again in your despair, to the records of those happier years, and reconstruct from them the truer likeness of your beloved.'"[94] But even as he did so, and as the modern century took on a full steam, such an embrace was becoming harder and harder for American authors. It was an embrace that his good friend Mark Twain found impossible to duplicate—try as he might.

4

Mark Twain's Grief

Susy, Theodicy, and "Systemless System"

> It is an odious world, a horrible world—it is Hell; the true one, not the lying invention of the superstitious. . . . We have lost her, & our life is bitter. We may find her again—let us not despair of it.
>
> Twain to wife Livy, August 1896, in *Love Letters*, 328

> Howells was here yesterday afternoon, and I told him the whole scheme of this autobiography and its apparently systemless system—only apparently systemless, for it is not that.
>
> *Autobiography of Mark Twain*, 441

If Howells came to such a full embrace of the bonds with the dead, it was a lesson hard earned, and one that took him almost twenty years. But even by the summer of 1889, just months after Winny's death, he could write to his friend Mark Twain about something he had read in a strange book, "that consoled a little, namely: we saw and felt the Power of Deity in such fullness that we ought to infer the infinite Justice and Goodness which we did not see or feel."[1] Some might be surprised at reading Twain's complicated and largely religious response to Howells's gestures toward the transcendent in the face of his daughter's demise, as in a letter he wrote to his wife Livy: "this that Howells speaks to appeals to one's reason; it sounds like sense. We do see & feel the power of what we call God; we do see it & feel it in such measureless fullness, that we 'ought to infer' . . . that there is a large element of Justice & Goodness in His creature, man; & we may also infer that He has in Him Injustice & Ungoodness . . . Well, since what we call God made that preponderance of Goodness, he must have done it because he admired it, & he must have admired it because he discovered it to be his own principal feature. . . . I arrive at this result: I am plenty safe in *his* hands; I am not in any danger from that kind of Deity. The one that *I* want to keep out of the reach of is the caricature of him which one finds in the Bible." In effect, Twain's response broaches key questions about the justice of God, thus entering the territory of what theologians consider "theodicy": how we envision and defend God in light of the "problem of evil"—the widespread and often innocent pain and suffering in our world. For Twain, his friend Howells's grief was immediately contextualized in his own mind as a profoundly theological problem. Twain pictures God as containing justice and injustice, goodness and ungoodness, but having a "preponderance" of the better impulses. It amounts to a decidedly mixed bag, a rather Manichaean view of the world, and yet later in this letter, he assures Livy, "I don't know anything about the hereafter, but I am not afraid of it"—one of the strongest appeals to a belief in an afterlife that he would ever make, especially after this late date (1889).[2]

But along with this rather hopeful sort of confession, Twain's writings during the 1890s became mixed with heavy doses of what we can call "horror." Certainly fictions prior to 1890 contained strong images of horrific violence and death; for example, *Adventures of Huckleberry Finn* depicts the young Buck face down and dead in the Mississippi River, and *Connecticut Yankee* shows us unrelenting images of modern warfare, with piles of bodies and pools of blood. Such horrific images, and the philosophical consideration of them, would take a more prominent role in Twain's thinking as the 1890s proceeded. Twain's depictions of and meditations on "horror" have affinities with a long history in Western culture. And with the rapidly changing conditions of a "secular age" dawning, philosophical encounters with horror were capable of inducing a deathblow to any remaining concepts of transcendence. In other words, by the 1890s, intellectuals were primed and ready to receive in full the implications for theology of horrendous acts.[3]

The intellectual history of these concepts has roots as far back as the massive earthquake in Lisbon, Portugal, in 1755, an event that shook Europe literally and intellectually. One historian has called that moment the birth of the modern temperament: "The eighteenth century used the word Lisbon as we use the word Auschwitz today. . . . It takes no more than the name of a place to mean: the collapse of the most basic trust in the world."[4] Indeed, it was in the shadow of Lisbon that European attempts to forge a satisfactory theodicy emerged, chiefly from Leibniz, or the counterclaim of their inadequacies, as from Rousseau. Later, the so-called argument from horror, by which a concept of a benevolent God comes under severe attack due to the horrifying evils we confront everyday, was expressed in many ways throughout the nineteenth century. Perhaps this argument's most overwhelming version is stated by Ivan in Dostoyevsky's novel *The Brothers Karamazov* and features the extremes of cruelty and torture to question the goodness of God. David Bentley Hart has praised the genius of Dostoyevsky's argument, calling it "the only challenge to a confidence in divine goodness that should give Christians serious cause for deep and difficult reflection."[5] Hart's ingenious point is that most believers have not taken Ivan's (and Dostoyevsky's) argument from horror as seriously as they should: "Those Christian readers who have found it easy to ignore or dispense with the case Dostoyevsky constructs for Ivan have not fully comprehended that case."[6] Philip Tallon agrees with Hart in his account: "horror functions, in its expression of revolting disvalue, as the sharpest critique of divine providence that any aesthetic theme could offer."[7] Twain certainly engaged the poetics of horror, and used the word itself, in just these ways, as in his inclusion in the *Autobiography* of a report on an anti-Jewish riot in Kishinev, Russia, he reads in the *Jewish Daily News* (the report sounds like one of Ivan's lurid stories out of *Brothers Karamazov*): "The scenes of horror attending this massacre are beyond description. Babes were literally torn to pieces by the frenzied and blood-thirsty mob. The local police made no attempt to check the reign of terror. At sunset the streets were piled with corpses and wounded."[8] Among other things, Twain's invocation of horror goes well beyond lament or shame; as the theologians suggest, horror presents the strongest argument imaginable against the benevolence and justice of God. As such, the horrific encounter with a child's death, as in the case of the subjects of this volume, could produced a response experienced by many Victorian parents of limited or dissipated belief; in effect, the death of a child could destroy any remaining belief, becoming a final coup de grace against any serious loyalty toward God. And as we'll see, the deaths of not only US soldiers but also hundreds of children in the Philippines as casualties of war, became a real-time horror for Twain and his good friend Howells.

In these contexts, Twain's rather hopeful yet at times extrabiblical claim to depend on a certain "kind of Deity," especially in light of the multiplied "horrors" of the modern age, would be tested soon enough. When Mark Twain's lovely, highly intelligent adult daughter Susy died suddenly after days of delirium and an awful fever in the summer of 1896, he and Howells could easily see the clear links between their two daughters—and between themselves, as grieving fathers. Both daughters died at almost the exact same age, both shared the same precocious, artistic temperaments, and both died without parents at their side. Twain immediately recognized these similarities; in the coming days he looked to Howells (and then to other grieving parents) for consolation and for strategies of survival. Twain noticed how Howells remained deeply tied to his daughter Winny, and how he had incorporated into his written work a gentler and more sympathetic tone. As Howells later wrote: "Return in your tenderness, turn again in your despair, to the records of those happier years, and reconstruct from them the truer likeness of your beloved."[9] Twenty years after Winny passed, Howells was able to counsel the bereaved in such a tender matter.

But Twain's journey into the bowels of grief and despair was long and hard, if not traumatic. And it became even harder for his wife Livy, as it had for Elinor Howells. By late 1896, Mark Twain wrote to Livy: "It is an odious world, a horrible world—it is Hell."[10] The bad times, financial and otherwise, had deepened throughout the 1890s: financial distress due to the failure of the Paige typesetter; Twain's mother Jane suffered a stroke in Illinois and then died in October 1890; Livy's mother died a month later; and their youngest daughter Jean suffered intense epileptic seizures. Overall, the numbers of premature deaths Twain had suffered in his life by the mid-1890s are truly shocking: four siblings, a son, a niece, and a nephew. By the early 1890s, Twain himself began suffering chronic pain from rheumatism in his arm while Livy experienced increased problems with her heart, and the family as a whole closed the Hartford home in the summer of 1891 (for good, as it turned out) and relocated to Europe for most of the next nine years. Soon enough, the physical pain in his heart brought on by angina began to grow, affecting his thought processes and his mood, as Victor Doyno explains: "When elderly men suffer from angina, indicative of congestive heart failure and cardiac insufficiency, as Sam did, they usually do not get enough oxygen to the brain and accordingly may become confused and behave erratically, without normal inhibitions. Without pharmacological relief, congestive heart failure and angina can be painful, frightening, and disorienting. Mental confusion often accompanies cardiac subfunction, systemic depressants such as alcohol are actually not a person's friend, and the chest pain reminds the person in lucid moments that he is dying."[11] As Twain physically experienced decline and the onset of death, the dream of hearth and home seemed to be similarly disintegrating for the genteel family of Hartford. And his heart ached over the loss.

But a new day seemed to be dawning with the completion of his around-the-world tour of 1895–96, undertaken to pay off the massive debt. Twain was tired but optimistic, excited at the prospect of seeing the return of his financial fortunes, perhaps even living again in the beloved Hartford

Olivia Susan (Susy) Clemens (died 1896), far right, with family. Left to right: Clara, Mark Twain, Jean, Livy (mother), and Susy. Courtesy of the Mark Twain Papers and Project, Bancroft Library, University of California at Berkeley.

home. Just before the beginning of the journey, he had paid a visit to the house, after which he wrote to Livy of the experience, and of his great desire to reunite his family in the beloved home: "It seemed as if I had burst awake out of a hellish dream, and had never been away, and that you would come drifting down out of those dainty upper regions with the little children tagging after you. . . . I was seized with a furious desire to have us all in this house again and right away, and never go outside the grounds any more forever—certainly never again to Europe."[12] The "furious desire" of Twain's aging and, by now, literally aching heart, and the reason for all the hard work of paying off his extensive debts, was in fact a triumphant return to Hartford to live out the rest of his years, surrounded by a dear and loving family.

Sadly, it was not to be. In the hot summer of 1896, while resting in Great Britain near the journey's end, Twain anticipated with some joy and satisfaction the arrival of his two daughters Susy and Jean from America, neither of whom had accompanied him on the yearlong tour. But then in early August, around the time when they would be preparing to sail for England, a telegram brought Twain the news that Susy was ill. According to a later message, however, she apparently would recover given enough time. Twain decided to stay in England and send his wife Livy across the sea to nurse Susy back to health.

It was one of the decisions he bitterly regretted for the rest of his life. Many biographers have considered Susy to be the favored daughter, their most prized production. Indeed, it may not be too much to say her mother Livy nearly worshipped her: Livy's letters to Susy are filled with tender affections unlike those notable in letters to the other two daughters. Clara later wrote, "[my parents] must have loved and admired my elder sister, Susy, by far the most, which made it all the more wonderful that they could so completely disguise the fact."[13] Although the matter of Susy being the definite "favorite" of her father remains a vexed question, we can be assured that her death provoked profound and lifelong effects on the Clemens household.[14] On one level, Susy's demise constituted for Twain the sudden death of hope's most tangible expression—the hopes embodied in our children. His narration of the episodes surrounding her death in the *Autobiography* includes some of the most poignant lines he would ever compose. The passage is worthy of lengthy quotation:

> At the hour when my wife and Clara set sail for America, Susy was in no danger. 3 hours later there came a sudden change for the worse. Meningitis set in, and it was immediately apparent that she was death struck. That was Saturday, 15 August.
>
> That evening she took food for the last time. (Jean's letter to me.) The next morning the brain fever was raging. She walked the floor little in her pain and delirium, then succumbed to weakness and return[ed] to her bed. Previously she had found hanging in a closet again a gown which she had seen her mother wear. She thought it was her mother, dead, and she kissed it, and cried. About noon she became blind (an effect of the disease) and bewailed it to her uncle. From Jean's letter I take this sentence, which needs no comment:
>
> About one in the afternoon Susy spoke for the last time.
>
> It was only one word that she said when she spoke that last time, and it told of her longing. She groped with her hands and found Katie, and caressed her face and said "mamma."
>
> How gracious it was that in that forlorn hour of rack and ruin, with the night of death closing around her, she should have been granted that beautiful illusion—that the latest vision which rested upon the clouded mirror of her mind should've been the vision of

> her mother, and the latest emotion she should know in life the joy and peace of that dear imagined presence.[15]

Twain, remembering the events years later, evidently did find some consolation in the disturbed hallucinations of his dying daughter. But mainly these lines illustrate a sense of the sheer terror that even a great writer found hard to articulate. Twain also wrote extremely accurate lines about the emotionally numbing first encounter with this disaster, lines coming soon after his loss: "It is one of the mysteries of our nature that a man, all unprepared, can receive a thunderstroke like that and live. There is but one reasonable explanation of it. The intellect is stunned by the shock and but gropingly gathers the meaning of the words. The power to realize their full import is mercifully wanting. The mind has a dumb sense of vast loss—that is all. It will take mind and memory months, and possibly years, to gather together the details and thus learn and know the whole extent of the loss."[16] But when Mark Twain said these words in February 1906, he was speaking from the experience of almost ten full years since the death of Susy—and eighteen months after Livy's death.

In these poignant comments, we have an almost perfect expression of what trauma encompasses: a severe shock, seeming to be almost an act of nature or of God, a jolt that takes some amount of time to process and comprehend. This aspect of trauma is called "latency" or belatedness. Here is how psychologist Shelly Rambo describes the latency phenomenon: "trauma has a double structure: the actual occurrence of violent event and a belated awakening to the event. Trauma is not solely located in the actual event but, instead, it encompasses the return of that event(s), the ways in which the event is not concluded . . . an inability to fully process an event means that it returns. This return distinguishes trauma and suffering. Suffering is what, in time, can be integrated into one's understanding of the world. Trauma is what is not integrated in time; it is the difference between a closed and an open wound. . . . The experience of survival is one in which life, as it once was, cannot be retrieved."[17] Similarly, Cathy Caruth describes latency this way: "the pathology consists, rather, solely in the *structure of its experience* or reception: the event is not assimilated or experienced fully at the time, but only belatedly, its repeated *possession* of the one who experiences it . . . the impact of the traumatic event lies precisely in its belatedness, in its refusal to be simply located, in its insistent appearance outside the boundaries of any single place or time."[18] Long before psychologists standardized the term and the experience, Mark Twain set down on paper a striking account of latency. He refers to the lengthy period after a traumatic event until the full realization of that event—a period that can take months or even years. In the case of parental grief, the latency period typically runs two to three years or more, with much evidence to suggest that it is in the fourth year that many grieving parents actually bottom out.[19]

The concept of latency helps explain why some of Twain's friends and family thought he looked fine in the months after Susy's death. For instance, nearly a full year after Susy's death, Susan Crane wrote to Samuel Moffett, July 22, 1897, from Weggis: "I now wish to tell you that I find your uncle Sam looking well, and seeming quite himself. He is cheerful and full of work, and never more gentle and lovely. It is a joy to see him, and hear him talk. This moment I hear him singing, always a sweet sound."[20] There is an indication here, eleven months after Susy's death, that Twain is still struggling with latency and belatedness. The description by his sister-in-law Susan Crane indicates that he's just fine, "seeming quite himself." Although outwardly he appears to be joyful and happy, a clinical reading of these accounts suggests that he hasn't quite yet bottomed out, or fully grasped the loss. It is also striking that Twain seemed to understand this latency period, when he spoke of it a decade after Susy's death: "It will be years before the tale of lost essentials is complete, and not till then can he truly know the magnitude of his disaster."[21] This remark also suggests a lengthy period of continuing bonds with Susy, to the extent that "truly knowing" what has been lost refers to his daughter, and the "lost essentials" some version of her legacy, which require completion.

Despite numerous outward indications, Twain and his wife found it difficult to process the trauma. Twain's inability is seen in several letters; for instance, he tells Susan Crane on September 30, 1896: "Oh, oh, oh, dear Sue, I cannot believe it, cannot realize it, cannot accept it! It is a dream, & will pass, & Susy will come again."[22] This inability to "realize" a death was a common trope of the nineteenth century; the word "realize" is defined in the 1828 *Webster's Dictionary* in several germane ways: "to impress on the mind as a reality," and "to feel in all its force." The latter definition describes an inability to feel the fullness of an emotion; it suggests it takes some time to do so, and Twain recognized early on that "it will be years [to realize] the magnitude." Twain had noted in earlier works, including in *Connecticut Yankee*, a sense of language's inability to impress upon the mind the reality of a matter. In a well-known passage, he writes: "it was only just words, words—they meant nothing in the world to him, I might just as well have whistled. Words realize nothing, vivify nothing to you, unless you have suffered in your own person the thing which the words try to describe."[23]

More specific to the issue of grieving, it is intriguing that the verb "realize" as an idiom for latency was in common usage before the concept became a standard psychological term. Drew Gilpin Faust explains in more detail, regarding a delayed response to a loved one's death: "Civil War letter and journal writers confronting the news of loss repeatedly proclaimed their inability to 'realize' a death—using the word with now antiquated precision to mean to render it real in their own minds. . . . Making a death real, feeling and accepting its certainty, required effort. After her brother James was killed at Second Bull Run, Sarah Palmer wrote in anguish to her sister Harriet, 'I can't realize that I am never to see that dear boy again . . . it is too hard to realize.'"[24] Mark and Livy often used the verb "realize" in this rather antiquated way, in describing the elusive nature of the death of Susy. In a letter to Laurence Hutton, dated September 6, 1896, Twain writes: "[Next week] I shall know how our incredible & unrealizable disaster came about."[25] Fairly early in the process, he seems to sense that it will take much time to process and thus to "realize" the full extent of the loss. In October 1896 he writes to Ned Bunce: "The sense of our stupendous disaster grows, day by day, instead of diminishing."[26] Remembering the news of her death a full decade later, he wrote: "The power to realize their full import is mercifully wanting."[27] And Livy, in 1899, writes regarding the old Hartford house and its memories: "Generally the mere thought of the place nearly breaks my heart when I faintly realize that I shall not find her there."[28] The loss is still not completely grasped, in this construction, over three full years after Susy's death. Racked with guilt and hearing contested accounts, Twain and Livy struggled to process the horror, and perhaps, never truly did so. And if anything, Livy's letters to family and friends document an even more unrelenting traumatic grief, and document as well her own battles with latency and the realization of the death of Susy.

The story of Mark Twain as caregiver for his wife Livy, and the couple's joint experience of grief, horror, and perhaps trauma, has yet to be fully narrated. Perhaps most moving of all are the scores of letters Livy wrote in the years afterward to a few, select friends. As late as January 1898, nearly eighteen months after Susy's death, Livy writes to a friend, "Constantly she visits me in my dreams and I feel that if I were to go to the Hartford house or to Elmira I should certainly find her. Friends say that time softens trouble: I do not know, I hope it may be so, I have not found it yet."[29] In April 1897, she writes, "The air seems full of voices telling me that Susy is dead, yet I cannot take it in. . . . How terrible it seems that mothers live to bury their children."[30] If we hesitate to call Susy the favorite daughter of her father, we can certainly state that there was a very deep and special relation between her and her mother that transcended whatever we can perceive with the other two, Clara and Jean. Twain recognized this exclusive connection—and the horror the death visited in particular upon Susy's mother—making his caregiving even more grievous.

There is great sorrow in letters like these: a parent's slow recognition that as long periods pass, not only does the pain not subside but it might even become more severe. Even as friends often seem to suggest to Sam and Livy that "time will heal the wounds," like many grieving parents they begin to discover that this is clearly not the case, and the really dark secret they reveal to intimates is that in fact time aggravates the horror. Indeed, much recent research has shown that for grieving parents, it is often three or more years after a child's death that the pain and grieving enter their lowest points, and become often most horrific. This reality is due to a large extent on the latency period of grieving, often quite lengthy. And so about three and a half years after Susy's death, Livy seems to recognize that the healing myth is not working for her. She writes in December 1899 to Grace King: "I could not go back to Hartford. The heartbreaking associations there and all the changes. I still find it very difficult to live without Susy, of course I shall always find it very very difficult. In the old place would it not be still more nearly impossible? Generally the mere thought of the place nearly breaks my heart when I faintly realize that I shall not find her there."[31]

Meanwhile, as Livy was writing such heartbreaking material, her husband loomed nearby, watching her struggle in her agonies. It is just prior to this time, in June 1899, that Twain writes to Joe Twichell about his own recognition that the pain may never subside, and that his experience of Susy's death three full years earlier would become, as it had with Howells, a permanent wound. The letter simultaneously records his mental confusions and his brokenness of memory, also common among bereaved parents. This unpublished letter suggests that Twain's experience had become, in other words, what we now call trauma, and further, that he had somehow become cognizant of some of these features of trauma: "In some ways time does not merely fly, now, it vanishes; it takes little or no account of intervals that are actual abysses. It seems only a few weeks since I last saw Susy—yet that was 1895, & this is 1899. On the other hand it seems many, many years since I saw those two fine Whitmore lads that have been taken away—but it is not many, at all. I think I perceive, by Howells' letters, that to him Winny's death is still recent."[32] There is an element of dread here, as Twain notices that Howells is still haunted by Winny, though she had by then been dead over ten years. It is a sobering moment in the letters of Mark Twain, regarding his powerful perceptions of his own grieving. Such personal letters suggest that the philosophical problem of evil—and the necessity of tailoring one's vision of God according to this acute, modern problem, or of dismissing God completely—haunted the thoughts of Mark Twain and Livy after Susy's death.

One consolation for Twain was his understanding that at the moment of her death, Susy believed her mother to be nearby, though in fact Livy was still crossing the Atlantic on a ship. (Livy suffered tremendous guilt over not being at her side, however, as did Twain.) Another consoling idea was that Susy died young and innocent; she would not have to face life's most dreary trials. Her innocence and purity had been maintained. "Susy died at the right time, the fortunate time of life; the happy age—24 years. At 24, such a girl has seen the best of life—life is a happy dream. After that age the risks begin; responsibility comes, and with it the cares, the sorrow, and the inevitable tragedy."[33] Twain's mind and his heart were telling him competing stories. For example, he wrote to Livy not long after the death of Susy, "I pitied you in this awful trouble that my mistakes have brought upon you. You forgive me, I know, but I shall never forgive myself while the life is in me."[34] Feeling tremendous guilt (as they had at the sudden death of their firstborn, Langdon), and hearing contested accounts of what had actually transpired, Twain and Livy grew extremely bitter about the lack of proper medical care and the negative influence of spiritual healers.[35] Twain wrote to Henry Rogers on December 18, 1896: "We are bearing Susy's wholly unnecessary death as well as we can. The hard part to bear is the knowledge that if she had been with wise and thoughtful friends instead of with [fools here scratched out] the other sort, she would be with us to-day."[36] Daughter Clara went even further: she writes to Alice Day that Susy "was simply killed by mental science & spiritualism, without the least exaggeration. A murder it was, a demented cold-blooded unforgivable murder!"[37] Surely Clara's views were influenced by the bitterness and regret of her parents. Soon enough, Twain turned his bitterness against a concrete figure: Mary Baker Eddy, founder of Christian Science.

All in all, Twain's material on Susy's death includes some of the most emotional and distressing passages ever written by one of America's great authors. It often features nostalgia saturated in pathos and sentiment, evoking some of Twain's most tender moments. Likewise, Susy's death prompted some of the bitterest screeds ever recorded by an American as well. The cauldron of Twain's genius was now set to boiling with nostalgia and rage, sentiment and fury. In effect, Twain's grief experiences produced a deeply divided response that has not been fully recognized as such—one of the predictable patterns of bereaved parents. With Mark Twain's grief, we begin to encounter in full force what might be considered a more "modern" response, especially in contrast with the narratives of the writers described earlier. Twain's experience forty years after Stowe's is deeply informed by the spiritual crisis of his age, including the effects of a lengthy "death of dying" in the general culture and the shift toward skepticism and often rejection of a Christian frame of reference. Again, the culture of Twain's time was unprecedented in the sheer number of plausible options among the intelligentsia. The "conditions of belief" had become compromised by the "nova effect" of the nineteenth century: an expanding, highly contested field of cross-polemics that resulted from so many new and compelling options for belief, making unbelief fully viable—even though such unbelief came with a strong dose of loss and malaise in the wake of disenchantment.[38]

Importantly, and in the midst of this nova effect, Twain's experience generally lacked the consolations of faith that marked the lives of earlier Americans, including those that had aided his neighbor Stowe. His experience enacts "the decline of sentimentalism and accordingly an increasing emphasis on the 'privatization of grief,'" as Peter Messent puts it.[39] And outside of a growing (and sometimes theological) correspondence with the Reverend Joe Twichell, he lacked a faith community in which to find solace and theological explanation (including any substantive appeals to theodicy). Under such conditions of the emerging "secular age," much different from the antebellum years in which Stowe suffered her loss, Mark and Livy's grief experience was surely even more grueling.[40] Twain's sister-in-law Molly, wife of the religious Orion, picks up on these important changes in an undated letter to an unnamed recipient: "I think it is very sad that Livy refuses to be comforted. Strange she cannot feel that Susie is hers just as much as ever. But that Susie was translated just a little before herself. I thank God always for my precious faith."[41] Molly discerns the dire emotional circumstances for parental grief in an increasingly skeptical age. Her unspoken assumptions come straight from such New Testament texts as I Thessalonians 4:13: that those who believe need not sorrow, "even as those with no hope." Molly's statement is a predictable response that illustrates the belief that the hope of the gospel and the consolations of faith could somehow lessen the pain. Without that hope, the suffering might become unimaginable. As Pat Jalland claims, "for those Victorian agnostics who doubted the existence of God and were unconvinced by the concept of an afterlife, the trauma of the death of a loved one could be overwhelming."[42]

In lieu of a religious community, Twain drew some solace from those who had suffered a similar fate; he recognized himself as full member of the fraternity of fathers who had lost their grown-up children, and thus can understand each other in ways that "outsiders" cannot. Obviously Howells provided wise experience and their friendship deepened, about which more below. His good friend Henry Rogers had lost his seventeen-year-old daughter Millicent in 1890, and though there does not seem to be any written record of his response, Rogers committed extensive funds to prolonging her memory and legacy in the form of the Millicent Library in Fairhaven, Massachusetts. The stunning Italian Renaissance–style building began to rise in 1891–92, and features a memorial window of the deceased daughter that one can admire to this day. Mark Twain visited the Millicent Library at least twice, once in 1894 and again in 1901.[43] Similarly, he appreciated the note from Wayne MacVeagh, another unfortunate member of the club of bereaved fathers: "The solacing word from you, who have suffered the like disaster with us has value, & we thank you for saying it. . . . We two are now passing through what you two passed through before us—the daily shock, the ghastly shock which the morning brings, when we wake—and remember! And we live on. How, we do not know—nor why."[44] To another friend after the death of their second grown son, Twain later writes: "There is no office for words to perform, except to rejoice for Susy, & say no word more further, than to offer love & sympathy of this family, who know what you feel, we being Past Masters in grief."[45] As Livy writes to a friend whose husband has died, "when one has had a great trouble oneself it gives one a great feeling of tenderness for others that are suffering."[46]

Besides bitterness mixed with longing, Twain's letters often ask theological questions. For the Clemens family, Susy's demise becomes an overwhelming instance of the problem of evil in human life. We might call her suffering and death illustrations of a "horror" in the sense Philip Tallon describes: "Horror, in art or in life, violates our sense of proper order and thus undermines our ability to trust the order of the world or to positively relate ourselves to the world around us. . . . Horror, in these cases, works to stump theodicy into silence."[47] One result may be Twain's imagining of a "systemless system," as his *Autobiography* aims to illustrate, but another more general and clear outcome is Twain's growing obsession with (and ultimately, his bitter rejection of) the Christian search for theodicy: an explanation of why a good God would allow such unspeakable acts, examples of "horrendous evils," as had visited his innocent daughter.[48]

The letters of both parents reflect an engagement with horror and a quest to locate some kind of response to it—but the intuition that such a response may be, under present conditions, impossible. Livy beseeches her friend Grace King: "What a mystery it all is. What a heartbreaking mystery. . . . I cannot at all reconcile myself to going on in this world with Susy gone out of it." Several times Twain calls Susy's death "unnecessary," questioning the justice of it all.[49] In writing his condolences to Twain, Ned Bunce invokes the problem of evil in a letter of October 5, 1896: He sends "loving sympathy that I have for you all in the awful bereavements that you have suffered. So far as a poor finite mind can see, the blotting out of existence of a life so full of intellectual vigor and the many qualities that lent their aid to the making up of a lovely character—is a calamity and it is hard to believe that it is all for the best. Just before we went away for the summer Susie was at our house and we both remarked upon her wonderful mental attainments and had an opportunity to see a trait of her character that, if possible, endeared her to us more than ever. Then a little later when we called to see her at Mrs. [?] to say good bye—I had the fortune to take her away from the musical people in the house and had an old time talk with her on the piazza and I am thankful that my last sight of her was such that it remains with me as a loving memory—What can I say."[51] The difficulty of believing Susy's death was "for the best" is a response to a standard remark from friends and family, and gestures to a right belief in God's will and sovereignty. However, Bunce recognizes how unhelpful such a comment is to the grieving. In fact, as theologian David Bentley Hart puts it, it is an egregious remark that "only a moral cretin" might make, given the sheer experience of horror: "Most of us would have the good sense to be ashamed to speak such words."[52] The statement that a horrendous evil is somehow God's will is especially heinous. And yet, as any person grieving the dead knows, well-intended friends make such comments all the time. Twain's response indicates how Bunce's pondering of God's justice was a regular feature of his own meditations: "It is with me as it is with you, dear Ned: I cannot see the reason for it nor the justice of it. To me, there was no explicable pretext for taking her away & no apparent justification of the act. . . . The sense of our stupendous disaster grows, day by day, instead of diminishing. What a loss it was! It is as Livy says: 'Others that are bereaved try to comfort us, & say Be patient, & wait—time will heal the wound. What do *they* know? They have not lost a Susy Clemens.'"[53]

Twain appeals to divine justice—but confesses an inability to "see the reason for it nor the justice." His genuine desire seems to be to discover some kind of justification for Susy's death: an explanation of God's justice in the face of her seemingly needless suffering. Her demise seems unfair, since "there are plenty that wanted to go, plenty that would have paid a premium for her place; and she did not want to go." If Stowe's heroic and redemptive response represents an earlier, more conservative and sentimental worldview, then Twain's later response, tainted more by the conditions of the "nova effect" of growing unbelief, represents a sustained attack against such a view—with certain exceptions. When disaster struck his family, Twain was already well along the road toward a modern skepticism of all things religious. During the years he resided in Hartford, he had become a regular and even habitual practitioner of the town's pervasive social Christianity, under the wing of his good friend and pastor, the Reverend Joseph Twichell. For almost twenty years, he spent more time with Twichell than any of his other male friends, traveled with him, attended his church and supported it financially, and often prayed with him.[54] But their relationship changed dramatically when the storms of the 1890s hit, and the Clemenses moved away from Hartford and its edifying, strongly religious social milieu. Culminating with the death of Susy, the calamities represented too much spiritual turmoil, including doses of horror. Powerless to accept the horror of Susy's painful, seemingly "unnecessary" death, and unable to discern any meaning and purpose in it, Mark Twain's turn toward nihilism and a form of a deeply contested skepticism, one symptomatic of the emergent "secular age," had reached critical mass.

And yet despite these strong conditions of modern unbelief, in the months after Susy's death, Mark and Livy immersed themselves in older, romantic versions of the poetry of mourning. Most importantly, the Clemenses became absorbed in reading and re-reading Alfred Lord Tennyson's famous eulogy *In Memoriam* (1849). Both recalled that Tennyson was one of Susy's favorite poets as a young lady. Livy received a copy from her friend John McAlister, after which she wrote: "How can I thank you for the exquisite copy of *In Memoriam* which has just reached me. You must have divining power because it is exactly what I was wanting. I have been reading the poem a good deal this Winter."[55] Tennyson's poem is a long and profound meditation on loss and grief, and as one historian writes, "*In Memoriam* held great meaning for many Victorians in mourning . . . they were reassured to know that Tennyson's search for faith finally triumphed over doubt."[56] Twain wrote about the poem in a letter from Weggis, Switzerland, dated July 20, 1897—the month before the one-year anniversary of Susy's death: "I have read part of *In Memoriam* again. It *is* a noble poem. Mrs. Clemens reads it persistently, & thanks you all the time for the healing it brings her."[57] Twain's admiration for Tennyson's long elegy is worth noting, especially in its obsessive nostalgia for family, which he now associated with the irrecoverable Hartford home where they all were at their happiest together. Many passages in Tennyson's poem also describe the kinds of physical symptoms that plague the bereaved, and which certainly were major aspects of Twain's experience after the loss of Susy: the hauntings of the dead, the deep sense of feeling like a "guilty thing," and the persistence of sleeplessness.

Another volume of particular comfort for Twain and Livy, which they often read together, was *Palgrave's Golden Treasury of Songs & Poems* (1892). Twain's personal copy is filled with marginalia written during the initial period of grief, generally with reference to poems speaking of death and bereavement. The volume was inscribed to Clara on August 17, 1896, and was given to Twain by Carlyle Smythe, his lecture agent. Clara returned to her parents in London on September 9, and Twain would have presented the book to her relatively soon after her landing, so it is likely he read and marked up the poems in the several weeks following the news of Susy's death. From the many marginalia, it is evident that he favored the elegiac verse of Shakespeare, Wordsworth, Shelley, Keats, and Byron, among others. Twain was clearly drawn to expressions of despair and doom: "I feel like one / Who treads alone / Some banquet-hall deserted," writes Thomas Moore in "The Light of Other Days." He likes Keats's confession: "when I feel, fair Creature of the hour! / That I shall never look upon thee more, . . . / then on the shore / Of the wide world I stand alone." He is distinctly moved by intimations of immortality: inspired by the idea of "aerial kisses / Of shapes that haunt Thought's wilderness." He stresses lines like the "nurslings of immortality" in Shelley's "The Poet's Dream" as well as Wordsworth's "thoughts whose very sweetness yieldeth proof / That they were born for immortality" in his "Within King's College Chapel, Cambridge." Shakespeare is marked more than any other poet, including the transformative lines from *The Tempest* that would become important to T. S. Eliot later: "Those are pearls that were his eyes: / Nothing of him that doth fade, / But doth suffer a sea change." Most of all, the marginalia indicate that Twain was drawn especially to formal elegies like "Elegy on Thyrza" and "Elegy," both by Lord Byron, which feature lines of a style and tone similar to those found in the elegy he composed for Susy. "Elegy on Thyrza" is particularly highlighted, with more of Twain's markings than any other poem in the volume. Twain scored several of its stanzas, at times two or even three times, including themes such as the desire to have been at the deathbed, and the idea that it might be best she died young, and thus spared the horror of decay: "earthly eye but ill can bear / To trace the change to foul from fair."[58] Overall, the notations in this volume put to rest his own mockery of "cemetery poetry" from earlier days: in the darkest hours of his life, Mark Twain found elegies expressive of his own metaphysical fears and loneliness, and at times he found them deeply comforting.

The highlighted poems from *Palgrave's Golden Treasury*, Tennyson's *In Memoriam*, and Twain's first elegy for Susy attest to the growing attractions of a romantic sensibility after the death of a loved one, a sense that a bond continues with the dead, the person remains the same, and a loving relationship cannot be terminated by the death experience. Twain's first elegy for Susy, also called "In Memoriam," was written on the first anniversary of Susy's death, in August 1897 at Lake Lucerne in Switzerland. Surviving parents have regularly observed the anniversaries of a child's death, and the Clemenses did so for years. In his notebook, Twain writes: "One year to-day since the great disaster fell. Livy went away to be alone. She took the steamer & spent the day solitary in an inn in an unknown town up the lake—a village. I spent the day alone under the trees on the mountain side writing some lines—a lament for Susy in the form of an allegory."[59] This first elegy idealizes Susy and features the sentimental mode that Twain famously denounced in earlier writings; it insists the bond with Susy remains viable and constructive, and it features no irony or bitterness whatsoever. But on the second anniversary, he wrote another, dramatic poem: "Broken Idols." Compared with the sacred and hushed tone of "In Memoriam," Twain's "Broken Idols" (dated August 18, 1898) is filled with throbbing pain and near delirium. The main speaker of "Broken Idols" is a woman, patterned after his wife Livy. We know the neurotic wife to be Livy, based on a letter she wrote to a friend announcing the connection: "Shall I tell you a secret? . . . Mr Clemens wrote me an other poem on the 18th of August last. It gives, in a most beautiful way I think, three or four pictures of Susy's life from her young childhood until the day of her death."[60] What Livy passes over in this description (almost as if she is unable to "realize" it) is how the poem depicts her. "Broken Idols" is a terrifying account of a mother physically oppressed with grief, experiencing wild mood fluctuations and hallucinations, and near madness. If the first elegy is the sentimental Twain at his finest, then the second records the haunted mind of the far more commonly remembered "dark" Twain.[61]

When we consider the biographical accounts of the late Twain, which emphasize a mainly nihilistic mood that often manifests as fury toward God, it is clear which side of the divide has received the most critical attention. Unfortunately, for decades, Twain's final period was generalized as simply the "dark years," but more recent biographers have contested this view.[62] While such a revision is well overdue, it does not deny that a strong case can be made for those final years being filled with much darkness and despair. But as has now also become apparent, the darkness was interspersed with much light, laughter, nostalgic storytelling, appeals to sentiment, and flat-out joy. Thus a fuller and richer picture of the aging author has emerged, one showing a man of highly divided nature—in fact, divided almost to epic proportions. Nobody could be quite so sweet and nostalgic, or nearly so bitter and furious, as the late Mark Twain.

However, it also seems clear that Twain's "continuing bond" with Susy remained a major motivating factor in many of the most positive achievements for the remainder of his writing and public career—perhaps even the central factor—and that he was often able to exploit appeals to sentiment and sympathy with great sophistication. Twain's grief over Susy's death, including his rigorous role as caregiver and observer of Livy's torturous experience, seems to have enhanced Twain's sympathy for the downtrodden and the resulting growth in his social justice agenda in the years after 1896. And Susy's death also commenced a long train of meditations about religion and the nature of God and evil—themes that critics find compelling in the later writings. As has often been observed in clinical studies, grief can actually soften an otherwise hardened heart; it can reinvigorate emotional sensibilities that have lain dormant for a long time. The strong urge to begin dictating his *Autobiography*, filled with passages of remarkable nostalgia, reminiscence, compassion, and meditative beauty, can also be associated with the death of Susy, along with the prolonged suffering and then death in 1904 of Livy. And so I argue that constructive effects did emerge from Twain's experience with Susy's death, but that these effects were always immediately in tension with the more sinister effects of his own traumatic experience, as well as his intense suffering for nearly eight years as Livy's caregiver. His semiautobiographical picture of suffering is most memorably captured in "Broken Idols"—a minor masterpiece of Twain's final years.

"Broken Idols" illustrates that Twain exemplified one key category of the modern grieving parent: a deeply divided nature. The split tendency is certainly a plausible conclusion based on the data we have available. Clinical research indicates that bereaved parents often feel torn in half, torn in two directions, and have great difficulty reconciling themselves. This divided feeling is very common, as Dennis Klass explains: "When the symbols of affiliation of the parents' worldview are not useful, some live in a divided world. They maintain a *bond with the transcendent* that is linked to their children. In other parts of their lives, however, they feel cut off from the God in whom they still believe."[63] After Susy died, the most significant work Twain would accomplish came out of either of these two, competing impulses. I argue that the best and most moving work of it all emerged from his constructive response to his bonds with Susy. As he says so memorably in "Broken Idols": "The fires of grief! *They* lap the heart in flame, / *They* smelt the red gold free! It is the bleeding heart / That pays the due of woe in minted coin."[64] "Broken Idols" contains some of the most heartbreaking material Twain ever composed on the topic of loss and bears strong autobiographical witness to the pathos and mental horror of Twain's experience. But strikingly, the poem also depicts how the pain of the "bleeding heart" actually "pays the due of woe in minted coin." There is value to be reaped from this horror, Twain seems to admit. As such, his poem might remind us of Stowe's many appeals to her sentimental and religious readers that they must mindfully "kiss the rod" of afflictions, and thereby accept in hope the discipline of the Lord. To take Stowe's appeal back even further, we can quote Calvin's *Institutes*: Stowe embraced the idea that "the more we are afflicted with adversities, the more surely our fellowship with Christ is confirmed! By communion with him the very sufferings themselves not only become blessed to us but also help much in promoting our salvation."[65] "Broken Idols" shows that Twain was still open to a secularized version of this foundation of Reformed thinking—absent the communion in Christ, but nevertheless sensing intuitively that some constructive elements might arise out of our adversities.

Indeed, constructive growth did at times come out of his life's worst disaster. Surprisingly, Twain may have been most powerful and authentic, and finally perhaps most convincing, when his work derived overtly from the death of Susy, whose horrific death became symbolic of the great suffering and pain of human existence. Twain seemed to recognize that the horror of her death betrayed any attempt to explain it; he sensed it to be symptomatic of what Hart has written of such horrendous evils: they present "the only challenge to a confidence in divine goodness that should give Christians serious cause for deep and difficult reflection."[66] The divided response to grief that we have already outlined is similar to his divided theory of autobiography. After Susy's death, followed by Livy's eight years later, Mark Twain yearned for further immersion into the past. He had made many attempts at an autobiography over the years, for example, but as the new century began the project took on a renewed momentum in Twain's mind. It had been in the planning stages for many years, first in a number of botched beginnings, followed by approximately 450,000 words that were dictated in about 252 sessions, from January 1906 through most of 1909. Albert Paine had the bright idea of hiring a stenographer in order to help him record Twain's seemingly random, stream of consciousness efforts. And so when he dictated his *Autobiography,* Twain was usually lying in bed, dressed in his silk nightgown, and propped up against the pillows.

The *Autobiography* as we now have it is surely an unwieldy collection, and out of its half million words, what is a reader to make of it? For our purposes, a good place to begin is with Twain's theory of autobiography, which as he explained in his own words, involved his attempt to produce what he called a "systemless system." He famously described the concept to his literary mentor, William Dean Howells: "Howells was here yesterday afternoon, and I told him the whole scheme of this autobiography and it's apparently systemless system—only apparently systemless, for it is not that. It is a deliberate system, and the law of the system is that I shall talk about the matter which for the moment interests me, and cast it aside and talk about something else the moment its interest for me is exhausted. It is a system which follows no charge and course and is not going to follow any such course. It is a system which is a complete and purposed jumble—a course which begins nowhere, follows no specified route, and can never reach an end while I am alive."[67] Twain's theory of autobiography is deeply tied to his growing sense that life may simply be a random system without center, without purpose, possibly without meaning, a system dominated by evil and suffering, with no evident meaning or redemption from that suffering. In theological terms, we also should recognize the grieving parent wrestling with the age-old philosophical problem of evil, Twain's quest for theodicy—a defense of God in the face of radical evil. In effect, Twain was unable to come up with a satisfactory answer; he failed, like many intellectuals during that same period, to develop a satisfactory theodicy. The world itself, with the death of the innocent Susy, seemed more and more to be a "systemless system," run by an absentee landlord, and as a result, he moved deeper into nihilistic philosophy. The random and serendipitous form of the *Autobiography*, like much modern art and fiction, was a natural outgrowth of that movement.

In the context of his grief, we can analyze certain major themes of the *Autobiography*, in particular, what these dictations reveal about Mark Twain's theological and philosophical tendencies in the last years of his life. Two major themes in the *Autobiography* are related to this: Twain's struggles with the theological concept of theodicy and the problems he associated with pain and suffering; and his developing critique of American empire and what he labeled "Christendom" (a topic broaching both politics and theology, and a subject of reading and research he delightedly undertook with his good friend Howells after his return to America in 1900, about which more will be discussed later). Twain's embrace of futility is depicted in the form and method of his autobiographical plan. Twain's "systemless system" is reflective of how he came to view the "systemlessness" of the universe, a pointlessness that leads beyond a merely modern sensibility into the postmodern. He came to believe that God's alleged control and benevolence were a dangerous fiction imprisoning naive minds. As with many of his generation, and inspired by popular speakers like Robert Ingersoll, Twain came to believe that rejecting the superstitions of the past and facing the scientific realities of the modern world were moral necessities.[68] This process, he thought, was essentially a passage from innocence to maturity, a "growing up" that was one of the crucial insights of his age: "the stance of maturity, of courage, of manliness, over against childish fears and sentimentality."[69] In short, Twain's theory of autobiography had affinities with his emerging theory of the universe. And his theory of the world and of God was deeply affected by his experience of tragedy and suffering, and his dissatisfaction with Christian accounts of theodicy and biblical defenses of God's justice left him deeply alienated from the American church.

In Twain's autobiographical writings at the end of his life, several metaphors repeatedly occur, seeming to reflect an inability to integrate the trauma of Susy's death into his understanding of the world. The terms *disaster* and *catastrophe* recur, as they do in the mourning letters: Twain's horror is characterized as great disasters, life-altering traumas. In particular the images of horror often feature either a house burning down, or a ship lost at sea. For example, he writes: "A man's house burns down.

The smoking wreckage represents only a ruined home that was dear through years of use and pleasant associations. . . . It is irrevocable what he lost. He did not realize that it was an essential when he had it; he only discovers it now when he finds himself all, hampered, by its absence. It will be years before the tale of lost essentials is complete, and not till then can he truly know the magnitude of his disaster."[70] Both cataclysmic metaphors—ships dead in the water, houses burning to the ground—may suggest to us today the concept of latency in trauma theory. They also illustrate the mindlessly repetitive disasters of the human condition—what Friedrich Nietzsche famously dubbed the "eternal recurrence." These seemingly futile repetitions became associated in Twain's mind with the "systemless system" of humanity: randomness, aimlessness, and ultimately futility, all central themes of the *Autobiography*. In one typical passage, he writes: "a myriad of men are born; they labor and sweat and struggle for bread; they squabble and scold and fight; they scramble for little mean advantages over each other; age creeps upon them; infirmities follow; Shames and humiliations bring down their prides and their vanities; those they love are taken from them, and the joy of life is turned to aching grief. The burden of pain, care, misery, grows heavier year-by-year; at length ambition is dead; pride is dead; vanity is dead; longing for release is in their place. It comes at last—the only un-poisoned gift Earth ever had for them—and they vanish from a world where they were of no consequence; where they achieve nothing; where they were a mistake and a failure and a foolishness; where they have left no sign that they have existed—a world which will limit them a day and forget them forever. Then another myriad takes their place, and copies all they did, and goes along the same profitless road, and vanishes as they vanished—to make room for another and another and 1 million other myriads to follow the same area path to the same desert and accomplish what the 1st., And all the myriads that came after it accomplished—nothing!"[71] Similarly, in spring of 1903 he writes, "the coat of arms of the human race ought to consist of a man with an ax on his shoulder proceeding toward a grindstone. Or, it ought to represent the several members of the human race holding out the hat to each other. For they are all beggars. Each in his own way. . . . None of the lot is ashamed of himself, but he despises the rest of the mendicants. Each admires his own dignity, and carefully guards it, but in his opinion the others haven't any."[72]

Such ramblings become especially commonplace throughout the *Autobiography* as they do in his later fictional false starts, all after the death of Susy. It's as if Susy became associated in Twain's mind with the problem of evil, and the inadequacy of any idea of a good and benevolent God. As is common with bereaved parents, Mark and Livy idealized their dead daughter in their memories of her. At one point he laments, "Susy was a dreamer, a thinker, a poet and philosopher."[73] Several times in the *Autobiography*, Twain remembers Susy as working through the problem of evil philosophically, a problem that she noticed at a very early age. He writes, "unlike the average of children she was at times much given to retiring within herself and trying to search out the hidden meanings of the deep things that make the puzzle and pathos of human existence, and in all the ages have baffled the Inquirer and mocked him. As a little child aged 7, she was oppressed and perplexed by the maddening repetition of the stock incidence of our races fleeting sojourn here, just as the same thing has oppressed and perplexed mature minds from the beginning of time."[74]

In this passage, we see Mark Twain remembering his daughter in very flattering ways. Like the young Jesus speaking wisdom to the Temple inhabitants (see Luke 2:42–51), we are given the picture of a seven-year-old girl wise beyond her years. The main phrase describing this phenomenon features Twain speaking in a way that no seven-year-old could even comprehend: "the maddening repetition of the stock incidence of our races fleeting sojourn here" sounds nothing like any child would ever say or think. He is projecting back upon his daughter some of his own philosophical musings that arose out of her death and were heightened by the loss. In his mind, Susy brought up key questions about providence, theodicy, and the problem of evil, and she is sketched as actively seeking answers at a very early age. In the unpublished memoir of Susy and Clara begun in 1876 and titled "A Record of the Small Foolishness of Susie and Bay [Clara]," a curious feature is the frequency with which Twain associated Susy with the young Jesus, something that happens many times. The subtitle is telling: "And Mary Treasured These Sayings in Her Heart," alluding to Luke 2:51 and describing the mother of Jesus. Often throughout this early narrative, there are brief anecdotes of Susy saying wise words similar to those of Jesus, or explaining how deeply she loves Jesus. "Susie is an admirable character. There is not a coarse fibre in her; she is as fine as gossamer. She was born free of selfishness," he claims. Most significantly, it is in "A Record of the Small Foolishness," that we first encounter young Susy's contemplations on evil and suffering, and what became in Twain's memory her trademark phrases: "Mamma, what is it all for?" "Mamma, what *is* little things?" "Mamma, what does the world go on, for?"[75] From these and other jottings we can see that from a very early time, Twain observed something profound, exquisite, and nearly divine about his gifted daughter, suggesting that these were not merely postmortem exaggerations.[76]

Other passages in the much later *Autobiography* echo these earlier reminiscences, and often elaborate upon them. Twain frequently presents her as a young sage dealing with the problems of suffering and pain. After one particularly long diatribe about the meaninglessness of a circular life and the accomplishment of precisely nothing, he transitions to an anecdote about Susy: "'Mama, what is it all for?' asked Susy, preliminarily stating the above details in her own halting language, after long brooding over them alone in the privacy of the nursery."[77] When Susy is disturbed in hearing about the manners in which Native Americans worshiped God differently from Protestants, she is evidently perplexed enough to rethink her whole conception of what God might be like. In particular she seems to be disturbed by the fact that many adults seem unwilling to accept Native American beliefs as being true. They are forced to affirm only the truth of their own religion and to condemn the beliefs of others outside of it. And so she begins to pray and ask that "there may be a God and a heaven—or something better." This strikes her father as being exceptionally wise: "my reverence for it has grown with the years that have passed over my head since then. Its untaught grace and simplicity are a child's, but the wisdom and the pathos of it are of all the ages that have come and gone since the race of man has lived, and longed, and hoped, and feared, and doubted."[78] Twain liked it so much that he repeated it, nearly word for word, in the novel fragment "Which Was the Dream?" One key difference is that in the story, the girl ends by calling for "SOMETHING BETTER." After the girl makes this confident statement, the narrator makes an aside: "It is the garnered doubt—and hope—of all the centuries, compacted into a sentence. And by a child."[79] As Joe Fulton notes, such proclamations are firmly in the prophetic tradition, insofar as they "speak to . . . precisely this state of unknowing, of hoping amid doubts for 'SOMETHING BETTER.'"[80]

Just a few weeks later, Mark Twain recalls Susy saying similar things about the plight of man in an evil world. It is within the context of an anecdote about an old acquaintance called David Gray, who was mentioned by his friend John Hay during a dinner party. The mention of Gray's name brought the memory of Gray's father, whom Twain had known during his time in Buffalo in the 1870s. Gray had died a terrible death in a railway accident many years before, but Mark Twain remembers all about him as he sits there at the dinner table. Then another odd turn occurs. Twain describes his precise train of thought as he sits there at the dinner table in "the gay laughter-and-chatter fog": "what is the use of it?" And immediately his mind takes him back to Susy, again: "these tiresome and monotonous repetitions of the human life—where is there value? Susy asked that question when she was a little child. There was nobody then who could answer it; there is nobody yet."[81] Again we see Twain's mind turning from the futility and nihilism of man's bleak status to the question being asked by his daughter at a very early age. In this formulation, little Susy sounds a bit like a young Friedrich Nietzsche: she gives voice to the obvious lack of a satisfactory theodicy—and to the fact that even an innocent, observant young girl can recognize this theological deficiency. As such, she is similar to the three-year-old girl in the sketch "Little Bessie." Written in 1908 through 1909, these chapters are among the most devastating critiques of conventional Christian theodicy ever written by Mark Twain, and Bessie's innocent questions are strongly reminiscent to the questioning of faith Twain attributed to Susy.[82] And as Tom Quirk points out, "Little Bessie" is not merely a cynical attack on religion, "there is sympathy too—sympathy for the mother who cannot answer her daughter's questions or spare her from the doubts and pains of merely being alive; and sympathy for a child whose life in such a world is just beginning."[83] Twain is taking seriously the questions of Christian belief; he comprehends the argument from horror, to recall Hart's comments: "Those Christian readers who have found it easy to ignore or dispense with the case Dostoyevsky constructs for Ivan have not fully comprehended that case."[84]

Associating Susy with the problem of evil happens yet again, about a month later, as he remembers an old friend named Reuel Gridley, who enlisted to fight in the Mexican War when Twain was just a boy. The young Sam is moved to envy as he sees the marching company depart the small town: "I can almost feel again the consuming desire that I had to join it." The troop was led by a Mr. Hickman who at that time was "a tall, straight, handsome athlete of 25. . . . And had a sword by his side and a broad yellow stripe down the leg of his gray pants." It is a scene of pomp and military swagger, but then immediately Mark Twain remembers seeing "the splendid Hickman in his old age. He seemed about the oldest man I had ever seen—an amazing and melancholy contrast with the showy young captain I had seen preparing his warriors for carnage so many, many years before. Hickman is dead—it is the old story.

As Susy said, 'What is it all for?'"[85] So yet again, we note that in Twain's mind, there's a close relationship between a powerful nostalgia for the past and a sense of the futility of suffering in the world.

Both moods, nostalgia and futility, are evoked by the memories of his young and innocent daughter Susy, and the autobiographical dictations are a major source of evidence in support of this view. Her sister Clara was close to Susy and commonly called her "the spiritual one."[86] Numerous other laudatory appeals to Susy's "spiritual" qualities might seem surprising to us, given the way we tend to understand spirituality today; however, by that time it was already a well-established term used to denote one's transcendent qualities outside of the domains of an organized church. Susy as deeply spiritual, one who is "a poet and philosopher," is a key to unlocking Twain's memory of her, as well as Livy's.[87] It leads directly to our encounter with Susy as representative of Twain's dissatisfaction with the justice he sees all around him, in a world of pain and suffering. For it is precisely to see and witness this suffering, to "feel" that pain through an enhanced sympathy, and to give voice to it, that is the true mark of a spiritual person.

One might think, then, that focusing on futility and eternal recurrence would put an end to any attempt to foster hope and justice, but with Twain it was not the case. Again, the divided response is prominently on exhibition. Even as he dealt with the grief and the trauma, and a growing sense of hopelessness and evil in the world, he launched into his greatest period of social activism and prophetic conscience, speaking truth to power. The rise of American empire was fueled by claims for America as Christian nation and as exemplary model of Christendom. In the case of social justice, the timing of international events coincided with the period of grief and trauma for himself and Livy. His time in Europe throughout the 1890s had bred within him a strong sense of being a resident and citizen of the world. His travels abroad, including visits to imperial regimes in India and elsewhere, sparked his cosmopolitan imagination. The cosmopolitan, in Marshall McLuhan's account, "transcends national boundaries and . . . articulates the commonality of human suffering and human potential . . . sympathetic, engaged, yet also distanced from his subject," and as one critic has written, "[Twain's writing] evinces a progressive, modernist critique of American politics and history, a critique provoked by his life as an urban citizen."[88] Altogether, these factors helped kick-start a new level of Mark Twain's social agenda.

Never a fan of hypocrisy or patriotic cant, Twain found America's imperial designs on the Philippines to be particularly sickening. Having promised to help the Filipinos gain independence, the American administration of President McKinley went on to secure the nation as its Pacific outpost and betray the leaders of the independence movement there. All this was done in the name of benevolent assimilation, Christian moral principle, and helping little brother. In one interview, Twain explains his shock:

> We claim to be a democratic people—a square dealing people—but we have bought our way into the society of sceptered thieves by paying $20 million to a country that is on it for an island group [the Philippines] that we had no right to purchase. It was the stupendous joke of the century when the United States, after conquering Spain and acquiring the islands by right of conquest, gave Spain $20 million. What for? For the islands? Spain didn't own them. Then, what for? Why, just for this: an American goes abroad and sells his daughter to a title and buys his way into noble circles. Uncle Sam paid that $20 million for his entrance fee into society—the society of sceptered thieves. We are now on a par with the rest of them. We did to turn what should be a benevolent protectorate into an autocratic monarchy!

In another, he claims, "Honestly, when I read in the papers that this deal had been made, I laughed until my sides ached. There were the Filipinos fighting like blazes for their liberty. Spain would not hear to it [sic]. The United States stepped in, and after they had licked the enemy to a standstill, instead of freeing the Filipinos they paid that enormous amount for an island which is of no earthly account to us."[89]

In effect, the loss of Susy exacerbated Twain's sense of moral outrage, the hellish nightmare of man's own doings, thus helping to inspire some of the finest social criticism of his long career. As clinical research indicates, survivors of grief often become more sympathetic and compassionate human beings. In the months following Susy's death, Twain worked obsessively on the manuscript of *Following the Equator*, a narrative about the round the world tour with much of the focus on various developing parts of the world such as India and South Africa. For up to seventeen hours a day he labored over this project, priming the pump for serious consideration of colonialism and its effects on the colonized. So America's rise to imperial status presented the most pressing set of issues that could draw his greatest attention and ultimately contempt, just in the period in which he wrestled with Susy's death. Furthermore, Twain linked the writing of that book with the obsessive attempts to stifle his grief, for example in a letter to Twichell of January 1897: "I am working, but it is for the sake of working—the 'surcease of sorrow' that is found there. I work all the days; & trouble vanishes away when I use that magic."[90] The allusion is to Edgar Allan Poe's gothic meditation on bereavement, "The Raven," where the gloomy narrator tries to find "surcease of sorrow" for his dead lover in his books. His work alone brings him some measure of peace, says Twain—unlike his poor wife, who, he tells Twichell, has "nothing."

In the materials Mark Twain wrote about the Philippines, we see this sympathy at full bore, salted with burlesque and irony. And after nearly a decade living in European capitals, clearly Twain aspired to be a learned citizen of the world. But he was fully an American, and without question, he also had very high hopes for American ideology and belief. He simply abominated how American belief was being embodied and abused during the Philippine-American War, and raged at the insinuation that American adventuring there actually represented the truest American ideals. As Susan K. Harris has argued recently, it should not be concluded that Twain was completely unpatriotic. His comments in his anti-imperialist writings show that he completely "got" the hypocrisy of America's claim to be bringing benevolence to benighted peoples. But to recognize hypocrisy does not mean to cease to believe. People who don't believe in a doctrine don't get angry when they see it abused. They smile cynically & move on. The ones who get angry are those who feel betrayed. Like his compatriots, Twain was deeply invested in the American narrative. But he was also a citizen of the world, and he was keenly conscious, even jealous, of the U.S.'s reputation for fair dealing. He read the Treaty of Paris as evidence that the U.S. had sold out, traded its clean hands for a minor place in the Concert of World Powers.[91]

Twain vents bitterly, for example, in an essay called "The Philippine Incident": "And so, by these Providences of God—the phrase is the Government's, not mine— . . . We are a World Power . . . the kind of World Power that a prairie-dog village is . . . and it is the duty of our Government to stand sentinel, with solemn mien, and lifted nose, and curved paws, on top of our little World-Power mound, and look out over the wide prairie, and if anything suspicious shows up on the horizon, bark."[92] By critiquing America's use of its growing power, Twain was not rejecting America as an ideal, or being un-American. Quite the opposite: he was calling for American to live by its own grand ideals and standards. And we can say the same about his critique of Christendom and of the church. Certainly Twain excoriates the political leaders' wooden appeal to "Providence." He is not completely rejecting any appeal to God—an appeal he sometimes himself made. Rather he is calling those leaders to account by the very standards that they have claimed to be following. "The Philippine Incident" exemplifies Twain's brilliant critique of American empire and American appeals to God's endorsement and deserves to be regarded as one of Mark Twain's lasting achievements in the years after his daughter's death.

But his sustained critique was not undertaken, nor accomplished, alone. It emerged from the renewal of a vigorous, happy, and synergistic friendship with W. D. Howells. Besides their constructive conversations about the pros and (mostly) cons of American empire, these two old men also shared the horror of losing a beautiful, poetic, young adult daughter, one whom they both loved to idealize in memory. And both felt the continuing bonds with their daughters—and perhaps this accounts as well for the emergence of what I would like to call their "Anti-Imperial friendship." Blasting American imperialism became a task Twain shared fully and even joyfully with Howells, by now considered the "dean" of American letters. Frankly, it is surprising that major authors such as Howells and Twain have not been given more attention in terms of their joint investment in the critique of American empire.[93] Soon after Twain appeared on the docks of New York, these two stalwarts recommenced their long friendship by focusing much of their collective attention on matters of national politics and overseas adventuring. This sophisticated joint project had begun before Twain's return, especially in their correspondence. Initially Howells joined Twain as a member of the Anti-Imperialist League, founded in 1898 to criticize the annexation of the Philippines. In the fall of 1900, just as the presidential reelection of McKinley was reaching its climax, Twain returned to America from a long stay in Europe. He was filled with venom about the direction of American foreign policy, and these two friends spent countless hours together, reading and discussing the latest political maneuverings of the day.

Despite this truly interesting "anti-imperial" friendship, very little has been written about it, and in particular, Howells's disdain for American empire has received almost no sustained attention. The Anti-Imperialist League also enlisted other literary voices, such as Henry James, Ambrose Bierce, Jane Addams, Edgar Lee Masters, and William Vaughn Moody. And yet only rarely have scholars written about their art as somehow informed by, or expressive of, a sustained political opposition to empire. More relevant to this study, the joint anti-imperial project Twain and Howells devised can be analyzed as a further manifestation of the sympathies that arose and were heightened by their daughters' deaths. We know how strong of a kinship these two men felt for each other, having suffered the same horrific experience under similar situations. It is plausible to suggest that, together as two members of the "club" of bereaved parents, both having lost lovely daughters entering the primes of their lives to illnesses seemingly untreatable, and both having daughters representing a continuation of their own lofty literary ambitions, these two aging authors hoped to discover some redemptive fruit from all the suffering they had come to see in the world.

My claim is that Twain and Howells combined forces in an interesting way that illustrates the notion of posttraumatic growth (PTG) identified a century later by psychologists. This claim is admittedly hard to prove, but suggestive evidence abounds. Their common crusade against the rise of American empire often featured fictionalized crises faced by bereaved parents. Both composed notable critiques of American empire that rested firmly on the grounding of grief and trauma. To illustrate the rhetorical effects of grief as deployed in the multiple texts that Twain and Howells authored during their period of activity in the Anti-Imperialist League, we might consider two works written almost simultaneously, in 1904: Twain's "The War Prayer," which was published posthumously in 1916; and Howells's "Editha," published in January 1905 in *Harper's*. These two gems, considered by many readers among the greatest late achievements of both authors, have several things in common. I will briefly sketch out one common theme that was important to both, and which was a frequent subject in their personal exchanges: the collateral damage of empire, especially the resulting civilian casualties, but also the profound grief it engenders upon the dead soldiers' and civilians' survivors. Twain's "War Prayer" and Howells's "Editha" both give voice to an extreme horror toward America's puzzling apathy toward such casualties; each is also expert at "deploying the language of romanticism against itself."[94] In addition, both tales deploy irony in the face of the religious nature of the military actions, and both end with the opponents of war labeled as insane.[95]

Above all, both pieces are suffused with a powerful sense of lament: a biblical type that "refers to an irreparable, hopeless catastrophe," as is often illustrated in the Psalms.[96] Biblical lament typically features "various forms of struggle, including crying out precisely because we do not—and for the life of us, cannot—see how particular instances of human suffering are consistent with God's promises to protect, sustain, and care for God's people."[97] In the case of "The War Prayer," lament is illustrated in the words of the prophet, but in the case of "Editha," lament is seen in the anger and despair of the grieving mother. "The War Prayer" is set in a church service during a time of war, and a mysterious stranger arrives to speak prophetically to his captive audience. Ironically, the stranger's tirade follows the singing of a hymn called "God the Omnipotent," which invokes God's grace to live in peace and harmony for all people: "Give to us peace in our time, O Lord." Much of the stranger's speech centers on the nature of the congregation's prayers for victory, and what their prayers actually entail: "When you have prayed for victory you have prayed for many unmentioned results which follow victory—*must* follow it, cannot help but follow it. Upon the listening spirit of God fell also the unspoken part of the prayer."[98] Twain is cagily pointing out that when we pray for one thing, we are often praying also for other, "unmentioned results." You have prayed "unthinkingly"; you have not thought carefully about the "whole" consequences of your "pregnant" words. Among those results, the stranger explains, the most significant is the collateral damage of empire, including dismembered and dead civilians, some of whom are always women and children. He gives voice to the unmentioned content of the prayers for victory: "O Lord our God, help us to tear their soldiers to bloody shreds with our shells . . . help us to lay waste their humble homes . . . help us to wring the hearts of their unoffending widows with unavailing grief." Thus, in the "The War Prayer," Twain confronts his readers with the horrifying "unmentioned results" of their earnest prayers for victory, inventing a term for collateral damage decades before its emergence as a euphemism during the Vietnam War. It is telling that the rediscovery and revival of the popularity of Twain's "The War Prayer" was during the Vietnam War era—an incursion that made civilian casualties the fodder of the nightly news.

Similarly, Howells presents in "Editha" the pining desires of a young woman for her fiancé George to enlist immediately in the war at hand. The woman, named Editha, "had been puzzled by his want of seriousness" regarding the war. Without telling him, she knew that military service was required for "the completion of her ideal of him." Her view of the war is that it obviously has commenced through "Providence": "I call any war glorious that is for the liberation of people who have been struggling for years against the cruelest oppression. Don't you think so, too? . . . I call it a sacred war."[99] Indeed, she even breaks off the engagement and returns the ring because of his unwillingness to "be a man" and sign up for service. And thus, George Gearson is pressured to enlist—and is promptly killed in action. When she goes to visit the bereaved mother,

Editha is startled by Mrs. Gearson's indignation: "'No, you didn't expect him to get killed,' Mrs. Gearson repeated, in a voice which was startlingly like George's again. 'You just expected him to kill some one else, some of those foreigners, that weren't there because they had any say about it, but because they had to be there, poor wretches—conscripts, or whatever they call 'em. You thought it would be all right for my George, *your* George, to kill the sons of those miserable mothers and the husbands of those girls that you would never see the faces of.'"[100] After her emotional outburst, the grieving mother reaches up to tear the black mourning crepe from the face of Editha. The act symbolizes a moment of unveiling, and yet the story ends with the irony that Editha does not quite comprehend the bereaved mother's resentment and despair. Editha's silence is deafening.

To put their views in context, Howells and Twain were well aware of the massive collateral damage brought about by the United States in the Philippines, including most alarmingly the cost of countless Filipino lives—a modern-day "horror" that defies easy dismissal by a Christian sensibility. According to historian John Tirman, "Philippines casualties were 4000 U.S. soldiers, most by disease. Filipino mortality ranges from about 34,000 military and at least another 200,000 civilians dead, but might include the indirect deaths totaling 1 million or more due to the cholera epidemic. Separating out what was directly caused by the war and what was indirect is a vexing challenge: as in the case of the cholera epidemic amplified by a war, or how and when to stop counting war casualties, given the fact that several local insurrections continued in the Philippines until at least 1913. But it's accurate to say that for every U.S. soldier who died in the Philippines as many as 100 civilians and 10 Filipino soldiers died as well."[101] As Tirman argues, it's hard to understand "Christian America's" brazen disregard for the death tolls of civilians, many of whom were women and children: "The public's blasé attitude toward non-American casualties is the central mystery. . . . The apathy is particularly puzzling in view of a prominent, normative counter claimant (Christian ethics), the dominant cultural influence on Americans' thinking; given Jesus's teachings about compassion, one would expect deep sympathy in America for those who suffer in these wars."[102]

This "central mystery" of widespread apathy among an ostensibly Christian citizenry in light of such horror is brilliantly presented in these two minor masterpieces written by Howells and Twain. As Twain jotted down in a notebook entry around the time these works were composed: "From man's point of view patriotism is the noblest thing there is; from God's it is the meanest. . . . A Christian must labor for the breaking down of all walls that interrupt the fusion of the race into a common brotherhood, and one of the most formidable of these is patriotism."[103] Unfortunately, Christian America has overlooked the "meanest" side of patriotism, its multiplication of horrors—as both Editha and the congregation of the unnamed church in "The War Prayer" overlooked it." Twain and Howells illustrate how Americans struggled to confront their own imperial impulses and to admit to their global footprints.

These tales are among the highlights of their authors' nearly decade-long "anti-imperial" friendship, and both are steeped in the pathos of lament. Both men were deeply troubled by their nation's designs on establishing something very much like an empire, one often based on modes of conquest and violence, and they lamented America's military adventures that were grounded on invocations of God, progress, and the "benevolent" goals of "God's arbiters," appointed to mediate the destinies of mankind and to bring light to a darkened world. The writings of both authors on imperial topics were saturated with the grief of the survivors, the "unmentioned results" of our collective prayers for victory and vengeance. I am suggesting that Twain and Howells felt a solidarity with the bereaved parents of the fallen soldiers, a sympathy heightened by their own profound grief experiences, and that their rhetoric is commonly filled with lament, a form as old as the Psalms of the Hebrew Bible.

Given all this, it's hard not to consider how their bond together as bereaved parents somehow enhanced their obsession with announcing America's decline. Of course, one need not be a bereaved parent to protest a war. But it is also plausible that their common disaster produced an even stronger solidarity for the bereaved—and strengthened their common cause against further catastrophes. For at least half a decade, we can state firmly that theirs was, to a large extent, an anti-imperialist friendship. And perhaps we can even claim that Howells and Twain entered the arena of critiquing American foreign policy together, to whatever extent, in the lingering memories of their beloved daughters.

The story of Mark Twain in response to the death of his daughter illustrates the divided, hotly contested impulses at work in his experience of parental grief. The horror, despair, sense of futility, wandering in darkness, and guilt are all there, unrelieved and real. Twain records the dark side about as well as anyone, and an authentic account of parental grief must always start there. Sadly, for many parents, the experience begins and ends there; they cannot seem to get beyond it. And in certain ways, a darkened account of the late Twain has held critical sway. But the philanthropic side, energized in constructive ways by the "fires of grief," has been overlooked in favor of the "misanthropy" of these same years.

Assuredly, there were serious dissonances at work in the final years of Mark Twain, some of which he could never resolve. In short, he tried to have it both ways, but perceptive readers can discover his true leanings: a powerful social conscience that in many ways is the truest legacy of his lost daughter, Susy. As Abraham Lincoln once said, America will continue to progress as long as we pay attention to "the better angels of our nature." For Mark Twain, Susy represented the better angel. But Susy's spirit continued to haunt him, in not so unpleasant ways hovering around him. Such ghosts help us remember the good of the past and help us celebrate the hopeful sensibilities of the beloved dead. On occasion, Mark Twain succeeded in doing this. On other occasions, he didn't. But he did seem conscious of the struggle, as in the powerful lines from "Broken Idols":

> The fires of grief! <u>They</u> lap the heart in flame,
> <u>They</u> smelt the red gold free! It is the bleeding heart
> That pays the due of woe in minted coin.[104]

5

Du Bois's Grief

Burghardt and Cultural Trauma

It wasn't only American empire that angered Mark Twain in the years after Susy died. In a letter he wrote in 1901 to his editor, Twain explained that he was horrified by lynching, which was becoming acceptable social behavior. Twain was so appalled by the rising numbers of lynchings that he was preparing to write a book on it. Dated August 26, Twain's lengthy letter reported that he was now "full of" the topic and that the book would be titled "History of Lynching in America." He had a clear purpose in writing it: "Nothing but such a book can rouse up the sheriffs to put down the mobs and end the lynchings—which are growing in number and spreading *northward*. Last year there were 115; in 7 months of this year there were already 92. . . . Yesterday I wrote an acid article on the subject . . . [and in it] I *implore* the missionaries to come back from China and convert their own Christian countrymen."[1]

The book was never completed, but a long essay on lynching did come from the blistering "pen warmed up in hell" of Mark Twain. Although it was never published in his lifetime, likely because Twain decided it was too acidic and might turn some of his readers against him (especially southern whites), it remains available to us. Titled "The United States of Lyncherdom," it was a tough-minded assault on the sheer viciousness at the heart of the lynching culture. Twain was especially horrified that citizens of his home state had joined the ranks of the lynch mobs: "And so Missouri has fallen, that great state! Certain of her children have joined the lynchers, and the smirch is upon the rest of us," he wrote. "On a Sunday afternoon a young white woman who had started alone from church was found murdered. For there are churches there; in my time religion was more general, more pervasive, in the South than it was in the North, and more virile and earnest, too, I think; I have some reason to believe that this is still the case. The young woman was found murdered. Although it was a region of churches and schools the people rose, lynched three negroes—two of them very aged ones—burned out five negro households, and drove thirty negro families into the woods. . . . Let us import American missionaries from China, and send them into the lynching field."[2]

The irony is thick: Twain appeals to the supposedly Christian character of his home state and wonders how such a religious environment had developed a widespread culture of lynching. He believed it was the height of religious hypocrisy to send missionaries overseas to "Christianize and civilize" the savages, while at the same time such savagery that manifested itself in lynching practices went uncriticized and unprosecuted throughout America. He felt that the lynching culture betrayed a disturbing violence, rooted in a racist hatred for blacks that was corrupting the heart of America at the turn of the century. He also perceives, and exploits, the religious roots of much of the rhetoric surrounding lynch culture and virulent hatred of African Americans. Perhaps it sounds odd today, but Twain's views were actually progressive in 1901. Forward looking, even controversial and revolutionary, his anti-lynching stance foreshadowed the noise that was about to be made by the twentieth century's most ardent crusader against the lynching culture, W. E. B. Du Bois. Although Twain and Du Bois almost certainly never met, their strategies and arguments about the mainstream American ideologies and beliefs at the turn of the twentieth century had much in common. Both understood lynching to be a manifestation of the dark side of a powerful American civil religion. At the heart of this civil religion, they believed, were elements of empire, conquest, and racial hierarchy. Both perceived the sheer irony of declarations of America as "Christian nation," given the widespread practices of the lynching mobs and the oppression and hatred of black people. Both jabbed sarcastically at the bold proclamations of the civil religious establishment, which preached confidently of bringing the "light of civilization" to the rest of the world, as in the recent annexations of Hawaii (1898) and the Philippines (1899). Both were powerfully moved by the cultural trauma of public lynching in the land of the free—lynchings mostly of young males, a horrific practice that left behind their traumatized parents.

Most importantly in the context of my topic, both were survivors of the loss of a child. But it is especially difficult to track Du Bois's grief experience due to a general lack of personal writing or letters about it, similar to what we've seen already in the case of Lincoln, who also wrote very sparingly about his personal feelings on his son's death. As Ryan Schneider has noted, Du Bois's grief was similar to that of Emerson in his essay "Experience," in that both of them understood "the difficulty, if not the impossibility, of arriving at the meaning of loss through the sharing of feelings."[3] And it is admittedly hard to prove the importance of "continuing bonds" in the life of one who remains virtually silent about that experience—as many traumatized or grieving individuals do. In this final chapter, such are the challenges for dealing with Du Bois's parental grief, and they make this perhaps the most debatable chapter of the book. Nevertheless, certain conclusions seem plausible. For one, it is clear that instead of focusing on his personal struggles with his son's death, Du Bois channeled his grief into an opportunity to represent the traumas of a people, and so Du Bois became a spokesperson for the grief of others, like himself, who had suffered life's darkest moment. Rather than supernatural, the bonds with the dead became symbolic and aesthetic. One of Du Bois's great achievements in the realm of continuing bonds was his ability to transform these tragic events into an opportunity to erect a glorious and redemptive memorial for the living. If Du Bois did not believe literally in the bonds as supernatural and transcendent, he exploited their cultural power in his writings in such a way that the bonds could have significant and perhaps even world-changing symbolic weight. And beyond literary works, Du Bois also seemed to understand what two legal critics have recently argued: collective memory can have its strongest and most long-lasting effects in the culture through judicial intervention, and that in the modern era, it is often through legal proceedings that collective memories are established and violence is reduced.[4] In these ways, Du Bois exemplifies elements of the modern shift that brings my historical narrative to a close: his artistic reformulations of his bonds with his dead son, in tandem with the legal exposure of atrocities, in the context of a world that is leaving behind the religious foundations of an earlier period. But before the personal tragedy of Du Bois came the context of the culture of lynching in which countless black sons were unjustly murdered, mocked, and left in public spaces.

Almost all people endure individual sufferings, but sometimes certain traumatic events affect larger groups, either at a local, statewide, national, or even international level. Such events have been called "cultural traumas" because of their effect on widespread dissemination and their far-flung effects on multiple populations.[5] Sometimes, if these events target certain groups, it is the members of that group that are most powerfully traumatized, as with the experience of African Americans in slavery and then systematic oppressions through Jim Crow and segregation.[6] Other obvious examples include the Holocaust, which mainly targeted Jews in Nazi Germany and throughout occupied Europe. And yet, although clearly the Jews were traumatized more than non-Jews, the lingering effects of trauma on such a massive scale have reverberated across the globe, so much so that we can say that the Holocaust may be the most traumatic social phenomenon in human history. Thus one need not be Jewish to have been traumatized by the Shoah: it affected entire cultures and peoples. In all such cases, cultural trauma occurs "when members of a collectivity feel they have been subjected to a horrendous event that leaves indelible marks upon their group consciousness, marking their memories forever."[7] Again, the category of horror is invoked. Cultural trauma also calls for witnesses who can give firsthand testimony. As Mamie Till-Mobley said over fifty years later, after the senseless lynching of her own fourteen-year-old son Emmett Till in 1955: "After all, we had averted our eyes far too long, turning away from the ugly reality facing us as a nation. . . . People had to face my son and realize just how twisted, how distorted, how terrifying, race hatred could be. . . . They would have to see their own responsibility in pushing for an end to this evil. People had to consider all that as they viewed Emmett's body. The impact was like being hit with a sledgehammer."[8] Mamie's description of how the images of her dead son affected those who saw them is similar to the psychological effects of individual trauma as "a blow to the psyche that breaks through one's defenses so suddenly and with such brutal force that one cannot react to it effectively," and of collective trauma as "a blow to the basic tissues of social life that damages the bonds attaching people together."[9] For Du Bois, these two phenomena happened almost simultaneously: a terrifying confrontation with a local lynching, followed quickly by the senseless death of his only son due largely to a failed and biased medical establishment, both in the spring of 1899.

Nobel Prize winner Elias Canetti once wrote, "in the face of life's horror—luckily most people notice it only on occasion, but a few whom inner forces *appoint* to *bear witness* are always conscious of it—there is only one comfort: *its alignment with the horror experienced by previous witnesses*."[10] Canetti's idea that one might find comfort in the fact that others have shared the same distress seems strange at first. However, as we've seen with Twain and Howells, intimacies often arise when individuals suffer similar tragedies. Some psychologists argue that "trauma shared can serve as a source of communality in the same way that common languages in common backgrounds can. There is a spiritual kinship there, a sense of identity even when feelings of affection are deadened and the ability to care numbed."[11] For those who share a common trauma, there is no need to explain most things about it, because everyone has been marked by the same pain and understands the basic feelings. In the cases of lynching, Du Bois recognized that the victim is someone else's child. The parents of a lynching victim were forced to witness their own child made into a spectacle: mocked, spit upon, chastised, and publicly humiliated, much the same as Jesus Christ. And so throughout his work, Du Bois frequently portrays the pain and suffering of the surviving parent. More generally, the lynching victims become for Du Bois symbolically the children of the race, the hope of a new generation—an observation he often made as well. In effect, Du Bois sketched lynching victims as the children of all African Americans, and Christlike in their glorious potential to change history.

Another Nobel laureate, the Holocaust survivor Elie Wiesel, once wrote that his generation "invented a new literature, that of testimony." The concept of testimony is in many ways a legal concept: testimony most often occurs during a trial, which seeks to settle a disagreement about truth. There is, in other words, a crisis of evidence that the verdict must resolve: "Testimony is provided, and is called for, when the facts upon which justice must pronounce its verdict are not clear, when historical accuracy is in doubt, and when both the truth and its supporting elements of evidence are called into question."[12] As such, Wiesel recognized the rise of testimony in the middle of the twentieth century as a crucial moment in history. As civilization became more mature, and as media became more sophisticated, the news of injustice and atrocity became common knowledge in the world. Simultaneously, new ways of voicing injury and grievance also became more widely available, especially through modern forms of media. Out of the rubble of World War II and the evidence of the Holocaust and other atrocities arose such unprecedented truth-telling testimony as the Nuremberg trials, America's civil rights movement, and the Truth and Reconciliation Commission in South Africa.

Testimony as a rhetorical mode came of age in the twentieth century, especially with the advent of mass media, but important illustrations of this process happened long before the events of the Holocaust. Du Bois noticed early on how communal trauma fostered sympathy for the victims of atrocity, not only among African Americans but also often among Caucasians. He also recognized how the survivors of atrocity must lead the way in bearing witness against American injustice, racial and otherwise, and how a sophisticated use of new media could help the cause. Not only did Du Bois perceive these things but also as an African American educated at Harvard he developed an extremely important voice that could "testify" as an intellectual and as a member of the traumatized group itself. Finally, he had experienced the ultimate sorrow: the loss of his only begotten son. The deep memories of loss and trauma actually ended up fostering communal solidarity; in an odd twist, the cultural trauma of lynching, augmented by parental grief searching for something redemptive to come out of these senseless killings, actually brought people together. Du Bois mastered the exploitation of these emotions and the spirit of generativity, as seen in his masterpiece *The Souls of Black Folk*, and later in his other writings and his somewhat unheralded role as editor of *The Crisis*, with its comprehensive coverage of the lynching culture. Out of the tragedy of lynchings—coupled with the anguish of the death of his son Burghardt—Du Bois worked to find redemption and hope for a people, and to a large extent, he succeeded.

Cultural trauma, "mediated through various forms of representation and linked to the reformation of collective identity," marked the lives and identities of African Americans after emancipation, and especially during the era that many historians claim was the low point of race relations in America: roughly 1890 through 1910.[13] During these years, African Americans were terrorized in any number of ways, beginning with the Jim Crow laws and institutionalized segregation. Not only was lynching used to terrorize black people, it also was rarely prosecuted by the law and was often condoned by civic leaders and law enforcement officers. Law enforcement figures sometimes even participated in the ghoulish spectacles, which were often attended by thousands of citizens. These spectacles were well documented through the emerging art of photography. Professionals moved in with cameras to create postcards and other memorabilia of the lynching, which sold like hotcakes to those in attendance. Several recent scholars have published scores of photos from these eager businessmen, in books and on the web.[14] Many feature the blasé and even joyful responses of onlookers in sharp contrast to the object of their gaze: the grisly, desecrated black bodies. As mentioned, it was usually young black males hanging from a tree. The deep-seated fears of black male sexuality often spurred the angry crowds onward. The association of sexual prowess of black males with degenerate, criminal behavior is revealed by a common practice: castration of the naked body, often placing the genitals in the mouth of the victim (if not fought over or sold to attendees). Body parts in general were often cut off and kept as mementos. It was a gruesome practice undertaken with ritualistic fervor throughout the nation, not just in the Old South; sometimes it was even justified in terms of God and country. And since mobs typically targeted young black males, the practice of lynching left a long line of grief-stricken and traumatized parents in its wake.

In effect, those who participated in lynching desired to enforce the exclusion and segregation of African Americans. These were acts of terrorism designed to keep the black man down, as it was often put. Author Richard Wright wrote years later that just the threat of violence modified his behavior. "The things that influenced my conduct as a Negro did not have to happen to me directly; I needed but to hear of them to feel their full effects in the deepest layers of my consciousness. Indeed the white brutality that I had not seen was a more effective control of my behavior than that which I knew."[15] But in an odd turn of events, the lynching culture came back to haunt the perpetrators. A handful of heroic persons refused to play that game. In effect, the unjust violence and horror motivated certain key individuals to work to convince society to enact the very changes the terror was actually meant to repress. Unjust violence perpetrated against African Americans produced what Du Bois, in *Souls of Black Folk*, would call a "vague unrest"[16] just underneath the African American experience. But this unrest was in fact, for Du Bois, a function of "divine discontent": it could inspire citizens to action and protest.[17] Du Bois and other likeminded cultural pioneers after him perceived a possibility of redemption even in the most horrific violence, as in the aftermath of what became one of America's most notorious lynchings, in southern Georgia just before the turn of the twentieth century.

On the night of April 12, 1899, Sam Hose—also known as Sam Holt, Sam Wilkes, and Tom Wilkes (his birth name)—was accused of a series of horrific crimes in Coweta County, Georgia. A woman named Mattie Cranford rushed to the home of her father-in-law to report that Sam Hose had murdered her husband Alfred with an ax, that he had violently assaulted two of her young children, and that Hose had raped her next to the body of her dying husband in the presence of her children. News of the crime spread immediately, and during the course of the ten-day manhunt for Hose, local and national newspapers repeated and sensationalized the details of the story. "DETERMINED MOB AFTER HOSE;

HE WILL BE LYNCHED IF CAUGHT" is how the headlines read in the *Atlanta Constitution* on April 14, 1899.[18] Not surprisingly, Sam Hose was portrayed by the media as a beastly and cold-blooded killer, and the governor of Georgia offered a reward for his capture. Historian Joel Williamson has studied the change in white thinking about black people in the South between 1889 in 1915: increasingly during this period, white southerners considered black men as reckless beasts that had been held in check by slavery. As a result, lynching was recognized by many to be a vital method of maintaining control over these out-of-control animals. Black men were understood to be "supersexual creatures, uninhibited and possessed by large, almost insatiable appetites. In particular black men were considered to have freakishly large sexual organs and a lust for white women."[19]

Given this widespread view, southern masculinity simply could not allow even the appearance of a black male approaching a white woman, let alone touching her, one of the great taboos of the period during and after the Civil War. The allegation of rape against a white woman would have been viewed by many conservative southern men of the time as an atrocity deserving of harsh punishment. Officials decried the criminal tendencies of black males, reaching even as high as the US Congress. In 1907, South Carolina congressman Ben Tillman railed in Congress against such deviance: "White women of the South are in a state of siege. . . . Some lurking demon who has watched for the opportunity seizes her; she is choked or beaten into insensibility and ravished, her body prostituted, her purity destroyed, her chastity taken from her. . . . So far as I am concerned he has put himself outside the pale of the law, human and divine. . . . Civilization peels off us . . . And we revert to the impulses . . . To kill! kill! kill!"[20] The white male image of the so-called "black-rapist" became a staple of southern ideology by the end of the nineteenth century, largely due to a sustained attack against the concept of miscegenation as the ultimate sin of integration.[21] For many southerners, Sam Hose represented proof of the heartless criminal tendencies of African Americans, and his lynching signaled "a new and horrifying pattern" of modern lynching as public spectacle.[22]

After an extensive search involving scores of volunteers, Sam Hose was found on the morning of April 23, over ten days after the murder and nearly one hundred miles from the scene of the crime. Upon hearing the news of his capture, more than six thousand white Georgians came to witness the lynching, two thousand of them traveling to the small town of Newnan on special excursion trains from Atlanta. After the sheriff went through a brief ceremony of legal formalities, the mob overtook control of Sam Hose, processed down the streets of Newnan, and brought him to a small field outside of town. Once there, they mutilated him, chained him to a tree, doused him in kerosene, and set him on fire. "Don't make it too hot," someone in the crowd shouted as the pyre ignited, fearful that the victim's agony would be cut short. As reported in one newspaper: "Before the torch was applied to the pyre, the Negro was deprived of his ears, fingers, and other portions of his body with surprising fortitude. Before the body was cool, it was cut to pieces, the bones were crushed into small bits and even the tree upon which the wretch met his fate was torn up and disposed of as souvenirs. The Negro's heart was cut into small pieces, as was also his liver. Those unable to obtain the ghastly relics directly, paid more fortunate possessors extravagant sums for them. Small pieces of bone went for 25 cents and a bit of liver, crisply cooked, for 10 cents."[23] When the lynching was over, spectators rummaged through the charred remains for souvenirs, which they shared with neighbors the next morning. It was a Sabbath afternoon, a "Black and Bloody Sunday" a local newspaper called it, and many in the crowd had come from church services to the meadow where the ritual was enacted.[24] The mob included many prominent citizens of the region, including the presidents of Capitol Bank and the *Atlanta Constitution*.

Despite the lack of clear evidence, Sam Hose was immediately found guilty in the court of public opinion, even though questions still remained as to the motive behind the killing and the validity of Mattie Cranford's accusations.[25] The distortion and sensationalizing of the reported details in the media soon made it impossible to determine the "facts" of the case, and the lack of any formal investigation or judiciary process prevented Mrs. Cranford from swearing to the truth behind her claims. Closer to home, the reaction to the lynching of Sam Hose was surprisingly insensitive. A poem published in the May 12 edition of the *Newnan Herald and Advertiser* titled "Sam Holt" absolved those involved in the lynching from any guilt they may have felt:

> The monster fiend of all the fiends
>   That ever cursed the earth;
> The blackest devil of all his kind—
>   A devil from his birth!
>
> Then boldly say, "We've done no wrong
>   To burn the monster at the stake;

"But join in peans [*sic*] and in song
For all that's dear—for woman's sake. . . .

'Twas but right that he should die
With lurid fire to light the same
'Twill teach these brute beasts to know
That vengeance dire will quickly come;

God's righteous wrath is never slow
To avenge the Christian home
And so 'twill be till cause shall cease
To blight with crime our Southern land.[26]

The poem judges the cause of lynching "right," the result of "God's righteous wrath" in protecting the "Christian home," thus validating the act as a work of Christian justice.

At the same time as this awful series of events unfolded, a young professor of sociology at nearby Atlanta University, sixty miles to the north, was about to come into his own. The "justice" rendered upon Sam Hose became one of life's most profound wake-up calls for W. E. B. Du Bois, just turned thirty-one years old. His intimate observation of racism in Atlanta was profoundly influenced by the atrocities unleashed by the fierce white crowds. For Du Bois, the Sam Hose lynching was a decisive turning point and a direct call to action. Consistent with his belief in the "double consciousness" of the African American, Du Bois recognized that despite his Harvard education and his many distinctions, for all practical purposes he was himself still "the embodied equivalent of Samuel Wilkes in the eyes of white supremacist Georgians."[27] He was struck most powerfully by the swiftness of the white southern violence and by the inability of reason or civil justice to stop the anger of the mob. He responded immediately to the lynching of Sam Hose, writing a letter on the day of the lynching that he planned to publish in the editorial page of the *Atlanta Constitution*. On his way to drop off the letter, however, Du Bois learned that Hose had been barbecued, and that his burned knuckles were on display in the windowed storefront of a white man's business. He never published the letter. Du Bois wrote that almost immediately after the reports of the Sam Hose lynching, he abruptly "began to turn aside from my work," recognizing, "one could not be a calm, cool, and detached scientist while Negroes were lynched, murdered and starved." In a speech following the event, Du Bois said, "I suddenly saw that complete scientific detachment in the midst of such a South was impossible."[28]

Du Bois would always recall the lynching of Sam Hose as the most substantive, early contact with the vicious, blood-lust side of white racism. He considered it nothing short of a flagrant display of white hatred for black people. Later, Du Bois wrote elegantly in his book *Darkwater* (1920) about how that particular event shook him, allowed him to find himself, and helped form a new identity that would propel him forward for the rest of his career:

> My real life work was done at Atlanta for thirteen years. . . . They were years of great spiritual upturning, of the making and unmaking of ideals, of hard work and hard play. Here I found myself. . . . It took but a few years of Atlanta to bring me to hot and indignant defense. I saw the race-hatred of the whites as I had never dreamed of it before,—naked and unashamed! The faint discrimination of my hopes and intangible dislikes paled into nothing before this great, red monster of cruel oppression. I held back with more difficulty each day my mounting indignation against injustice and misrepresentation.
>
> With all this came the strengthening and hardening of my own character. The billows of birth, love, and death swept over me. I saw life through all its paradox and contradiction of streaming eyes and mad merriment. I emerged into full manhood, with the ruins of some ideals about me, but with others planted above the stars; scarred and a bit grim, but hugging to my soul the divine gift of laughter and withal determined, even unto stubbornness, to fight the good fight.[29]

The facts surrounding the assault, rape, and murder Sam Hose was alleged to have perpetrated are far from established. In an interview as late as 1960, when Du Bois was in his nineties, he still believed that the charges against Sam Hose were false: "They started then to find Sam Hose and they couldn't find him. And then, suddenly, there was the accusation that Sam Hose had raped (Cranford's) wife. Now, everybody that read the facts of the case knew perfectly well what had happened. The man wouldn't pay him, so they got into a fight, and the man got killed—and then, in order to arouse the neighborhood to find this man, they brought in the charge of rape. Even from the newspapers you could see there was no foundation for it."[30] But the horrific extent of racial hatred had suddenly become more than an idea or an abstract problem for Du Bois—it was a "great, red monster of cruel oppression." The term "monster" turns the tables on the white racists who had labeled Sam Hose a monster, and such a rhetorical act exemplifies the writer's new way of seeing this and other atrocities. As a result, he believed, even though he felt "hardened" by the experience, he also "emerged into full manhood, with the ruins of some ideals about me, but with others planted above the stars; scarred and a bit grim, but . . . determined, even unto stubbornness, to fight the good fight." Du Bois draws upon New Testament language to signal the spiritual impact of the traumatic events: "fight the good fight" is an idiom from Paul, in which he connects discipleship to the ascetic focus and practice of an athlete (I Timothy 6:12). But just beneath this pious statement was the same rage that had come fully to life in the scathing prose poem *A Litany at Atlanta*, composed in the aftermath of the Atlanta race riots in September 1906:

> A city lay in travail, God our Lord, and from her loins sprang twin Murder and Black Hate. Red was the midnight; clang, crack, and cry of death and fury filled the air and trembled underneath the stars where church spires pointed silently to Thee. And all this was to sate the greed of greedy men who hide behind the veil of vengeance!
>
> *Bend us thine ear, O Lord!*
>
> In the pale, still morning we looked upon the deed. We stopped our ears and held our leaping hands, but they—did they not wag their heads and leer and cry with bloody jaws: *Cease from Crime!* The word was mockery, for thus they train a hundred crimes while we do cure one.
>
> *Turn again our captivity, O Lord!*
>
> Behold this maimed and broken thing, dear God: it was a humble black man, who toiled and sweat to save a bit from the pittance paid him. They told him: *Work and Rise!* He worked. Did this man sin? Nay, but someone told how someone said another did—one whom he had never seen nor known. Yet for that man's crime this man lieth maimed and murdered, his wife naked to shame, his children to poverty and evil.[31]

The diction and style of the King James version of the Bible—as in word choices like Thee, Behold, nay, lieth—heightens the solemn and prophetic tone. As with other of his works, the tone situates Du Bois's argument in a religious frame and lends it a somber seriousness. The setting of the poem is clearly a Christian city, "where church spires pointed silently to Thee." The passage articulates a full-blown prophetic anger declaring the wrath of God on the perpetrators, many of whom populate the churches on Sunday morning.

Du Bois carried the memory of Sam Hose's lynching with him his entire life, claiming that each subsequent lynching scarred his soul. The magazine of the NAACP, *The Crisis,* founded in 1910 and edited by Du Bois for twenty-four years, regularly covered lynchings, thus documenting his long-term preoccupation with these spectacles. *The Crisis* provided extensive coverage of images from the lynchings as they occurred and prepared statistics about the numbers of lynchings on a yearly basis. Some of its most important coverage came in the form of investigative reporting about specific cases. For example, in the July 1916 issue, Du Bois and the NAACP capitalized on the grisly and notorious public lynching of Jesse Washington in Waco, Texas, known as the "Waco Horror," by printing firsthand accounts and horrifying pictures of the charred body, images that quickly gained national exposure. As the historian James SoRelle has written: "in lynching Jesse Washington, the mob in Waco unwittingly provided the NAACP with a *cause célèbre* that the national association could utilize to invoke support for a systematic campaign to halt lynchings."[32] Oswald Villard, treasurer of the NAACP at that time, stated that such brutal mob scenes called into question the meaning and purpose of American society: ""The crime at Waco is a challenge to our American civilization, yes, to every American."[33] Numerous photographs of the gruesome scene, witnessed in person by perhaps fifteen thousand Texans, circulated widely, showing Washington's badly burned remains hanging by a chain from a tree out in front of the courthouse. The savage spectacle as captured in these photographs (which the photographer hoped to use in producing postcards for sale to the crowd) became the object of widespread condemnation. Many civic leaders of the city could be identified in the photos, and yet no one was even arrested or questioned. Almost immediately Waco became known as "Barbecueville." The brutality of Washington's lynching became another influential episode in the American public's slow recognition of the hideous nature of the practice.[34] Again, the memories of the dead, like Washington, ended up motivating the survivors, spurring them forward toward progressive reform. Public lynch victims came to represent one more opportunity for the survivors to draw upon their continuing bonds with the dead, including Du Bois.

Still, if the cruel public lynchings of the likes of Sam Hose were the extent of the horror, perhaps the spring season of 1899 would not have left such an indelible imprint upon the character of W. E. B. Du Bois. But it was not to be the only tragedy to rock his world—sadly, his only son would die just a few weeks after the lynching of Sam Hose. As such these two episodes, occurring as they did only a month apart, should be examined together as a double-barreled traumatic cluster of events in this crucial season of change in Du Bois's long life: one cultural and public, the other personal and private. Together, the horrors of spring 1899 would mark a new epoch in the life of W. E. B. Du Bois—a turning point, after which the way of seeing his world could never be the same.

Burghardt Gomer Du Bois was born on October 2, 1897, in Great Barrington, Massachusetts, the birthplace of his father. Du Bois was finishing his second book, *The Philadelphia Negro*, at the time of his son's birth, and spent much of Burghardt's first year splitting time between his work in the seventh ward of Philadelphia and his home in Great Barrington. During the weeks he spent at home, Du Bois doted over his young son, firmly believing that Burghardt was destined to become a leading voice in the future progress of his race. But the dream was not to be—less than two years later, Burghardt contracted nasopharyngeal diphtheria, and his symptoms grew steadily worse over the next ten days, eventually leading to his death on May 24, 1899. After initially downplaying the severity of his son's illness, Du Bois spent the final day of his firstborn's life in a futile search for an Atlanta physician willing to treat a black child. The death of the firstborn son hung heavily over the heads of Du Bois and his wife Nina. Their relationship was never the same, and while Du Bois suffered greatly, "it was Nina's emotional health that was permanently affected," a fact Du Bois himself recognized; "In a sense my wife died too. Never after that was she quite the same in her attitude towards life and the world."[35] While his wife went to Great Barrington to grieve, Du Bois would go on to preside over a conference in Atlanta only six days after burying his son.

Du Bois had met his first wife Nina in the classroom at Wilberforce University in Ohio, where she was one of his students. Nina was the daughter of a hotel chef in Cedar Rapids, Iowa; "she was not sophisticated, but she had excellent manners and was well spoken."[36] Nina was very beautiful, light skinned, and was idolized by many of her classmates at Wilberforce. Du Bois was not a wealthy man when he married—a source of great anxiety for him—but he and his young bride were happy and in love when they left the chapel in Cedar Rapids on May 12, 1896. Many considered them to be well matched, and their future looked bright; shortly after their marriage, Du Bois was offered a position at the Uni-

Burghardt Du Bois (died 1899) and his parents, Nina and W. E. B. Du Bois, in 1897. Courtesy of the W. E. B. Du Bois Papers, University of Massachusetts-Amherst.

versity of Pennsylvania, a position that carried with it a raise of one hundred dollars a month.

By all accounts, the early years of Du Bois's marriage to Nina were joyous and loving. Speaking about his wife, Du Bois wrote, "Her great gift was her singularly honest character, her passion for cleanliness and order and her loyalty."[37] The first two years of their marriage, spent in Philadelphia and Atlanta, "were probably the happiest of Nina's married life."[38] In a letter written four months after her wedding, Nina wrote to Du Bois, "I'm feeling real good. I think I'll be good and well when I come home to you."[39] Du Bois relates a story of their first Christmas as a married couple in his *Autobiography*, painting a vivid picture of the simple joy they found in each other. Du Bois awoke on Christmas morning to find his wife "in her little gown secreting bundles in and around my socks." They celebrated the holiday as a honeymoon couple might, until "Finally the whole day melted away in misty happiness."[40]

The birth of their first son was arguably the high point in the relationship between Will and Nina. Du Bois was thrilled to have a son, and the experience of giving birth seemed to have signaled a positive change in his young wife. Prior to Burghardt's birth, Nina observed sex as "fundamentally indecent,"[41] but Du Bois saw Nina as a "transfigured woman"[42] after giving birth, and "the lustful lover experienced a powerfully deepened affection."[43] Du Bois spent most of Burghardt's life dividing his time between home and work, with the majority spent on the latter. Nina was a dutiful mother, however, and the dynamic they had created in their home life sustained them for the time being. But even though many believed them to be a good match, Will and Nina Du Bois were very different people. Nina was considered a bright girl, but there was always a significant intellectual gap between the young couple, a gap that often rendered them incapable of communicating about the issues in their relationship and in the world around them. Du Bois's writings about his first wife illustrate a widening gulf between them: "Du Bois would tend to write about her with brevity and a tinge of condescension."[44] The growing alienation, commonly accentuated among couples who lose children, was easy for Will and Nina to ignore during the honeymoon phase of their marriage, but it became painfully clear in the wake of the sudden loss of their son.

Burghardt's death left a wound within the Du Bois family that would never be overcome, one that came to define both parents for the rest of their lives. For Nina, Burghardt's death began a lengthy decline in physical and mental health. For Will, trauma and parental grief became a key focus of much of his thought and writing, as best seen in his solemn chapter "The Passing of the First-Born," one of the final sections of the book that would seal his literary reputation, *The Souls of Black Folk*. Du Bois connects his own grief powerfully to the atrocities carried out against countless other black sons, and to the suffering of the black race in America more generally. Du Bois sketches his son's glorious potential as "stillborn," as Robert Gooding-Williams puts it: "[he] fantasized that his child was a prophet. . . . But Du Bois's fantasy is thwarted, for his child dies. . . . [Du Bois] remains haunted by the worry that, like a child dead before it is born, it will inspire them with nothing new, and so fail to transform the world-wilderness."[45]

Gooding-Williams is correct to note the discouragement, of course. Burghardt symbolizes "the persistent thwarting of black men's desire to give birth to a future rather than the past."[46] And yet, like him, I also argue that the burden of the chapter in *Souls* is to go beyond this haunting, to reveal, or conjure, some redemptive element to the death of his son, who in Du Bois's tender portrait is transformed into a messianic symbol for the sufferings of an entire oppressed people. But Du Bois also writes briefly of Nina's reaction, saying, "in the chamber of death writhed the world's most piteous thing—a childless mother."[47] While Du Bois was able to project the death of his son onto the world of his work, Nina was left alone, and it was "Nina's emotional health that was permanently affected."[48] Burghardt's death certainly altered the marital relationship between Du Bois and Nina: "Whether Burghardt's death wedged between them or whether they allowed it to push them apart because there was so little holding them together in the first place, each felt increasingly alienated from the other."[49] This alienation increased throughout the course of their marriage; it affected Nina's treatment and raising of their second child, Yolande. Yolande was born on October 21, 1900, and her birth "brought (Will and Nina) closer together than they had been since Burghardt's death." Nina obsessed over the day-to-day raising of her daughter, "niggardly apportioning Yolande's playtime with the few children approved for contact, and having her clothing washed over and over." Nina had always been a meticulous manager of the household affairs, "but the care of Yolande was compulsive—a prophylactic regimen to assure to Yolande what in their inexperience she and Will had failed to give Burghardt."[50] Ultimately, Atlanta, with its darkest memories, proved impossible for Nina as a place to live. She obviously associated the city with the avoidable death of her son, but more generally she felt the oppressing weight of an apartheid she had never known during her previous life in the North. While Will could escape to his work, Nina was left to raise her daughter nearly alone, and "She behaved as though the hated city were only waiting to strike Yolande down and take her away like Burghardt."[51] It wasn't until the Atlanta race riots of 1906, a time of unprecedented and widespread upheaval, that Du Bois agreed to have Nina move with Yolande back to her home in Great Barrington.

As the years passed, Du Bois became increasingly detached from life at home. Between 1900 and 1910, Du Bois spent months away from his family, sometimes in places as far off as Paris and London. This separation was significant in the shaping of his daughter's psyche; Yolande "would repeatedly try to capture his love and attention by becoming sick or refusing to do what was expected of her." Nina wrote frequently to the absent Will, and these letters often expressed a desperate attempt to reach out to her husband, "to engage Du Bois somehow and make him recognize her as a person in her own right, rather than as an abstraction and a significant, though uninteresting, extension of himself."[52] As much data confirms, spouses often have wildly different ways of dealing with the deaths of their children. These massive differences often spell doom for relationships, and divorce is a common solution for bereaved parents. It certainly appears that Du Bois and his wife Nina were unable to find common ground as they tried to make sense of the death of Burghardt. As such, the death of Burghardt greatly exacerbated what was already an irreparable breach. Like many marriages, Will and Nina Du Bois were unable to overcome the trauma of parental bereavement, and sadly their marriage ended in divorce.

The traumatic impact on Du Bois of the lynching of Hose and the death of his son has been commonly underappreciated.[53] Scholars have tended to see Du Bois as responding in an ambivalent manner to his son's death: for some Burghardt is a sign of hope (of immortal life, of life beyond the Veil) who prefigures a better life despite his death; for others, Du Bois's loss and/or his response are negative consequences of a disordered society, in which death is perhaps the best fate for the child. Most surprising is that until recently, serious consideration of his son's death has most often been ignored. Similarly, Du Bois's religious beliefs have largely remained ambiguous in this process; his belief in the afterlife remains an uncertainly expressed hope rather than a certainty, and the loss of his son is linked more to social realities than to a search for religious truth. And yet his elegy for Burghardt, writes Ryan Schneider, "creates a space for emotional intimacy in which the warmth and affection of the father-son bond can be represented even as anguish over its loss can be fully expressed."[54]

And yet, we might ask, is that bond indeed lost? Or does the bond continue—and if so, how for Du Bois? Later in the same essay, Schneider describes how Du Bois "includes soaring and majestic tributes to his son's virtue, talent and potential as a leader, counting his death as a loss not just to himself but to a larger world."[55] Paradoxically, however, Du Bois is suggesting that this loss can become a gain, redemptively, and that the father-son bond, though lost in one sense, might become found again; through the work of his art a new kind of bond might continue. Other recent scholars have also seen Du Bois as attaching a mystical significance to his son as a prophetic figure, identifying Burghardt with the recurring image of "the immortal child," which came later in Du Bois's literary career. Burghardt's significance for Du Bois's spiritual beliefs is as a sign of hope within the suffering caused by life behind the Veil—though perhaps a highly conflicted and ambiguous sign. In this way, Burghardt became the prototype of all black victims transformed into redemptive figures in Du Bois's imaginative writing, especially lynching victims. Biographer Edward Blum argues that Du Bois chose instead "to associate the black victim with the biblical Christ. . . . [He] sought to convert the lynched African American from an object of disdain into a paragon of virtue. . . . By characterizing lynchings as crucifixions and by linking the lives of embattled blacks with that of the biblical Christ, African American writers reversed the religious and theological universe of whites. In these narratives, blacks were not soulless or subhuman evildoers. Rather, they were the very flesh, figuratively and literally, of God—and, in some cases, God incarnate."[56]

This association is crucial to Du Bois's sketch of his dead son: a victim of an uncaring system, Burghardt is transformed into a powerful symbol of hope and incarnation. As he writes poignantly in *Souls*: "We were not far from worshipping this revelation of the divine, my wife and I. . . . heard in his baby voice the voice of the Prophet that was to rise within the Veil. . . . A perfect life was his, all joy and love. . . . The world loved him." In this formulation, the loss is incalculable and of lasting importance: "he might have borne his burden more bravely than we."[57] The loss described is saturated in pathos and hope, and we are to leave this meditation with the memory of the dead inspiring us forward into the promised future. And Du Bois insisted that his readers focus directly on his lost child; he trains our gaze on his dead son, as he does with the victims of spectacle lynching later in the pages of *The Crisis*.

In his lifelong attempt to influence public perception of African Americans, Du Bois often sketched them as beautiful, holy and godlike, as in his championing of the their physical appearance and their music. Besides popularizing the horrifying images of black lynchings, Du Bois was also a leader in the presentation of an alternative vision of African Americans that featured their beauty and courage. Du Bois understood the power of images and was a pioneer in the publicizing of more flattering images of black Americans than had been common before 1900, believing it could be politically useful. For example, Du Bois shifted his attention to the Exhibit of American Negroes at the Paris Convention of 1900, augmenting his reliance on the written word with visual images: he put together an impressive collection of charts, maps, and graphs recording the economic and literary growth of the African Americans in Georgia. Most profound, however, was his inclusion of a variety of photographs of what he called "typical Negro faces." These images portrayed African Americans in their homes, businesses, and churches, and were aimed at combating the stereotype of the lazy and ignorant Negro: "Above all, the photographs Du Bois chose exemplified dignity, accomplishment, and progress."[58] Historian Shawn Michelle Smith argues that the use of these images was largely his attempt to own and testify to his blackness, "reclaiming an affirmative African American identity in the face of brutally dehumanizing forces."[59] Thus it was a tactic in the war against demonizing views of black folk. Just as white Georgians used the images of lynching, African American mug shots, and the bloody souvenirs as reminders of their supremacy, Du Bois turned to positive images to build pride in the progress of the African American race.

Similarly, the wail of injustice and pain depicted in *The Souls of Black Folk* is counterbalanced by the songs of the spirit, the "Negro spirituals," filled as they were with hope and beauty. Admiration of the slave songs, or "jubilees," was another aspect of African American experience that united antilynching crusaders like Du Bois and Mark Twain. Du Bois would famously call them the "sorrow songs," filled as they were with the pain and sadness brought about by the sufferings of his people. Although filled with sorrow and pain, the spirituals, said Du Bois, were his people's gift of the spirit—and the most sublime and beautiful cultural expression black people of America had yet achieved. They were the manifestation of a deep cultural trauma that marked the history of African Americans in America, he claimed. Du Bois associated this trauma with "the tragic soul life of the slave," and he believed it continued to mark African Americans well into the twentieth century. For Du Bois, this tragic soul of the slaves manifested most prominently in the slave songs, "the one true expression of the people's sorrow, despair and hope."[60] The songs reflect a "double consciousness" that is experienced by all people of faith: despair and hope, the tragic and the victorious. The dynamics of religion always include belief and doubt, hope and despair, a perception that complicates the traditional understanding of Du Bois's famous concept of the double consciousness by extending it to include the normal experience of a follower of Jesus, who was simultaneously a member of this world community and yet not of it. Double consciousness can also be related to the complex notion of redemptive suffering, according to which pain and grief can bring about goodness and redemption. Such is the everyday consciousness of the spiritual life, says Du Bois, and such is the tone and content of the Negro spirituals. As Terrence Johnson argues, Du Bois seeks to "define justice and freedom in relation to human suffering, death, despair and hope—the moral vocabulary Du Bois discovers in the Negro spirituals. . . . We must wrestle with death before we can truly address the legacy of American slavery."[61] Thus, again, as with Howells, Du Bois denies the denial of death, and the spirituals constantly force us to confront the reality of death all around us—as do the ghastly lynching photos published in *The Crisis*.

The grief and trauma, as well as the hope and promise, inherent in these songs had long been described by historians and ethnographers, but the greatest influence on Du Bois's understanding of the songs was probably Frederick Douglass. As P. Sterling Stuckey has written, Douglass was for Du Bois "his primary intellectual and spiritual mentor, and very likely the prose stylist who influenced him most," though not enough has been made of this obvious connection.[62] In fact, a large portrait of Douglass was hung above the fireplace in the Du Bois home in Brooklyn, and visitors were sometimes invited to admire the picture with their hosts. In *Souls*, Du Bois referred to Douglass as "the great form," and "the greatest of American Negro leaders."[63] Douglass said in his *Narrative* that the slave songs "told a tale of woe," and "breathed the prayer and complaint of souls boiling over with the bitterest anguish."[64] Again we see the double consciousness of the believer in God; there is simultaneously complaint and prayer, despair and hope. Similarly, the spiritual songs brilliantly project a double consciousness of belief: deep sorrow and tragic pain balanced by the hope and beauty of transcendence.

After the Civil War, the Negro spiritual tradition was promoted nationally by several individuals, especially Thomas Wentworth Higginson, longtime abolitionist, Harvard graduate, Union officer, and commander of the first regiment of freed slaves fighting against the Confederates. During the war, Higginson became fascinated with the songs his soldiers sang, and he began collecting them. He published his findings and his meditations on the music after the war ended, first in an article called "Negro Spirituals" in the *Atlantic Monthly* of June 1867, and then in book form as *Army Life in a Black Regiment* (1869). These songs, Higginson believed, were "a stimulus to courage and a tie to heaven. . . . By these they could sing themselves, as had their fathers before them, out of the contemplation of their own low estate, into the sublime scenery of the Apocalypse. . . . There is no parallel instance of an oppressed race thus sustained by the religious sentiment alone. These songs are but the vocal expression of the simplicity of their faith and the sublimity of their long resignation."[65]

By the time Du Bois wrote *The Souls of Black Folk*, Negro spirituals were already widely considered the greatest cultural achievement of African Americans up until that time. In a letter of March 1875 from London, for instance, Mark Twain wrote, "I am expecting to hear the Jubilee Singers to-night, for the fifth time."[66] The Fisk Jubilee Singers were a group of eleven young African Americans, eight of whom were former slaves, whose initial purpose was to raise funding for Fisk, a new college for freed slaves in Nashville, Tennessee. Twain was present both times they performed in Hartford in 1872, the first performances on January 28, 1872, at the Asylum Hill Congregational Church pastored by his good friend Joseph Twichell. The next day, the *Hartford Courant* claimed that the Jubilee Singers created "a sensation rarely equaled. . . . It is the first time that we at the north have heard the genuine songs of their race, executed with their faith and their feeling. It was like a revelation. . . . One heard in those strange and plaintive melodies the sadness and the hope of a trusting and a really joyous race."[67] As late as 1897, just days before the one-year anniversary of the death of his daughter Susy, Twain found great comfort in hearing one last time the Jubilee Singers, as he grieved in Switzerland: it was "diviner, even, than in their early days, 26 years ago. They came up to the house this morning & sang for us. They are as fine people as I am acquainted with in any country."[68] Rooted in tragedy and pain, the spirituals were yet somehow deeply consoling to the bereaved family.

Higginson's and Twain's attraction to this music, filled with both sadness and hope, rested largely on its power to engender sympathy for the oppressed victims of slavery, especially among whites. But the black spirituals left a deep impression on Du Bois as well. As a student at Fisk University from 1885 to 1888, he knew the Fisk Singers well and heard them perform. Many of their stock songs became important in his formation as a moral thinker, and would later become keys to unlocking the secret power of his masterpiece. *Souls* begins with an annotation from "Nobody Knows the Trouble I've Seen," indicating that the book will locate and meditate on such troubles. But it is precisely through these troubles that the spirituals live and breathe. He writes in *Souls*, "little of beauty has America given the world saved the rude grandeur God himself stamped on her bosom. . . . The Negro folk song—the rhythmic cry of the slave—stands to-day not simply as the sole American music, but as the most beautiful expression of human experience born this side the seas. It has been neglected, it has been, and is, half despised, and above all it has been persistently mistaken and misunderstood; but notwithstanding, it still remains as the singular spiritual heritage of the nation and the greatest gift of the Negro people."[69] In chapter 14 of *Souls*, titled "The Sorrow Songs," Du Bois penned some of the most heightened and beautiful expressions of religious belief found in his entire corpus. Often the prose echoes the King James version of the Bible as he analyzes the spirituals: "They are the music of an unhappy people, of the children of disappointment . . . they grope toward some unseen power and sigh for rest in the End. . . . My children, my little children, are singing to the sunshine."[70] These biblical echoes indicate a level of profundity and mystery that colloquial language is unable to convey; the songs describe "misty wanderings and hidden ways"; they speak of "trouble and exile, of strife and hiding," and articulate humankind's "infinite longing for peace."[71] Significantly, it is with these meditations that Du Bois brings his great volume to a close. The final word of *Souls*, like in the Bible's book of Revelation, is given to the hope of heaven and the courage to see it fulfilled. By ending *Souls* with this tribute to the spirituals, Du Bois seems to agree with Higginson (whom he quotes several times); these songs stimulated courage and provided a "tie to heaven," or at least, the justice that heaven represented.

For Du Bois, the spirituals also exemplified what he called "the gifts of the Spirit." In these songs, he recognized a source of unity: "Our song, our toil, our cheer, and warning have been given to this nation in blood-brotherhood. Are not these gifts worth the giving?"[72] His perception is much like Lord Shaftesbury's idea that these songs can "excite a like sympathy, and stir the hearts of the English people to join them."[73] These comments betray a theological sensitivity to the work of music in the spiritual life of believing communities. One theologian suggests that "the work of the Spirit is to create a new human and that the creation of the new human means the restoration of peace and right relationship among human beings. . . . When the church sings together, it announces the new community the spirit has created in Christ. But the church's singing not only announces this new community, it enacts it. When the church sings together, the creation of 'one new humanity in place of the two' (Ephesians 2:15) becomes an aural reality."[74] In some cosmic way, the singing of the spirituals, especially in group settings, fosters the imaginative work necessary for two communities to come together as one. Twain and Du Bois evidently recognized and personally experienced this phenomenon. The spirituals enabled them, at least partially and briefly, to enter into the pain and sorrow of the oppressed slaves, thus manifesting a kind of solidarity based in common experiences of trauma. For fleeting moments, the two communities, black and white, were experienced as coming together in a kind of "aural reality."

Each chapter of *Souls* is headed with a musical notation from one of the old spirituals. The final chapter gives reference to several others as well. Yet the theological content and meaning of these songs, or the specific reasons that each song was chosen for each specific chapter, have rarely been discussed. This may be largely due to the fact that Du Bois assumes the reader knows the songs by these notations alone: each heading consists only of a line of music, without the lyrics. Easily overlooked, they are recognizable by those with a musical knowledge, thus creating a community according to certain skills and experience. Unity, indeed, is at the heart of many of the spirituals featured in *The Souls of Black Folk*. In "There's a Great Camp Meeting in the Promised Land," we are urged "O, Walk together children, / Don't you get weary, / Walk together children, / Don't you get weary." The song depends upon an image of all believers being happy together at the camp meeting. Similarly, "March On" presents the image of an army: "March on, and you shall gain the victory, / March on, and you shall gain the day." In "The Rocks and the Mountains," an appeal is made to all people, regardless of rank or race, to admit to the plain fact that all will be judged according to righteousness. Security is found only in God's grace: "Oh the rocks and the mountains shall all flee a-way, / And you shall have a new hiding place that day." God's justice will rule that day, a source of comfort and a reference to the impending defeat of evil: "And the kings of the earth, and the great men, and the rich men, and the chief captains, and the mighty men, and every bondman, and every free man, hid themselves in the dens and in the rocks of the mountains; and said to the mountains and rocks, Fall on us, and hide us from the face of him that sitteth on the throne" (Revelation 6:15–17). Finally, the spirituals celebrate a cosmic community that mystically joins the dead and the living via the continuing bonds, so that throughout all eternity the circle may remain unbroken.

Besides their roots in spiritual unity, the "groanings too deep for words" (Romans 8:26) featured in the spirituals represent the divine discontent and the deep yearning of the oppressed minorities of America. One critic calls this spiritual malaise a "lurking dis-ease," and Du Bois invents his own term in the story "Of the Coming of John": a "vague unrest."[75] This discontent, for Du Bois, explains the naming of the sorrow songs: "Through all the sorrow of the sorrow songs there breathes a hope—of faith in the ultimate justice of things. The minor cadences of despair change often to triumph and calm confidence. Sometimes it is faith in life, sometimes of faith and death, sometimes assurance of boundless justice in some fair world beyond. But whichever it is, the meaning is always clear: that sometime, somewhere, man will judge man by their souls and not by their skins. Is such a hope justified? Do the sorrow songs sing true?"[76] Those difficult questions signify the author's doubts about the religious realm. And yet lines like these also show that Du Bois constantly framed his argument in a deeply religious context. He writes, "Christianity means sympathy; the realization of what it costs a human being to live and support a family in decency. . . . Christianity means unselfishness; the willingness to forgo in part one's personal advantage." In *Souls*, Du Bois venerates sympathy above all else, even though he is highly educated and speaks most comfortably in a rationalistic mode. As a result, the structure of the book indicates that logical arguments can only go so far. Instead of rational logic, the final five chapters of *Souls* rely most heavily upon emotional and spiritual arguments and aim to develop within readers a strong sense of sympathy for the plight of black Americans. Du Bois writes, "the nineteenth was the first century of human sympathy—the age when half wonderingly we began to descry in others that transfigured spark of divinity which we call Myself; when clodhopper and presence, and tramps and thieves, and millionaires and—sometimes—Negroes, became throbbing souls whose warm pulsing life touched us so nearly that we have gasped with surprise, crying, 'Thou to! Hast thou seen sorrow and the dull waters of hopelessness? Hast thou known life?'"[77] For Du Bois, religion is most usefully understood as a form of social criticism fueled by sympathy, which is by definition a force binding together individuals in solidarity. We might recall the era's most trenchant, foundational theory of the practice of realism: William Dean Howells in 1886 affirmed realism's ability to extend social awareness and "widen the bounds of sympathy."[78] What Du Bois disliked the most is any religion that diverted attention away from the real world, or that worked to dissolve the bonds between people. During the time period in which he wrote, much of the American church was doing just that: moving away from the social world, or separating people, especially white from black. This was common, despite the rise of literary realism and the "social gospel," two emerging movements deeply engaged in providing a real response to the growing poverty and oppressions of the "reality" of a rapidly expanding industrial and urban landscape.

The social Christianity and literary realism at the end of the nineteenth century both appealed strongly to Du Bois. Similarly, his prophetic proclamations appealed to fostering a sympathy that would face life's problems and begin developing solutions in the real world. As he told the graduates of his alma mater, Fisk, in 1898: "I cannot promise you happiness always but I can promise you divine discontent with the imperfect."[79] Du Bois recited a poem to end his lecture to these promising, young black educators:

> Truth forever on the scaffold,
> Wrong forever on the throne.
> Yet that scaffold sways the future,

And behind the dim unknown
Standeth God within the shadow,
Keeping watch above his own.[80]

His concept of discontent is very much a religious sensibility. The scaffold invokes the crucifixion of Jesus and the lynching of countless young black men. Du Bois's concept of "divine discontent," much like his idea of "vague unrest," is rooted in the Hebrew prophets such as Isaiah and Amos, and it exists with the intention of transforming the world, including not only the hearts of men and women, but also the existing social conditions.[81] These prophets appealed to the concept of *shalom*: the idea that things "ought" to be a certain way, and that justice and equality conform to this "oughtness." Human discontent results when the world is simply not the way it ought to be.[82] As such Du Bois presents discontent as the source of Christian hope. This idea anticipates the later work of Martin Luther King Jr., who spoke of the "creatively maladjusted." It also resembles the "theology of hope" made famous in the 1960s by the German theologian Jürgen Moltmann, who wrote: "Hope does not calm the unquiet heart, but is itself the unquiet heart in man. . . . Peace with God means conflict with the world, for the goad of the promised future stabs inexorably into the flesh of every unfulfilled promise."[83] Divine discontent is a goad; it forces us to reject the status quo and work for a better world. Our discontent about the world urges us on toward action and change; our "vague unrest" is prophetic in pushing us forward to the achievement of America. True religion, for Du Bois, was about social hope leading to change for all.

The black spirituals, brimming with discontent and unrest, are not to be understood as accommodating or apathetic toward change. Instead the spirituals are agents for renewal: rooted in trauma, filled with sorrow, yet insistent upon the final victory of justice over evil. For Du Bois, the spirituals also presented a cosmic vision of God's power and provision in overcoming evil and resurrecting a new creation of beauty, justice, and peace. Like the final lines of the poem quoted above, Du Bois appeals to the "God within the shadow." In the lyrics of the spirituals, the most prominent theme is the appeal to the comedic ending of the Bible narrative—an appeal to a day and time when all things are brought together in God's provision and set right according to God's justice and beauty.[84] This culminating work of God's spirit is the *eschaton*: meaning, the ultimate goal toward which all of creation is moving. Du Bois's vision of progressive history was rather mainstream at this time, featuring as it did "a belief in inherent, inevitable spiritual progress, in the gradual tendency of the physical universe and of human history toward the good, the process that determined the manner in which God achieved his will." For example, the *Encyclopedia Americana* of 1903 stated as empirical fact that "progress governed the whole natural and moral universe."[85] In religious terms, a millennial eschatology is one focused on God's triumph and the vision of all things finally being made according to righteousness and justice for all. The British theologian N. T. Wright describes the New Testament concept of the power of resurrection as the driving force for progress in human history, a force that permeates human effort and culture. Wright argues that this concept has deep roots in nineteenth-century Britain and America, when it arose to new heights. He draws upon major expositions of Christian hope, such as Romans 8 and 1st Corinthians 15, claiming that "hope, for the Christian, is not wishful thinking or mere blind optimism. It is a mode of knowing, a mode within which new things are possible, options are not shut down, new creation can happen."[86] Wright suggests that his concept of "an epistemology of hope" found its greatest expressions at the turn of the twentieth century. That timing coincides perfectly with the basic message of the extremely popular Negro spirituals in general, as it does with Du Bois's understanding of their impact in his masterpiece.

The spiritual characteristics of Du Bois's career have often been overlooked, but our understanding of Du Bois has changed a lot in recent years. Today, the deeply spiritual side of this great African American leader is being depicted with more sophistication than earlier critics seem to have detected. These spiritual aspects are rooted biographically in Du Bois's traumatic grief—primarily in the death of his son, but also in the widespread social practice of lynching, which he came to associate with the loss of his son. In the most formative period of his life, when he was forced to suffer the death of Burghardt, witness the atrocities of lynching, and complete the writing of his greatest book, the consolation and hope represented in the black spirituals helped Du Bois get through it all. Those sorrow songs ended up becoming a fundamental aspect of his prophetic message. And so we should no longer be surprised that he prayed the following, with his students at Atlanta University, at the beginning of a new century: "Give us in our day, O God, to see the fulfillment of Thy vision of Peace. May these young people grow to despise false ideals of conquest and empire and all the tinsel of war. May we strive to replace force with justice and armies of murder with armies of relief. May we believe in Peace among all nations as a present practical creed and count love for our country as love and not hate for our fellow men. Amen."[87] Edward Blum draws the following conclusion: "Du Bois's God was a God of the oppressed. His Christ was a black man who befriended the marginalized. His heaven was a place with no rich people. Hidden in the American landscape of lynching and horror, of rape and neglect, Du Bois found dramas of redemption. Looking into eyes of the sorrowful, the mourning, and the enraged, Du Bois found a way to conceive of songs of grace. This was the gospel according to W. E. B. Du Bois."[88]

If Blum's account is accurate, and Du Bois does give us a gospel of redemption founded on a cosmic hope, then he is more like a prophetic preacher than a secular heretic. His was a gospel firmly founded on a "present practical creed" of facing injustice and changing the world to conform to how it "ought" to be. But it was also a gospel steeped in grief and trauma, and the continuing bonds with the dead. The roots of his gospel were surely in the traumatic events of 1899, the deaths of two young black males, one his only son, and the other a victim he never met. The trauma of these events continued to haunt him, especially as each new lynching made the daily news and reminded him, once more, of these twinned initial tragedies. Thus rooted in personal tragedy and cultural trauma, the horror became almost an obsession in his public journalism and always brought back for Du Bois the callous and indifferent responses of the white people of Atlanta, many of them professing to be Christians. Du Bois became a witness to the cultural trauma of the south: he testified to the suffering of all Americans, black and white, who had together been "subjected to a horrendous event that leaves indelible marks upon their group consciousness, marking their memories forever."[89] And he proclaimed the sheer beauty he saw in the faces, and songs, of the oppressed, as testimony to some kind of spiritual reality bigger than any one person.

In doing so, Du Bois drew deeply from the Christian prophetic traditions of *shalom*, justice, and hope in providing a responsible new interpretation of active faith. Far from denying Christianity, he marshaled the power of the songs of grace, believing that they might alleviate pain and provide courage to move forward. Du Bois recognized that these songs were "a stimulus to courage and a tie to heaven," as Higginson put it. Certainly not all observers could "hear" the spirituals; as Nietzsche's character Zarathustra complained at roughly the same time, Christians "have to sing better songs."[90] Du Bois disagreed: it wasn't the singer's problem alone, but also the listener's need to hear what is truly being sung. He challenged his readers to listen carefully to the music of the spirituals as a prophetic utterance, and through them he called for a newer and purer form of Christian faith. His early radicalism was founded in the fires of grief and solidified by the continuing bonds with the dead, carried out in response to the cultural traumas of his day but also cemented in the loving memory of his only begotten son.

Admittedly, his deployment of black spirituals and the Christ-like lynch victims, while deeply dependent on biblical themes, veered ever more toward the modern temperament. Du Bois was indeed beholden to the sentimental grief so powerful for Stowe and her antebellum readers. But Du Bois remained stubbornly resistant to the orthodox Christian doctrine of an earlier era. If the divided mind of grieving parents has been identified as perhaps the major theme of this study, perhaps none of the authors covered exemplifies the agonistic bitterness of the rivalry more than Du Bois. Perhaps even more than Mark Twain, Du Bois was drawn powerfully to the despair and the sheer hopefulness of both poles of the paradox. The great thinker known most famously for his account of "double consciousness" illustrates as well the double consciousness of the bereaved. As Emily Dickinson so capably described this emerging, modern religious sensibility, "We both believe and disbelieve a hundred times an hour, which keeps believing nimble."[91]

Du Bois was indeed nimble in his believing, and he was also politically savvy. It seems that, in his lifelong agonies over his lost son, and the countless lost sons of others, especially those lost through lynching, Du Bois found some consolation in the bonds with the dead as best he could, even while entertaining serious doubts about Christianity and the afterlife. But the bonds for him may or may not have been "real": solving that puzzle, or even showing his hand to a curious public was not initially his interest. Rather, he embraced the widespread public sympathies for a belief in the continuing bonds as a sacred doctrine. And the traumatized subject of grief, Du Bois expertly recognized, may need to be reckoned as an entire group, or even culture. So we conclude with a self-reflexive transformation of the sentimental bonds into a more "modern" version that would become the mainstay of the more secular age of the twentieth century, a version that illustrates the shift from the literal and supernatural to the figurative and rhetorical. Du Bois demonstrates the masterful exploitation of the residual power of the bonds—even as his own faith in their existence became, at best, "nimble." If those "bonds" with the dead are indeed man-made, rather than transcendent, so be it. Du Bois would expertly deploy them either way, reaping their redemptive fruit.

Epilogue
"Surrounded by a Cloud of Witnesses"
Recovering the Bonds with the Dead

> We are surrounded by a cloud of witnesses.
>
> Epistle to the Hebrews, chapter 12

This book has considered the history of American authorship in the context of parental grief. As Emily Dickinson put it, believing in the afterlife became very nimble for many writers well before the modern literary movement and the advent of World War I. Nimble believing often resulted from a questioning or loss of faith, including sincere doubts about the bonds with the dead. Such is the commonplace narrative of faith in America, before the twentieth century: a time, in Dickinson's memorable phrase, when many intellectuals could "believe and disbelieve a hundred times an hour."

In recent years, however, a reaching out to grasp at the sentimental bonds with the dead is making a bit of a cultural comeback. This grasping is seen in the growing mania for memorialization, the spectacle of massive crowds with lighted candles and teddy bears. Many consider such ritualistic spectacles to be maudlin, but they seem deeply consoling for the surviving parents and many others, as in the horrific anniversaries of murdered schoolchildren at places like Newtown's Sandy Hook Elementary in 2013. At *Newsday*'s website, one can still gaze at the images of the twenty children murdered at Sandy Hook Elementary in December 2012; the digital world is now allowing even more commemoration of the dead.[1] But clinical findings support a belief in a comeback for the bonds with the dead as well; research shows that survivors are often "surprised at the extent to which their deceased loved ones continued to influence and form part of their ongoing lives." As researcher Christine Valentine reports, "contemporary continuing bonds are flourishing, taking highly idiosyncratic forms rather than being grounded in traditional or religious structures."[2] These idiosyncratic responses have found new methods of expression, especially on the Internet. Meanwhile, in Ferguson, Missouri, not far from my home, the grieving parents of Michael Brown are still hoping for some kind of redemptive justice to come from the death of their son in August 2014. The sheer spectacle and rage of Ferguson might remind us of Gavin Stevens's great line in Faulkner's *Requiem for a Nun*: "The past is never dead. It's not even past."[3]

In this book, I've shown and analyzed some of the horrors a handful of our most famous writers experienced, horrors very familiar to me. But I've also documented the constructive ways that these deaths affected the worldviews and the writings of the surviving parent. I've considered how a child's death may have influenced the direction and content of the writer's production afterward, perhaps much more than has previously been thought. However, I certainly realize that a focus on the "posttraumatic growth" an author experiences, as opposed to the more common posttraumatic stress disease, should never allow us to diminish the pain and suffering of the bereaved.

In this regard I also speak from experience. The issues of bereavement and trauma covered in *Continuing Bonds with the Dead* are important for America culturally, but they're important also for me personally. In fact, I am myself a bereaved parent. My son Daniel died in 1999, at age six, so I know that a truthful reckoning of these phenomena must begin with the sheer disaster and horror of the experience for the surviving parents. There is nothing simple or easy about the process, and brief introductions like this one, emphasizing the "positive" or "constructive" outcomes of loss, run the risk of sounding glib, if not entirely offensive, to grieving parents. In this book, I have tried hard not to underestimate the awfulness of losing a child. I believe my own membership in "the club" allows me to speak with some intimacy about such horrors, and it may have helped me understand a little better than most readers what all of these heroic Americans were up against, as they tried to make something redemptive out of their horrible experiences.[4] Indeed, as more than one person has suggested, perhaps this book is itself the result of my own desire that something good might emerge from the rough-edged, sheer hell of parental grief.

I had been working on the life and times of Mark Twain for the better part of a decade when my own greatest tragedy struck, in summer 1999. In my descent into depression and near madness, I came across Twain's striking comments, some of the most accurate I've ever read about a parent's emotionally numbing encounter with a child's death, which he wrote soon after the loss of Susy: "It is one of the mysteries of our nature that a man, all unprepared, can receive a thunderstroke like that and live. There is but one reasonable explanation of it. The intellect is stunned by the shock and but gropingly gathers the meaning of the words. The power to realize their full import is mercifully wanting. The mind has a dumb sense of vast loss—that is all. It will take mind and memory months, and possibly years, to gather together the details and thus learn and know the whole extent of the loss."[5] Twain's description floored me, but thereafter we were kindred spirits, both members of the club nobody wants to join.

And so I began researching these phenomena, largely out of self-interest, as I tried to figure out what was wrong with me. It was a means of self-diagnosis and possibly therapy. One day, it suddenly dawned on me that perhaps some of the clinical data I was learning about parental grief could be used to help scholars understand the travails of major writers. Oddly, until my own tragedy, it had never occurred to me that so many major American authors had been similarly visited, including many of my all-time favorites: Harriet Beecher Stowe, Abraham Lincoln, and W. D. Howells, for example. Despite such sad experiences, all these literary superstars managed to live steady, productive lives that helped shape the rise of a mighty nation. That thought alone intrigued me and gave me some hope and consolation. Perhaps if they found a way to survive, I could as well.

I plunged ahead, genuinely curious as to how they did it. My first attempt to apply what I was learning to a literary life focused on Mark Twain, for two reasons. First, I was already fairly experienced in and knowledgeable about the field of Mark Twain studies. I'd written about him in my dissertation and then in my first book, and over the years had become familiar with the vast, ungainly field of Twain scholarship, so I already knew the terrain fairly well. Second, I identified closely with his travails, especially admiring his sense of humor in the face of life's greatest tragedies.

The project began with Twain but quickly migrated to other, equally intriguing bereaved parents. Like Harriet Beecher Stowe, my own encounters with Lincoln also relied heavily upon personal visits to Washington. I'd done work on Lincoln long ago, but somehow the poignant fact of his son Willie's death had never seemed important in my mind.

But in the midsummer of 2004, five years after Daniel's death, and on the very weekend that I was strolling around Washington, DC, among the many monuments and historic sites that direct a citizen's attention to the meaning of our nation, I marveled at the newly opened World War II

Memorial, smack dab in the center of the mall. It was hot and sunny, and yet thousands of tourists and I were struck by the sheer scale of the memorial, and our mutual bonds with the dead. My father, a pilot in the US Army Air Corps during the war years, loomed in the back of my mind as I viewed the grounds of the new memorial. For almost all of these tourists, the World War II Memorial stood not for the deaths of children, but for the deaths and legacies of their elders: fathers or even grandfathers. But for those of the previous generations, those who lived through those years, the dead were most often brothers, cousins—or sons. Less than a mile away, the scene was being supervised by the most famous monument in America, the Lincoln Memorial. Etched into the marble of that edifice were some of Lincoln's most enduring words: "It is for us the living, rather, to be dedicated here to the unfinished work which they who fought here have thus far so nobly advanced. It is rather for us to be here dedicated to the great task remaining before us . . . that from these honored dead we take increased devotion to that cause for which they gave the last full measure of devotion." Lincoln's grand memorial specifies the "honored dead" of the Civil War, invoking their ghosts as a means to carry onward toward fulfillment of that vague "unfinished work" of the American people.

It's hard for any American not to be impressed by the hardscrabble life and times of our sixteenth president, whose legendary failures are often listed as an encouragement to all of us to keep running the course. Another tragic aspect of Lincoln's life is often overlooked: the loss of two sons, one named Eddie who died in Illinois, and another named Willie who died in the White House at one of the lowest moments of the Civil War. And so when Lincoln spoke of "us the living," he must have surely recalled on some level the two sons of his own who were mystically present with him at the massive cemetery at Gettysburg.

I felt a tug of sympathy, reading those words scratched into the stone that day, as dozens of tourists pressed in for a photo. The solemn tone of my Independence Day weekend reminded me of an anecdote John Steinbeck told about his own visit to the Lincoln Memorial with his son. After they both stood for some time in the shadow of the great president, Steinbeck's son blurted out in awe, "Oh! Lord! We had better be great."[6]

What is a legacy, or myth, if not a constant reminder of the dead? What are those stone buildings on the National Mall, if not the living memorials, like Tom's cabin, of our continuing bonds with the ones who preceded us? Recently one historian wrote persuasively about America's "manic"

Eleanor Roosevelt explaining the Lincoln Memorial to Diane Hopkins, left, daughter of a WPA administrator, and Chandler Roosevelt, daughter of Elliott Roosevelt, while attending ceremonies on Lincoln's birthday, February 12, 1938. Courtesy of the Library of Congress, Prints and Photographs Division.

fascination with the building of more and more memorials, as mentioned in the introduction. But perhaps this obsession with memorials—if it does indeed exist—is merely a symptom of our communal sense of a growing disconnection with the past.[7]

The concept of an American mission and identity goes back way before Lincoln was born in 1809, of course—roughly two hundred years before his birth, in fact. Even prior to the birth of an "America," people believed that there was something special about the "virgin" landmass that came to be denoted simply as America—a designation that remains somewhat controversial. Poets throughout American history have sung the praises of that American "something," often with bravado and sometimes with obsession.

But none have sung America's praises as melodically, or as mythically, as Abe Lincoln (unless it would be his contemporary acolyte, Walt

Whitman). Maybe most Americans do not think of Lincoln's speeches as "songs," but I sometimes do—even as hymns, or "carols," one of Whitman's favorite terms. "America is the greatest poem," said Whitman, and Lincoln wrote some of the best songs. Lincoln's deeply spiritual memorial in Washington, where it is possible to imagine that visitors will still be strolling in a thousand years, is America's permanent testimony to one man's memory, but also, as I now believe, to our continuing bonds with him.

Besides the martyred president, and as I've argued, perhaps Willie Lincoln should also be remembered in that sacred site. When the theologian Jürgen Moltmann describes children as the "incarnate hopes" of their parents, it sums up very well how Lincoln felt about Willie, how Hattie Stowe felt about Charley, and indeed, how I felt about my son Daniel. Children, says Moltmann, are "original, unique, and incomparable. . . . Every child is also a new occasion for hope . . . we see children not only as the incarnation of our hope for life, but also perceive in them embodiments of God's hopes for us."[8]

Lincoln had very high hopes for his Willie, probably unreasonably high. And yet, one thing I've argued in *Continuing Bonds* is that even the most horrific traumas cannot kill all the music in the world, and that hope can live on. It is true that there are plenty of people among us whose hopes and dreams for their lives have been destroyed, whether by the loss of children, or the illness or death of a spouse, or by being thrust into a war zone, or by the "acts of God" with which our chaotic world seems littered: Katrina, tornadoes, the tsunami in Japan. But it need not always be so. The subjects of this book testify to a kind of inspired steadfastness that should be a great consolation to us all, whether traumatized or not.

Perhaps my work is, after all, one more example of how the continuing bonds with the dead can bear constructive and beneficial consequences—the "peaceable fruits of righteousness"—in the lives of others. And in a scholarly volume like this, perhaps some readers may dislike the fact that I've brought my own life story into the mix. I suggest that writers always do just that, either overtly or not—as this volume shows. But in fact, the major reason that I'm declaring my personal experience of grief is to assure the reader that I am not just some daydreaming romantic whose redemptive vision for a better world is sadly out of touch with reality. I have studied the nature of grief, from the inside out; like the writer of Ecclesiastes: "I directed my mind to know, to investigate and to seek wisdom and an explanation, and to know the evil of folly and the foolishness of madness" (Ecclesiastes 7:25). Or as Robert Frost once put it: "I have been one acquainted with the night."[9] And so have all the subjects of this book.

In his Nobel Prize acceptance speech of 1950, William Faulkner complained about younger American authors: "the young man or woman writing today has forgotten the problems of the human heart in conflict with itself which alone can make good writing. . . . His griefs grieve on no universal bones, leaving no scars. He writes not of the heart but of the glands."[10] Hopefully, *Continuing Bonds* has been a book about those "universal bones," and the "scars" left behind. The wound, we must remember, is the root of the Greek word for trauma: that which marks a body, and always remains. In this sense, and rephrasing Faulkner, the traumas of the past truly are not dead; they aren't even past. It is an expert definition of trauma, in fact.

But beyond Faulkner's universal bones is the yearning for more: a desire to touch and be touched by what Lincoln called our better angels. Or like Du Bois: we yearn for that vague unrest provoked in us by the lovely, lamenting voices of the lost. The stories told here suggest that the bonds with the dead continue, along with the wounds, and they also suggest that death can in fact be "swallowed up in victory" (I Corinthians 15:54). If this book has inspired even a few readers with that message, then I will have counted it a success.

Notes

Introduction

1. On "continuing bonds" theory, I have been most influenced by Klass, Silverman, and Nickman, *Continuing Bonds: New Understandings of Grief*; Klass, *Spiritual Lives of Bereaved Parents*; Stroebe, "Coping with Bereavement: A Review of the Grief Work Hypothesis"; Rosenblatt, *Bitter, Bitter Tears: Nineteenth-Century Diarists and Twentieth-Century Grief Theories*; Neimeyer, *Meaning Reconstruction and the Experience of Loss*; and Valentine, *Bereavement Narratives*.

2. This website is still available at http://www.remembrance.vt.edu/2007/, accessed June 7, 2014. A similar website that CNN initiated could also still be viewed online as of summer of 2014.

3. A transcript of Giovanni's oration is on the web at www.remembrance.vt.edu/2007/archive/giovanni_transcript.html, accessed June 7, 2014.

4. See www.reemasamaha.org/, accessed June 7, 2014.

5. Lincoln, *Collected Works of Abraham Lincoln* (hereafter *CWAL*), 7:23.

6. Harriet Beecher Stowe to Eliza Cabot Follen, December 16, 1852, quoted in Boydston, *Limits of Sisterhood*, 75–76.

7. From Carson, *Autobiography of Martin Luther King, Jr.*

8. See Taylor, *Secular Age*, 299–310 and passim.

9. Bregman, *Preaching Death*, 4.

10. Ibid., 17, 20–21, 22–23.

11. Ibid., 44.

12. On the "weightlessness" of the modern soul, see Lears, *No Place of Grace*.

13. In my account of the "American way of death" and the "death of dying" during this period, I have found most helpful the following studies: Laderman, *Sacred Remains*; Schantz, *Awaiting the Heavenly Country*; Bregman, *Preaching Death*; Kete, *Sentimental Collaborations*; Morley, *Death, Heaven, and the Victorians*; Mitford, *American Way of Death*; Farrell, *Inventing the American Way of Death*; and Luciano, *Arranging Grief*. This account will be developed in much greater detail below.

14. For an illuminating reading of public grief as expressed in memorials, see Doss, *Memorial Mania*, 61–116; for Doss's comments on Princess Diana, see esp. 67–68.

15. Bowditch, *Life and Correspondence of Henry Ingersoll Bowditch*, 2:14.

16. Faust, *This Republic of Suffering*, 168.

17. Ibid., 90.

18. Bowditch, *A Brief Plea*, opening page (n.p.).

19. Ibid., 5–6, 8–9 (emphasis his).

20. Bowditch, *Life and Correspondence of Henry Ingersoll Bowditch*, 2:16, 22.

21. The term was originally coined by Dennis Klass, Phyllis Silverman, and Steven Nickman in their influential volume *Continuing Bonds: New Understandings of Grief*.

22. Bregman, *Preaching Death*, 44.

23. From Whittier, *Voices of the True-Hearted*, 101.

24. See Grossman, *Reconstituting the American Renaissance*, 199. The first critic is Sharon Cameron, as claimed in her important essay, "Representing Grief: Emerson's 'Experience,'" reprinted in her book *Impersonality: Seven Essays*, 53–78. For the quote in Emerson, see "Experience."

25. Fern, *Ruth Hall*, 55, 56.

26. On this approach, and for a critique of the conclusions of Freud and his followers, see for example Klass, Silverman, and Nickman, *Continuing Bonds: New Understandings of Grief*; Klass, *Spiritual Lives of Bereaved Parents*; Stroebe, "Coping with Bereavement"; Bush, "Broken Idols"; Rosenblatt, *Bitter, Bitter Tears*; and Neimeyer, *Meaning Reconstruction and the Experience of Loss*.

27. Valentine, *Bereavement Narratives*, 4.

28. Ibid.

29. See for example Caruth, *Trauma: Explorations in Memory*; and Herman, *Trauma and Recovery*.

30. Florian, "Meaning and Purpose in the Life of Bereaved Parents Whose Son Fell during Active Military Service."

31. See Caroll and Hardt, "Bereaved Parents and Divorce."

32. Erikson, *Childhood and Society*.

33. Faust, *This Republic of Suffering*, 169–70.

34. See McAdams, *Redemptive Self*, esp. 3–14.

35. Ibid., 7.

36. Calhoun and Tedeschi, *Handbook of Posttraumatic Growth*.

37. This vast topic is covered by scores of excellent volumes. A good, brief summary is in Ahlstrom, *Religious History of the American People*, 805–15. My own understanding of America's spiritual crisis has been most influenced by the following volumes: Carter, *Spiritual Crisis of the Gilded Age*; Hutchison, *Modernist Impulse in American Protestantism*; Turner, *Without God, Without Creed*; Delbanco, *Death of Satan*; Kuklick, *Churchmen and Philosophers*; Menand, *Metaphysical Club*; Szasz, *Divided Mind of Protestant America*; Roberts, *Darwinism and the Divine in America*; Russett, *Darwin in America*; Cummings, *Mark Twain and Science*; Greene, *Death of Adam*; and Noll, *America's God*, among others.

38. Farrell, *Inventing the American Way of Death*, 4–5.

39. See Ariès, *Hour of Our Death*, 473.

40. Ibid.

41. See Mitford, *American Way of Death*. Besides the titles mentioned above in note 13, my account also depends on such works as Ariès, *Hour of Our Death*; Ariès, *Western Attitudes towards Death*; Landy and Saler, *The Re-Enchantment of the World*; and Kellehear, *A Social History of Dying*.

42. Farrell, *Inventing the American Way of Death*, 5, 44.

43. Wigglesworth and Bradford, *Encyclopedia Americana*, 4:137.

44. Ibid., 6:n.p.

45. Farrell, *Inventing the American Way of Death*, 66–73.

46. See ibid., 66–67.

47. Ibid., 70, 71.

48. See for example 1 Timothy 5:3–4; Acts 6:1; and James 1:27.

49. Mitford, *American Way of Death*, 16–17.

50. Farrell, *Inventing the American Way of Death*, 158.

51. See Laderman, *Sacred Remains*, 114–15.

52. Ibid., 160. On the Lincoln autopsy and embalming in the White House, see ibid., 158–59.

53. Farrell, *Inventing the American Way of Death*, 150–51.

54. Bledstein, *Culture of Professionalism*, 55.

55. Howells, *Hazard of New Fortunes*, 28, 62, 65.

Chapter 1

1. See Rosenberg, *Cholera Years*; and Rosenberg, "Cholera Epidemics."

2. Hedrick, *Harriet Beecher Stowe: A Life*, 94.

3. Ibid., 95.

4. Ibid., 96.

5. Fields, *Life and Letters of Harriet Beecher Stowe*, 280.

6. Hedrick, *Harriet Beecher Stowe: A Life*, 96–97.

7. See Jones, *Trauma and Grace*, xiv.

8. Rambo, *Spirit and Trauma*, 2, 7.

9. Hedrick, *Harriet Beecher Stowe: A Life*, 151.

10. HBS to Thomas Beecher, quoted in McFarland, *Loves of Harriet Beecher Stowe*, 44.

11. Hedrick, *Harriet Beecher Stowe: A Life*, 152.

12. Rosenberg, *Cholera Years*, 115.

13. Hedrick, *Harriet Beecher Stowe: A Life*, 189.

14. Ibid., 186.

15. Quoted in Rosenberg, *Cholera Years*, 41.

16. Quoted in McFarland, *Loves of Harriet Beecher Stowe*, 228.

17. Shurr, *Rappacini's Children*, 30.

18. On the growing ideology of belief in God as immoral, see Turner, *Without God, Without Creed*, 203–25. On the movements away from more traditional Calvinism during this period, see Noll, *America's God*, esp. 293–329.

19. Davis, "Rhetorical War and Reflex."

20. Ibid., 14n3.

21. An excellent account of how Stowe and the Beecher family were implicated in this schism is in Koester, *Harriet Beecher Stowe: A Spiritual Life*, 55–104 and

passim. A magisterial account of the internal divisions of antebellum Calvinism is in Noll, *America's God*.

22. Trueman, "Calvin and Calvinism," 226.

23. Gerrish, "Place of Calvin in Christian Theology," 290.

24. Little, "Calvinism and American National Identity," 47, 60.

25. Hodge, "Professor Park's Remarks," 308–9.

26. Valeri, "Calvin and the Social Order in Early America," 22. An excellent account of these principles as crucial to Calvinism is in Boulton, *Life in God*.

27. Quoted in Thuesen, "Geneva's Crystalline Clarity," 219.

28. Ibid., 219–20.

29. Ibid., 226.

30. Foster, *Rungless Ladder*, 111.

31. See Applegate, *Most Famous Man in America*, 44–45.

32. Beecher, *Common Sense Applied to Religion*, xix–xx.

33. Ibid., xxiv. This point and its connection with *Minister's Wooing* are well explained in Noll, *America's God*, 327–29.

34. Hedrick, *Harriet Beecher Stowe: A Life*, 189; Stowe and Stowe, *Harriet Beecher Stowe: The Story of Her Life*, 121–22.

35. Quoted in Boydston, *Limits of Sisterhood*, 76–77.

36. Hedrick, *Harriet Beecher Stowe: A Life*, 190–91.

37. HBS to Sarah Beecher, July 29, 1849, Stowe-Day collection.

38. Quoted in Foster, *Rungless Ladder*, 131.

39. Quoted in Reynolds, *Mightier Than the Sword*, 29.

40. HBS to Sarah Beecher, July 29, 1849, Stowe-Day collection.

41. Quoted in Belasco, *Stowe in Her Own Time*, 64.

42. Unless otherwise noted, all quotes from Scripture will come from the text most common for the educated reader of the nineteenth century: the King James Version (KJV).

43. Quoted in Reynolds, *Mightier Than the Sword*, 29.

44. See Hedrick, "'Peaceable Fruits': The Ministry of Harriet Beecher Stowe," 315.

45. Henry, *Commentary on the Whole Bible*, 797.

46. Foster, *Rungless Ladder*, 26. Further coverage of the biblical metaphor of the "rod" of discipline in the context of fiction during Stowe's career is found in Brodhead, "Sparing the Rod: Discipline and Fiction in Antebellum America."

47. Harriet Beecher Stowe to Eliza Cabot Follen, December 16, 1852, quoted in Boydston, *Limits of Sisterhood*, 75–76.

48. Ibid.

49. Haltunnen, *Confidence Men and Painted Women*, 130–31.

50. Boydston, *Limits of Sisterhood*, 75–76.

51. McAdams and Logan, "What Is Generativity?" 26.

52. Quoted in Stowe and Stowe, *Harriet Beecher Stowe: The Story of Her Life*, 149.

53. See for example Klass, *Spiritual Lives of Bereaved Parents*; Wheeler, "Role of Meaning and Purpose in Life in Bereaved Parents"; Stroebe, "Coping with Bereavement: A Review of the Grief Work Hypothesis."

54. Hedrick, *Harriet Beecher Stowe: A Life*, 201.

55. Cited in Dieter, *Holiness Revival of the Nineteenth Century*, 4. For general introductions to Wesleyan and subsequent Holiness theology, see ibid., 1–156;

Synan, *Holiness-Pentecostal Movement in the United States*, 13–76; Smith, *Revivalism and Social Reform in Mid-Nineteenth Century America*; and White, *Beauty of Holiness: Phoebe Palmer as Theologian, Revivalist, Feminist, and Humanitarian.*

56. Calvin Stowe to Harriet Beecher Stowe, April 30, 1842, Acquisitions, Stowe-Day Library.

57. Schmidt, *Restless Souls*, 5.

58. Quoted in ibid., 5; see also Wuthnow, *After Heaven*, and Roof, *Spiritual Marketplace*, for historical uses of the term *spirituality in America*.

59. See Hatch, *Democratization of American Christianity*.

60. See Smith, *Bible Made Impossible*.

61. See Schmidt, *Restless Souls*; Hutchison, *The Modernist Impulse in American Protestantism*; and Dorrien, *Making of American Liberal Theology*.

62. Lincoln, "Second Inaugural Address," *CWAL*, 4:271.

63. Schmidt, *Restless Souls*, 48.

64. On Stowe's fascination with Roman Catholicism and its aesthetics, see Gatta, *American Madonna*.

65. Palmer, *Promise of the Father*, 62–63. I am indebted to Professor Patricia Ward of Vanderbilt University for her unpublished paper on the Palmer-Stowe connection.

66. See Wheatley, *Life and Letters of Phoebe Palmer*, 606; and Hedrick, *Harriet Beecher Stowe: A Life*, 143, 145, 149.

67. Synan, *Holiness-Pentecostal Movement in the United States*, 28.

68. Quote on Finney in McLoughlin, *Revivals, Awakenings, and Reform*, 123, 125; on Emerson's address as cultural declaration of independence, see Bush, *American Declarations*.

69. From a letter dated July 1844 and quoted in an unpublished paper on the Stowe-Palmer connection, written by Patricia Ward, Vanderbilt University.

70. Stowe and Stowe, *Harriet Beecher Stowe: The Story of Her Life*, 133.

71. Hovet, "Christian Revolution," 538. Stowe's essay was "The Interior or Hidden Life." Elsewhere, Hovet has discussed other influences on Stowe's conception of mystical religious experience, including Thomas Upham, Horace Bushnell, and James B. Walker; see Hovet's essay "Modernization and the American Fall into Slavery in *Uncle Tom's Cabin*."

72. Boardman, *Higher Christian Life*, 128–29. Patricia R. Hill presents a convincing argument that the unnamed lady described by Boardman is Stowe; see her excellent article, "*Uncle Tom's Cabin* as a Religious Text," online at utc.iath.virginia.edu/interpret/exhibits/hill/hill.html, accessed April 30, 2015.

73. Reynolds, *Mightier Than the Sword*, 16.

74. Stowe, *The Key to "Uncle Tom's Cabin,"* excerpts reprinted in Ammons, *Uncle Tom's Cabin: A Norton Critical Edition*, 421.

75. Quoted in Belasco, *Stowe in Her Own Time*, 166.

76. Reynolds, *Mightier Than the Sword* 17, 18–19.

77. McFarland, *Loves of Harriet Beecher Stowe*, 232.

78. In Belasco, ed., *Stowe in Her Own Time*, 165.

79. Rambo, *Spirit and Trauma*, 11,15, 17.

80. See Jasper, *Sacred Body*; also Wright, *Jesus and the Victory of God*.

81. Quoted in Belasco, *Stowe in Her Own Time*, 122.

82. Noble, "The Ecstasies of Sentimental Wounding in *Uncle Tom's Cabin*."

83. Ammons, *Uncle Tom's Cabin: A Norton Critical Edition*, 227–28. All quotes from this novel come from this edition, hereafter cited as *UTC*.

84. Quoted in Douglas, *Feminization of American Culture*, 108.

85. *UTC*, 381, 385, 388.

86. Boydston, *Limits of Sisterhood*, 75–76.

87. *UTC*, 34, 43, 75.

88. Hedrick, *Harriet Beecher Stowe: A Life*, 275.

89. *UTC*, 115.

90. Fields, *Life and Letters of Harriet Beecher Stowe*, 149.

91. *UTC*, 111, 114.

92. *UTC*, 190.

93. On this theme see Schantz, *Awaiting the Heavenly Country*, 126–62.

94. *UTC*, 319.

95. *UTC*, 266–67.

96. *UTC*, 266.

97. *UTC*, 303.

98. Stowe, "On the Ministration of Departed Spirits in the World," 2–3.

98. *UTC*, 303.

100. See Channing, *Memoir and Writings of James Handasyd Perkins*.

101. Quoted in Hedrick, *Harriet Beecher Stowe: A Life*, 92.

102. See ibid., 92.

103. In Channing, *Memoir and Writings of James Handasyd Perkins*, 1:372.

104. Haltunnen, *Confidence Men and Painted Women*, 130.

105. Quoted in ibid., 130.

106. Stowe, "On the Ministration of Departed Spirits in the World," 1.

107. Letter of July 14, 1852, Elizabeth Dickerman to "Mrs. L.," in Dickerman, Dickerman, and Dickerman, *Sisters: A Memoir*, 133.

108. Jenkins, *Character of God*, 57.

109. *UTC*, 380.

110. *UTC*, 18.

111. See, for example, Christina Zwarg's essay, "Fathering and Blackface in *Uncle Tom's Cabin*"; Zwarg's discussion of the portrait of Washington is especially concentrated in 572–74.

112. On "romantic racialism," see Frederickson, *Black Image in the White Mind*.

113. On the reasons for memorials, see Kosselleck, *Practice of Conceptual History*; and Doss, *Memorial Mania*.

114. Quoted in Belasco, *Stowe in Her Own Time*, 165.

115. Quoted in ibid., 120.

116. Stowe, *The Minister's Wooing*, 211. All quotes within are from the Penguin edition, edited by Susan K. Harris, and hereafter referred to as *MW*.

117. *MW*, 196.

118. *MW*, 17.

119. *MW*, 197.

120. Stowe, *Oldtown Folks*, 1249.

121. *MW*, 195–96.

122. See Weinstein, *Family, Kinship, and Sympathy in Nineteenth-Century American Literature*; and Crane, *Race, Citizenship, and Law in American Literature*.

123. *MW*, 201–2.

124. *MW*, 163.

125. On humor as spiritual dynamite, see Dark, *Everyday Apocalypse*, along with Bush, "Mark Twain's American Adam: Humor as Hope and Apocalypse."

126. Quoted in McFarland, *Loves of Harriet Beecher Stowe*, 250.

127. Hedrick, *Harriet Beecher Stowe: A Life*, 283.

128. McAdams, *Redemptive Self*, 7.

Chapter 2

1. For the "official" Stowe family account of this episode, see the material presented in Belasco, *Stowe in Her Own Time*, 149–51. On the development (and historical problems) of the myth, see Vollaro, "Lincoln, Stowe, and the 'Little Woman/Great War' Story."

2. Quoted in Bush, ed., *Lincoln in His Own Time*, 110–11.

3. Quoted in ibid., 111.

4. Carpenter, *Inner Life of Abraham Lincoln: Six Months at the White House*, 17.

5. Quoted in Bush, *Lincoln in His Own Time*, 65.

6. Quoted in Mansfield, *Lincoln's Battle with God*, 137.

7. Quoted in Bush, *Lincoln in His Own Time*, 65.

8. Quoted in ibid., 68–69.

9. Quoted in ibid., 68.

10. Quoted in ibid., 65.

11. See Guelzo, *Abraham Lincoln: Redeemer President*, 387; and Hay and Burlingame, *At Lincoln's Side: John Hay's Correspondence and Selected Writings*, 20.

12. Quoted in Bush, *Lincoln in His Own Time*, 67–68.

13. Quoted in Burlingame, *With Lincoln in the White House: Letters, Memoranda, and Other Writings of John G. Nicolay*, 71.

14. See Shenk, *Lincoln's Melancholy*.

15. See Shenk, "Eureka Dept.: The Suicide Poem."

16. Quoted in Shenk, *Lincoln's Melancholy*, 178.

17. Quoted in Bush, *Lincoln in His Own Time*, 79.

18. *CWAL*, 7:18.

19. Lincoln, "Second Inaugural Address," *CWAL*, 8:332–33.

20. Similar analyses of these changes in mood and outlook are in Fredrickson, *Inner Civil War*; Saum, *Popular Mood of America*; Delbanco, *Death of Satan*; and Rose, *Victorian America and the Civil War*.

21. Blum, "God's Imperialism: Mark Twain and the Religious War between Imperialists and Anti-Imperialists," 35.

22. For examples of this scholarship, see Stout, *Upon the Altar of the Nation*; and Noll, *Civil War as a Theological Crisis*.

23. Miller, Stout, and Wilson, introduction to *Religion and the American Civil War*, 3–4.

24. See Goldfield, *America Aflame*.

25. The definitive edition is Davis and Wilson, *Herndon's Informants: Letters, Interviews, and Statements about Abraham Lincoln*.

26. Herndon to Jesse W. Weik, February 26, 1891, in Hertz, *Hidden Lincoln, from the Letters and Papers of William H. Herndon*, 266–67.

27. Ingersoll, "On Abraham Lincoln," in *Works of Robert G. Ingersoll*, 3:123. Reprinted in Bush, *Lincoln in His Own Time*.

28. On this topic, see most famously Ingersoll, *The Ghosts, and Other Lectures*.

29. Reed, "Later Life and Religious Sentiments of Abraham Lincoln," 340.

30. Ibid., 336, 342.

31. Davis and Wilson, *Herndon's Informants*, 549.

32. From Col. James Rusling, "Lincoln and Sickles," undated pamphlet of a speech given by Col. Rusling on May 5, 1910, at a Third Army Corps Reunion at the Hotel Manhattan. Parish Memorabilia of the Asylum Hill Congregational Church, in the Connecticut State Library.

33. Keckley, *Behind the Scenes; or, Thirty Years a Slave, and Four Years in the White House*, 99. Sections reprinted in Bush, *Lincoln in His Own Time*.

34. Chapman, *Latest Light on Abraham Lincoln and War-Time Memories*, 507.

35. Carpenter, *Inner Life of Abraham Lincoln: Six Months at the White House*, 186.

36. Further discussion is in Bush, "Abraham Lincoln and Spiritual Crisis"; also see Calhoun and Morel, "Abraham Lincoln's Religion: The Case for His Ultimate Belief in a Personal, Sovereign God."

37. Stowe, "Abraham Lincoln." Reprinted in Bush, *Lincoln in His Own Time*, 110–11.

38. Davis and Wilson, *Herndon's Informants*, 360. On Lincoln's romantic imagination, see Winger, *Lincoln, Religion, and Romantic Cultural Politics*.

39. Lowell, "Abraham Lincoln," 178–208. Reprinted in Bush, *Lincoln in His Own Time*.

40. Brooks, *Addresses*, 166–96. Reprinted in Bush, *Lincoln in His Own Time*.

41. Calhoun and Morel, "Abraham Lincoln's Religion: The Case for His Ultimate Belief in a Personal, Sovereign God," 38.

42. Reed, "Later Life and Religious Sentiments of Abraham Lincoln," 340. On the charge that Lincoln's words were simply political rhetoric without substance, see Calhoun and Morel, "Abraham Lincoln's Religion: The Case for His Ultimate Belief in a Personal, Sovereign God," 40–43.

43. Rambo, *Spirit and Trauma*, 17.

44. Among a large and growing body of important works about Lincoln's religion, two book-length studies are now mandatory starting places: Guelzo, *Abraham Lincoln: Redeemer President*, and Carwardine, *Lincoln: A Life of Purpose and Power*. In addition, the following works are of immeasurable value in beginning such a study: Diggins, *On Hallowed Ground: Abraham Lincoln and the Foundations of American History*; Fornieri, *Abraham Lincoln's Political Faith*; Morel, *Lincoln's Sacred Effort: Defining Religion's Role in American Self-Government*; Stauffer, *Giants: The Parallel Lives of Frederick Douglass and Abraham Lincoln*; Tackach, *Lincoln's Moral Vision: The Second Inaugural Address*; and Winger, *Lincoln, Religion, and Romantic Cultural Politics*.

45. Calhoun and Morel, "Abraham Lincoln's Religion: The Case for His Ultimate Belief in a Personal, Sovereign God," 41.

46. Reed, "Later Life and Religious Sentiments of Abraham Lincoln," 336, 342.

47. Jones, *Lincoln and the Preachers*, 37.

48. Trueblood, *Abraham Lincoln: Theologian of American Anguish*, 30.

49. Wolf, *Lincoln's Religion*, 123.

50. Quoted in Mansfield, *Lincoln's Battle with God*, 127.

51. Current, *Lincoln Nobody Knows*, 66.

52. Mansfield, *Lincoln's Battle with God*, 141.

53. *King John* (3.3.76–78; 93–105).

54. Weik, *Herndon's Lincoln*, 679.

55. Stephenson, *Lincoln*, 261, 257.

56. Wolf, *Lincoln's Religion*, 122–23.

57. Burlingame, *Abraham Lincoln: A Life*, 2:229.

58. Donald, *Lincoln at Home*, 337.

59. See Larsen, *Crisis of Doubt*, passim.

60. The best narrative yet to appear on the marks of a changing religious sensibility in Lincoln's thought and actions during the period after Willie's death is in Carwardine, *Lincoln: A Life of Purpose and Power*.

61. Webb, *American Providence: A Nation with a Mission*, 33.

62. Parrillo, "Lincoln's Calvinist Transformation: Emancipation and War," 229.

63. Niebuhr, "The Religion of Abraham Lincoln," 72–73.

64. Noll, "'Both . . . Pray to the Same God': The Singularity of Lincoln's Faith in the Era of the Civil War," 4, 13.

65. Hay, *Addresses of John Hay*, 239.

66. *CWAL*, 5:403–4.

67. Hay and Nicolay, *Abraham Lincoln: A History*, 6:341–42.

68. Basler's note is in *CWAL*, 5:404.

69. Hay, "Lincoln's Faith," in *Addresses of John Hay*, 239.

70. See for example Neely, *Last, Best Hope of Earth: Abraham Lincoln and the Promise of America*, 106–10.

71. Stauffer, *Giants: The Parallel Lives of Frederick Douglass and Abraham Lincoln*, 251.

72. Carpenter, *Inner Life of Abraham Lincoln: Six Months at the White House*, 17. Winger's discussion is in *Lincoln, Religion, and Romantic Cultural Politics*, 162–64. Lovejoy's and Stowe's comments are in Burlingame, *Abraham Lincoln: A Life*, 2:799.

73. Welles, *Diary of Gideon Welles*, 1:143.

74. Chase, *Inside Lincoln's Cabinet: The Civil War Diaries of Salmon P. Chase*, 149–50; Carpenter, *Inner Life of Abraham Lincoln: Six Months at the White House*, 90.

75. Guelzo, *Abraham Lincoln: Redeemer President*, 342; see also Guelzo, *Lincoln's Emancipation Proclamation*, 167–69.

76. See James McPherson's bracing account of this "miracle" in *Crossroads of Freedom: Antietam*.

77. Guelzo, *Abraham Lincoln: Redeemer President*, 153.

78. Guelzo, *Lincoln's Emancipation Proclamation*, 169.

79. Barton, *Soul of Abraham Lincoln*, 286.

80. On these three themes in Lincoln's work, see Noll, *America's God*, 426–32.

81. Tackach, *Lincoln's Moral Vision: The Second Inaugural Address*, 208.

82. See Winger, *Lincoln, Religion, and Romantic Cultural Politics*, 160, 166–67.

83. Noll, "'Both . . . Pray to the Same God': The Singularity of Lincoln's Faith in the Era of the Civil War," 13, 26.

84. See for example White, *Lincoln's Greatest Speech: The Second Inaugural*, esp. 127–28; as well as Wills, "Lincoln's Greatest Speech?"

85. All quotes from the second inaugural are from *CWAL*, 8:332–33.

86. Lowell, "Abraham Lincoln," 188–89. Reprinted in *Lincoln in His Own Time.*

87. On the cultural weight of the memorial and its status as symbol for the grandeur of American metaphysical beliefs, see Thomas, *Lincoln Memorial and American Life*. On wandering the mall more generally, see Percoco, *Summers with Lincoln: Looking for the Man in the Monuments.*

88. Noll, *America's God*, 426, 425.

Chapter 3

1. Reprinted in Bush, *Lincoln in His Own Time*, 30–1.
2. Howells, *Selected Letters*, 1:119–20.
3. Howells, *Winifred Howells.*
4. See Woodress, *Howells and Italy.*
5. Howells, *Winifred Howells*, 5, 7.
6. Ibid., 8.
7. In the *Century Magazine*, April 1886, 838.
8. In Stedman, *An American Anthology.*
9. In ibid.
10. Howells, *Selected Letters*, 3:228.
11. Crowley, *Dean of American Letters*, 15.
12. Cervetti, *S. Weir Mitchell, 1829–1914*, 1.
13. Howells, *Winifred Howells*, passim.
14. Goodman and Dawson, *William Dean Howells: A Writer's Life*, 296.
15. James and Howells, *Letters, Fictions, Lives: Henry James and William Dean Howells*, 199.
16. Goodman and Dawson, *William Dean Howells: A Writer's Life*, 296.
17. Crowley, *Dean of American Letters*, 100.
18. Howells, *Selected Letters*, 4:105.
19. Howells, *Winifred Howells*, 25.
20. Howells, *Selected Letters*, 3:231.
21. Quoted in Dolin, *Fur, Fortune, and Empire*, xv. The quote from the earlier historian is on the unpaginated frontis.
22. Goodman and Dawson, *William Dean Howells: A Writer's Life*, 296–97.
23. Howells, "Editor's Easy Chair," 475.
24. Crowley, *Dean of American Letters*, 14.
25. Dreiser quoted in Shi, *Facing Facts*, 213.
26. Howells, "Lyof N. Tolstoi," 851–52.
27. Crowley, *Dean of American Letters*, 10.
28. Howells, "Bibliographical" 4.
29. Goodman and Dawson, *William Dean Howells: A Writer's Life*, 120.
30. Howells, *Selected Letters*, 3:207.
31. Quoted in Carter, critical introduction to *A Hazard of New Fortunes*, xvi.
32. Howells, *Selected Letters*, 3:231.
33. Quoted in Crowley, "Unsmiling Aspects of Life," 88.
34. Howells, "Lyof N. Tolstoi," 738.
35. The cultural and historical significance of the Haymarket incident are covered well in Avrich, *Haymarket Tragedy.*
36. Shi, *Facing Facts*, 194.

37. Crowley, *Dean of American Letters*, 117–18.

38. James and Howells, *Letters, Fictions, Lives: Henry James and William Dean Howells*, 199.

39. Howells, *Selected Letters*, 3:270.

40. Ibid., 6:179.

41. Ferguson, *Trial in American Life*, 224.

42. Moody, "Religion and Realism in Late Nineteenth-Century American Literature," 112.

43. James and Howells, *Letters, Fictions, Lives: Henry James and William Dean Howells*, 196.

44. Bledstein, *Culture of Professionalism* 55.

45. Howells, *Hazard of New Fortunes*, hereafter *HNF*, 165.

46. *HNF*, 34.

47. Puskar, "William Dean Howells and the Insurance of the Real," 29, 30–31.

48. Kaplan, *Social Construction of American Realism*, 62.

49. *HNF*, 232.

50. *HNF*, 158.

51. Coverage of the social gospel as practiced in Hartford (and as it influenced Twain) is in Bush, *Mark Twain and the Spiritual Crisis of His Age*, 126–60.

52. Twichell Journal 6-13-1875, at Beinecke Library, Yale University.

53. Howells, "Editor's Study," 484–85.

54. Ely, *Social Aspects of Christianity* 1, 79.

55. Quoted in Carter, critical introduction to *A Hazard of New Fortunes*, xvi.

56. Gladden, *Recollections*, 116, 90.

57. Quoted in Puskar, *Accident Society: Fiction, Collectivity, and the Production of Chance*, 24.

58. See ibid.

59. *HNF*, 28.

60. *HNF*, 184.

61. *HNF*, 305.

62. *HNF*, 306.

63. *HNF*, 306.

64. See Wortham, "William Dean Howells's Spiritual Quest(ioning) in a 'World Come of Age.'"

65. *HNF*, 228.

66. Howells, *Selected Letters*, 3:253.

67. Anderson, Gibson, and Smith, *Selected Mark Twain–Howells Letters*, 2:606. The "strange book" was *Physical Theory of Another Life*, by Isaac Taylor.

68. See for example the group of eleven of the poems, in a very different order, in *Harper's New Monthly* of December 1894, 35–40.

69. Howells, "A Counsel of Consolation," 7.

70. Quoted in Long, *What Shall We Say?: Evil, Suffering, and the Crisis of Faith*, 44.

71. On Tennyson's elegies as gift books for mourners, see Jalland, *Death in the Victorian Family*, 282–83. The quotes from "Love and Duty" are in Tennyson, *The Works of Alfred Tennyson* (London, 1884), 94.

72. Howells, "A Counsel of Consolation," 3.

73. Milton, "Lycidas," in *John Milton: Complete Shorter Poems*, edited by Stella P. Revard. Malden, MA: Wiley-Blackwell, 2009, 80.

74. See for example Lynn, *William Dean Howells: An American Life*, passim. The major source of focused critical attention to this volume is Madsen, "Social Guilt and Private Suffering in W. D. Howells's *Stops of Various Quills*." The quotes are from Lynn, *William Dean Howells: An American Life*, 12, and Madsen, "Social Guilt and Private Suffering in W. D. Howells's *Stops of Various Quills*," 75.

75. Madsen, "Social Guilt and Private Suffering in W. D. Howells's *Stops of Various Quills*," 78.

76. Anderson, Gibson, and Smith, *Selected Mark Twain–Howells Letters*, 2:681; Howells, *Selected Letters*, 3:295–96.

77. *Stops of Various Quills*, VI; this volume includes no page numbers, but each poem is numbered in Roman numerals, which hereafter will be used for citation, in the body of the text.

78. *HNF*, 495.

79. Howells, "A Counsel of Consolation," 5.

80. Madsen, "Social Guilt and Private Suffering in W. D. Howells's *Stops of Various Quills*," 75.

81. Long, *What Shall We Say?*, 115–16.

82. Howells, "A Counsel of Consolation," 3, 4.

83. Anderson, Gibson, and Smith, *Selected Mark Twain–Howells Letters*, 2:842.

84. Howells, "A Counsel of Consolation," 6.

85. Ibid., 14–15.

86. Goodman and Dawson, *William Dean Howells: A Writer's Life*, 296–97; Clemens, Howells and Clark, *Mark Twain's Library of Humor*, 2:667.

87. Letter to Charles Dudley Warner, quoted in Anderson, Gibson, and Smith, *Selected Mark Twain–Howells Letters*, 2:662n3.

88. Kete, *Sentimental Collaborations*, 6.

89. Ibid., 146.

90. Anderson, Gibson, and Smith, *Selected Mark Twain–Howells Letters*, 2:670.

91. See for example Reinhold Niebuhr, *Moral Man and Immoral Society: A Study of Ethics and Politics*; *The Nature and Destiny of Man: A Christian Interpretation*; and *The Irony of American History*. For commentary and analysis see Lovin, *Reinhold Niebuhr and Christian Realism*.

92. Bush, "Broken Idols," 268.

93. See James, *Will to Believe and Other Essays in Popular Philosophy*.

94. Howells, "A Counsel of Consolation," 16.

Chapter 4

1. Anderson, Gibson, and Smith, *Selected Mark Twain–Howells Letters*, 2:606. The "strange book" was *Physical Theory of Another Life*, by Isaac Taylor.

2. Mark Twain to Olivia Langdon Clemens, hereafter MT and OLC, July 17, 1889, in the Mark Twain Papers and Project at the University of California at Berkeley, hereafter MTP. On the evidence of Twain's belief in the possibility of an afterlife, see Bush, *Mark Twain and the Spiritual Crisis of His Age*, 245–46.

3. My account of the conditions of a "secular age" is highly dependent on Taylor, *A Secular Age*.

4. Neiman, *Evil in Modern Thought*, 1.

5. Hart, *Doors of the Sea*, 42.
6. Ibid.
7. Tallon, *Poetics of Evil*, 182.
8. Twain, *Autobiography of Mark Twain* (hereafter *AMT*), 185.
9. Howells, "A Counsel of Consolation," 16.
10. Clemens and Wector, *Love Letters of Mark Twain*, 328.
11. See Doyno, "Samuel Clemens as Family Man and Father."
12. Quoted in Tuckey, introduction to *Devil's Race-Track* (hereafter *DRT*), x–xi.
13. Clemens, *My Father, Mark Twain*, 64.
14. I'm grateful to Professor Linda Morris for illumination on this topic of Susy as favorite; and for access to her unpublished paper, "When Did Susy Become Mark Twain's Favorite Daughter?"
15. *AMT*, 324–25.
16. *AMT*, 324.
17. Rambo, *Spirit and Trauma*, 7.
18. Caruth, *Trauma: Explorations in Memory*, 4, 9.
19. See Pine and Brauer, "Parental Grief: A Synthesis of Theory, Research and Intervention."
20. Susan Crane to Samuel Moffett, July 22, 1897, MTP.
21. *AMT*, 324.
22. MT to Susan Crane, September 30, 1896, MTP.
23. Twain, *Connecticut Yankee*, chapter 28.
24. Faust, *This Republic of Suffering*, 144, 145.
25. MT to Laurence Hutton, dated September 6, 1896, MTP.
26. MT to Ned Bunce, October 1896, MTP.
27. *AMT*, 324.
28. OLC to Grace King, December 1899, MTP.
29. OLC to Eliza N. Robinson, January 28, 1898, MTP.
30. OLC to Harriet Whitmore, April 22, 1897, MTP.
31. OLC to Grace King, December 1899, MTP.
32. MT to Joseph Twichell, June 1899, MTP.
33. *AMT*, 382–83.
34. Quoted in Willis, *Mark and Livy*, 237.
35. On the grief suffered at Langdon's death, see Snedecor, "'He Was So Rarely Beautiful': Langdon Clemens."
36. MT to Henry Rogers, December 18, 1896, MTP.
37. Clara Clemens to Alice Hooker Day, September 11, 1896, MTP.
38. These points, and the term "nova effect," are described in Taylor, *A Secular Age*, 299–304.
39. Messent, *Mark Twain and Male Friendship*, 162. Messent's entire section on the changing social circumstances of grief is enlightening; see 157–69.
40. My appeal to the idea of a "secular age" here and throughout this volume is highly dependent on the magisterial work of Taylor, *A Secular Age*.
41. Quoted in Morris, "When Did Susy Become Mark Twain's Favorite Daughter?"
42. Jalland, *Death in the Victorian Family*, 339.
43. This information is documented at the library's website, millicentlibrary.org, accessed May 1, 2015.

44. MT to Wayne MacVeagh, September 27, 1896, MTP.

45. MT to the Whitmores, December 19, 1898, MTP.

46. OLC to Mrs. Jonathan Curtis, April 23, 1897, MTP.

47. Tallon, *Poetics of Evil*, 177, 181.

48. On "horrendous evils," see Adams, *Horrendous Evils and the Goodness of God*.

49. See for example MT to Henry Rogers, December 18, 1896, MTP.

50. MT to Wayne MacVeagh, September 27, 1896, MTP.

51. Ned Bunce to MT, October 5, 1896, MTP.

52. Hart, *Doors of the Sea*, 100.

53. MT to Ned Bunce, October 10, 1896, MTP.

54. For much evidence of Twain as "practitioner" of Christianity see Bush, *Mark Twain and the Spiritual Crisis of His Age*, esp. 55–160.

55. OLC to John Y. McAlister, April 6, 1897, MTP.

56. See Jalland, *Death in the Victorian Family*, 283, 282.

57. Quoted in Gribben, *Mark Twain's Library: A Reconstruction*, 693.

58. All marginalia are recorded in Twain's copy of *Palgrave's Golden Treasury of Songs & Poems*. My thanks to Kevin MacDonnell, owner of the volume, and to MacDonnell Rare Books in Austin, Texas, for making these materials available to me and for helping me track down and transcribe Twain's original margin notations.

59. In Mark Twain's Notebook, 32b, p. 27, courtesy MTP.

60. OLC to Mary Cheney, October 7, 1898, MTP.

61. On the elegies and their deeply divided content, see Bush, "Broken Idols."

62. See for example Bush, *Mark Twain and the Spiritual Crisis of His Age*; and Shelden, *Mark Twain, Man in White*.

63. Klass, *Spiritual Lives of Bereaved Parents*, 142, emphasis mine.

64. Bush, "Broken Idols," 262–63.

65. Calvin, *Institutes of the Christian Religion*, 3.8.1.

66. Hart, *Doors of the Sea*, 42.

67. *AMT*, 333.

68. On the influence of Ingersoll on Twain, see Schwartz, "Mark Twain and Robert Ingersoll."

69. On the "growing up" metaphor of the secular age, see Taylor, *A Secular Age*, 362–65; quote is from 365.

70. *AMT*, 324.

71. *AMT*, 325–26.

72. *AMT*, 181–82.

73. *AMT*, 224.

74. *AMT*, 325.

75. All from "A Record of the Small Foolishness of Susie and 'Bay' Clemens (Infants)," [1876], 30–31. Typescript quoted with the permission of MTP.

76. All quotes here are from [Mark Twain], "A Record of the Small Foolishness of Susie and 'Bay' Clemens (Infants)," Benjamin Griffin, ed., typescript prepared by and held at the Mark Twain Papers and Project. My thanks to Ben Griffin for pointing out these similarities to me, and for providing me with a copy of the text.

77. *AMT*, 326.

78. *AMT*, 326.

79. Twain, "Which Was the Dream?" 50.
80. Fulton, *Reverend Mark Twain*, 171.
81. *AMT*, 375.
82. See Emerson, *Mark Twain: A Literary Life*, 292–93.
83. Quirk, *Nothing Abstract: Investigation in the American Literary Imagination*, 112.
84. Hart, *Doors of the Sea*, 42.
85. *AMT*, 419.
86. Lemaster and Wilson, eds., *Mark Twain Encyclopedia*, 649.
87. *AMT*, 224.
88. Ryan, "Mark Twain and the Cosmopolitan Ideal," 10, 4.
89. Quoted in Scharnhorst, *Mark Twain: The Complete Interviews*, 591–92, 595n16.
90. MT to Joseph Twichell, January 19, 1897, Twichell, *Journals*.
91. See Harris, *God's Arbiters: Americans and the Philippines*, especially 3–7.
92. Quoted in Zwick, *Mark Twain's Weapons of Satire: Anti-Imperialist Writings on the Philippine-American War*, 57–58.
93. For more detail on these matters, see Bush, "Christianity, Literature, and American Empire."
94. Edwards, "The Real Prayer and the Imagined: The War against Romanticism in Twain, Howells, and Bierce," 71.
95. Ensor, "Mark Twain's 'The War Prayer': Its Ties to Howells and Hymnology," 537.
96. Dunn and Rogerson, *Eerdmans Commentary on the Bible*, 366.
97. Boulton, *Life in God*, 198.
98. Twain, "The War Prayer," 652–53.
99. Howells, "Editha," 249.
100. Ibid., 257.
101. Tirman, *Deaths of Others: The Fate of Civilians in America's Wars*, 45.
102. Ibid., 12, 14.
103. Quoted in Phipps, *Mark Twain's Religion*, 209.
104. Bush, "Broken Idols," 262–63.

Chapter 5

1. Letter by MT to Elisha Bliss, August 26, 1901, MTP.
2. Twain, "The United States of Lyncherdom." The definitive text is in Oggel, "Speaking Out about Race: 'The United States of Lyncherdom' Clemens Really Wrote."
3. Schneider, *Public Intellectualism of Ralph Waldo Emerson and W. E. B. Du Bois*, 109.
4. See Savelsberg and King, *American Memories: Atrocities and the Law*, esp. 8–14.
5. On cultural trauma, see Caruth, *Trauma: Explorations in Memory*; and Alexander, *Cultural Trauma and Collective Identity*.
6. See especially Eyerman, *Cultural Trauma and the Formation of African American Identity*.
7. In Alexander, "Toward a Theory of Cultural Trauma," 1, in *Cultural Trauma and Collective Identity*.

8. Till-Mobley and Benson, *Death of Innocence*, 142. On Mamie's heroic deployment of her witness to the brutalization of her son's body, see Bush, "Continuing Bonds and Emmett Till's Mother."

9. Erikson, *Everything in Its Path*, 153–54.

10. Felman, "Education and Crisis," 14.

11. Erikson, "Notes on Trauma and Community," 186.

12. Felman, "Education and Crisis," 17.

13. Eyerman, *Cultural Trauma and the Formation of African American Identity*, 1.

14. See for example Allen, *Without Sanctuary*, and Apel and Smith, *Lynching Photographs*.

15. Wright, *Black Boy*, 190.

16. Du Bois, *Souls of Black Folk*, 189. All quotes from *Souls* will be from this edition, hereafter signified as *Souls*.

17. Kahn, *Divine Discontent: The Religious Imagination of W. E. B. Du Bois*.

18. Hale, *Making Whiteness*, 210.

19. Williamson, "Wounds Not Scars: Lynching, the National Conscience, and the American Historian," 1240.

20. Quoted in Kirschke, *Art in Crisis: W. E. B. Du Bois and the Struggle for African American Identity and Memory*, 51.

21. See Frederickson, *The Black Image in the White Mind: The Debate on Afro-American Character and Destiny*, 272–82.

22. Hale, *Making Whiteness*, 209.

23. Quote found online, www.americanlynching.com/infamous-old.html, accessed May 1, 2015.

24. Arnold, *What Virtue There Is in Fire*, 115, 132.

25. See Hale, *Making Whiteness*.

26. Quoted in Arnold, *What Virtue There Is in Fire*, 170.

27. Quoted in Smith, *Photography on the Color Line*, 114–15.

28. Du Bois, *Darkwater*, 13.

29. Ibid., 10.

30. Arnold, *What Virtue There Is in Fire*, 172.

31. Du Bois, *Darkwater*, 13.

32. SoRelle, "The 'Waco Horror': The Lynching of Jesse Washington," 536.

33. Ibid., 535.

34. See Carrigan, *Making of a Lynching Culture*.

35. Lewis, *W. E .B. Du Bois: Biography of a Race*, 227. Hereafter cited as Lewis.

36. Lewis, 178.

37. Du Bois, "I Bury My Wife," 37; as quoted in Lewis, 192.

38. Lewis, 192.

39. Nina Gomer Du Bois to W. E. B. Du Bois, September 4, 1896, W. E. B. Du Bois Papers, University of Massachusetts.

40. Du Bois, *Autobiography*, 196–97.

41. Du Bois, *Autobiography*, 57.

42. Du Bois, *Souls*, 208.

43. Lewis, 193.

44. Lewis,193.

45. Gooding-Williams, *In the Shadow of Du Bois*, 128, 127.

46. Ibid., 127.

47. Du Bois, *Souls*, 131.
48. Lewis, 227.
49. Lewis, 345.
50. Lewis, 251, 345, 252.
51. Lewis, 345.
52. Lewis, 437, 436.
53. Besides coverage in Lewis's biography, one of the best treatments of how violence affected Du Bois's spiritual and psychological transformation is in Capeci and Knight, "Reckoning with Violence: W. E. B. Du Bois and the 1906 Atlanta Race Riot."
54. Schneider, "How to Be a Sentimental (Race) Man," 109.
55. Ibid.
56. Blum, *W. E. B. Du Bois, American Prophet*, 179.
57. Du Bois, *Souls*, 171, 172, 174.
58. Lewis, 13.
59. Smith, *Photography on the Color Line*, 117.
60. On the concept of the tragic soul life, see Johnson, *Tragic Soul-Life: W. E. B. Du Bois and the Moral Crisis Facing American Democracy*.
61. Ibid., 8.
62. Stuckey, "Afterword: Frederick Douglass and W. E. B. Du Bois on the Consciousness of the Enslaved," 457.
63. Du Bois, *Souls*, 42.
64. Douglass, *Narrative*, 25.
65. Higginson, *Army Life in a Black Regiment*, 173.
66. *Mark Twain's Letters Volume 5: 1872–73*, 317n2.
67. Quoted in *Mark Twain's Letters Volume 5: 1872–73*, 316n2.
68. MT in Notebook #32b: 25. Courtesy MTP.
69. Du Bois, *Souls*, 205.
70. Ibid., 207, 210, 215.
71. See Alter, *Pen of Iron*, esp. 1–41; quotes from *Souls of Black Folk* are on 207, 210, 215.
72. Du Bois, *Souls*, 215.
73. Quoted in Stowe, *How Sweet the Sound*,114.
74. Guthrie, *Creator Spirit: The Holy Spirit and the Art of Becoming Human*, 79–80.
75. See Gooding-Williams, *In the Shadow of Du Bois*, 116; quote from *Souls* is on 189.
76. Du Bois, *Souls*, 213–14.
77. Ibid., 178.
78. Howells, *Criticism and Fiction*, 15. The quotation first appeared in an article published in *Harper's Magazine*.
79. Provenzo, *Du Bois on Education*, 212.
80. Ibid., 213.
81. See especially Kahn, *Divine Discontent*.
82. On "*shalom*" and oughtness see Plantinga, *Not the Way It's Supposed to Be*; and Wolterstorff, *Until Justice and Peace Embrace*.
83. Moltmann, *Theology of Hope*, 27.
84. On the Bible as comedy see Frye, *Great Code*, 105–38; and Buechner, *Telling the Truth*, 49–72.

85. On this view see Gamble, *War for Righteousness*, quotes from 30, 32.

86. Wright, *Surprised by Hope*, 72.

87. Du Bois, *Prayers for Dark People*, 58.

88. Blum, *W. E. B. Du Bois, American Prophet*, 180.

89. In Alexander, "Toward a Theory of Cultural Trauma," 1, in *Cultural Trauma and Collective Identity*.

90. Quoted in Nietzsche, *Portable Nietzsche*, 204.

91. Dickinson, *Letters*, 3:728; excellent meditations on this famous letter (and more generally Dickinson as religious thinker) are found in McIntosh, *Nimble Believing: Emily Dickinson and the Unknown*, and in Lundin, "Nimble Believing: Dickinson and the Conflict of Interpretations."

Epilogue

1. See Doss, *Memorial Mania: Public Feeling in America*; the website can be viewed at www.newsday.com/news/nation/newtown-shooting-victims, accessed May 1, 2015.

2. Valentine, *Bereavement Narratives*, 4.

3. Faulkner, *Requiem for a Nun*, 92.

4. Again, I found out the hard way, in June of 1999. And my own pain and trauma led me into the research, partly for selfish reasons. I couldn't figure out what was going on inside of me. I wanted to know more about what my wife and I were up against, and I happened to be a Mark Twain scholar already, so my investigations into this nightmare phenomenon began most earnestly with old Sam Clemens and poor Susy.

5. *AMT*, 324.

6. Quoted in Percoco, *Summers with Lincoln*, 175.

7. See Doss, *Memorial Mania: Public Feeling in America*.

8. Moltmann, *In the End—The Beginning*, 16–17.

9. Frost, "Acquainted with the Night," 255.

10. Available online (along with the actual recording of the speech) at http://www.nobelprize.org/nobel_prizes/literature/laureates/1949/faulkner-speech.html/, accessed May 1, 2015.

Bibliography

Adams, Marilyn McCord. *Horrendous Evils and the Goodness of God*. Ithaca, NY: Cornell University Press, 2000.

Ahlstrom, Sydney E. *A Religious History of the American People*. New Haven, CT: Yale University Press, 1972.

Alexander, Jeffrey C. "Toward a Theory of Cultural Trauma," in Alexander et al., *Cultural Trauma and Collective Identity*. Berkeley: University of California Press, 2004. 1–30.

Alexander, Jeffrey C., et al. *Cultural Trauma and Collective Identity*. Berkeley: University of California Press, 2004.

Allen, James, et al. *Without Sanctuary: Lynching Photography in America*. Santa Fe, NM: Twin Palms, 2000.

Alter, Robert. *Pen of Iron: American Prose and the King James Bible*. Princeton, NJ: Princeton University Press, 2010.

Ammons, Elizabeth, ed. *Uncle Tom's Cabin: A Norton Critical Edition*. New York: W. W. Norton, 1994.

Anderson, Frederick, William M. Gibson, and Henry Nash Smith, eds. *Selected Mark Twain–Howells Letters, 1872–1910*. New York: Athenaeum, 1967.

Apel, Dora, and Shawn Smith. *Lynching Photographs*. Berkeley: University of California Press, 2008.

Applegate, Debby. *The Most Famous Man in America: The Biography of Henry Ward Beecher*. New York: Random House, 2007.

Ariès, Philippe. *The Hour of Our Death*. New York: Random House, 2013.

———. *Western Attitudes toward Death: From the Middle Ages to the Present*. Baltimore: Johns Hopkins University Press, 1975.

Arnold, Edwin T. *What Virtue There Is in Fire: Cultural Memory and the Lynching of Sam Hose*. Athens: University of Georgia Press, 2009.

Avrich, Paul. *The Haymarket Tragedy*. Princeton, NJ: Princeton University Press, 1984.

Barton, William Eleazar. *The Soul of Abraham Lincoln*. Urbana: University of Illinois Press, 1920.

Beecher, Catharine Esther. *Common Sense Applied to Religion; or, The Bible and the People*. New York: Harper and Brothers, 1857.

Belasco, Susan, ed. *Stowe in Her Own Time: A Biographical Chronicle of Her Life, Drawn from Recollections, Interviews, and Memoirs by Family*. Iowa City: University of Iowa Press, 2009.

Bledstein, Burton J. *The Culture of Professionalism: The Middle Class and the Development of Higher Education in America*. New York: W. W. Norton, 1976.

Blum, Edward J. "God's Imperialism: Mark Twain and the Religious War between Imperialists and Anti-Imperialists." *Journal of Transnational American Studies* 1, no. 1 (2009): 35–38.

———. *W. E. B. Du Bois, American Prophet*. Philadelphia: University of Pennsylvania Press, 2009.

Boardman, William Edwin. *The Higher Christian Life*. Boston: H. Hoyt, 1859.

Boulton, Matthew Myer. *Life in God: John Calvin, Practical Formation, and the Future of Protestant Theology*. Grand Rapids, MI: Eerdmans, 2011.

Bowditch, Henry Ingersoll. *A Brief Plea for an Ambulance System for the Army of the United States; as Drawn from the Extra Sufferings of the Late Lieut. Bowditch and a Wounded Comrade*. Boston: Ticknor and Fields, 1863.

Bowditch, Vincent Yardley. *Life and Correspondence of Henry Ingersoll Bowditch*. Boston: Houghton Mifflin, 1902.

Boydston, Jeanne. *The Limits of Sisterhood: The Beecher Sisters on Women's Rights and Woman's Sphere*. Chapel Hill: University of North Carolina Press, 1988.

Bregman, Lucy. *Preaching Death: The Transformation of Christian Funeral Sermons*. Waco, TX: Baylor University Press, 2011.

Brodhead, Richard H. "Sparing the Rod: Discipline and Fiction in Antebellum America." *Representations* (1988): 67–96.

Brooks, Phillips. *Addresses*. Boston: C. E. Brown, 1893.

Buechner, Frederick. *Telling the Truth: The Gospel as Tragedy, Comedy, and Fairy Tale*. New York: Harper and Row, 1977.

Burlingame, Michael. *Abraham Lincoln: A Life*. Baltimore: Johns Hopkins University Press, 2013.

———, ed. *With Lincoln in the White House: Letters, Memoranda, and Other Writings of John G. Nicolay, 1860–1865*. Carbondale: Southern Illinois University Press, 2006.

Bush, Harold K., Jr. "Abraham Lincoln and Spiritual Crisis." In *The Cambridge Companion to Abraham Lincoln*, edited by Shirley Samuels, 126–40. New York: Cambridge University Press, 2011.

———. *American Declarations: Rebellion and Repentance in American Cultural History*. Urbana: University of Illinois Press, 1999.

———. "'Broken Idols': Mark Twain's Elegies for Susy and a Critique of Freudian Grief Theory." *Nineteenth-Century Literature* 57 (2002): 327–68.

———. "Christianity, Literature, and American Empire." *Christianity and Literature* 62, no. 3 (2013): 275–96.

———. "Continuing Bonds and Emmett Till's Mother." *Southern Quarterly* 50, no. 3 (2013): 9–27.

———, ed. *Lincoln in His Own Time*. Iowa City: University of Iowa Press, 2011.

———. "Mark Twain's American Adam: Humor as Hope and Apocalypse." *Christianity and Literature* 53, no. 3 (2004): 291–314.

———. *Mark Twain and the Spiritual Crisis of His Age*. Tuscaloosa: University of Alabama Press, 2007.

Calhoun, Lawrence G., and Richard G. Tedeschi. *Handbook of Posttraumatic Growth: Research and Practice*. Hillsdale, NJ: Lawrence Erlbaum, 2006.

Calhoun, Samuel W., and Lucas E. Morel. "Abraham Lincoln's Religion: The Case for His Ultimate Belief in a Personal, Sovereign God." *Journal of the Abraham Lincoln Association* 33, no. 1 (2012): 38–74.

Calvin, John. *Institutes of the Christian Religion*. Edited by John T. McNeil. Translated by Ford Lewis Battles. Philadelphia: Westminster, 1960.

Cameron, Sharon. "Representing Grief: Emerson's 'Experience.'" In *Impersonality: Seven Essays*, edited by Sharon Cameron, 53–78. Chicago: University of Chicago Press, 2009.

Capeci, Dominic J., and Jack C. Knight. "Reckoning with Violence: W. E. B. Du Bois and the 1906 Atlanta Race Riot." *Journal of Southern History* (1996): 727–66.

Caroll, Dannette, and Mark Hardt. "Bereaved Parents and Divorce." *Bereavement Magazine* (September–October 1999).

Carpenter, Francis B. *The Inner Life of Abraham Lincoln: Six Months at the White House*. Boston: Houghton Mifflin, 1894.

Carrigan, William. *The Making of a Lynching Culture*. Urbana: University of Illinois Press, 2006.

Carson, Clayborne, ed. *The Autobiography of Martin Luther King, Jr*. London: Abacus, 2001.

Carter, Everett. Critical introduction to *A Hazard of New Fortunes*, by William Dean Howells. Eds. David J. Nordloh et al. Bloomington, IN: Indiana University Press, 1993.

Carter, Paul Allen. *The Spiritual Crisis of the Gilded Age*. DeKalb: Northern Illinois University Press, 1971.

Caruth, Cathy, ed. *Trauma: Explorations in Memory*. Baltimore: Johns Hopkins University Press, 1995.

Carwardine, Richard. *Lincoln: A Life of Purpose and Power*. New York: Knopf, 2008.

Cervetti, Nancy. *S. Weir Mitchell, 1829–1914: Philadelphia's Literary Physician*. University Park: Pennsylvania State University Press, 2012.

Channing, William Henry, ed. *The Memoir and Writings of James Handasyd Perkins*. Cincinnati: Trueman and Spofford, 1851.

Chapman, Ervin, ed. *Latest Light on Abraham Lincoln and War-Time Memories*. New York: Fleming H. Revell, 1917.

Chase, Salmon Portland. *Inside Lincoln's Cabinet: The Civil War Diaries of Salmon P. Chase*. New York: Longmans, Green, 1954.

Clemens, Clara. *My Father, Mark Twain*. New York: Harper and Brothers, 1931.

Clemens, Olivia Langdon, and Dixon Wecter. *The Love Letters of Mark Twain*. New York: Harper, 1949.

Clemens, Samuel Langhorne, William Dean Howells, and Charles Hopkins Clark, eds. *Mark Twain's Library of Humor*. New York: Garrett Press, 1969.

Crane, Gregg D. *Race, Citizenship, and Law in American Literature*. Cambridge: Cambridge University Press, 2002.

Crowley, John W. *The Dean of American Letters: The Late Career of William Dean Howells*. Amherst: University of Massachusetts Press, 1999.

———. "The Unsmiling Aspects of Life: *A Hazard of New Fortunes*." In *Biographies of Books: The Compositional Histories of Notable American Writings*, edited by James Barbour and Tom Quirk, 78–109. Columbia: University of Missouri Press, 1996.

Cummings, Sherwood. *Mark Twain and Science: Adventures of a Mind*. Baton Rouge: Louisiana State University Press, 1988.

Current, Richard. *The Lincoln Nobody Knows*. New York: Hill and Wang, 1958.

Dark, David. *Everyday Apocalypse: The Sacred Revealed in Radiohead, The Simpsons, and Other Pop Culture Icons*. Grand Rapids, MI: Brazos Press, 2002.

Davis, Rodney O., and Douglas L. Wilson, eds. *Herndon's Informants: Letters, Interviews, and Statements about Abraham Lincoln*. Urbana: University of Illinois Press, 1997.

Davis, Thomas J. "Rhetorical War and Reflex: Calvinism in Nineteenth-Century Popular Fiction and Twentieth-Century Criticism." *Calvin Theological Journal* 33 (1998): 443–56.

Delbanco, Andrew. *The Death of Satan: How Americans Have Lost the Sense of Evil*. New York: Farrar, Strauss, and Giroux, 1995.

Dickerman, Elizabeth Hall, Abbie Ann Dickerman, and Sarah Frances Dickerman. *The Sisters: A Memoir of Elizabeth H., Abbie A., and Sarah F. Dickerman*, by Israel P. Warren. New York: American Tract Society, 1859. Print.

Dickinson, Emily. *The Letters of Emily Dickinson*. Cambridge, MA: Harvard University Press, 1986.

Dieter, Melvin Easterday. *The Holiness Revival of the Nineteenth Century*. Metuchen, NJ: Scarecrow, 1980.

Diggins, John Patrick. *On Hallowed Ground: Abraham Lincoln and the Foundations of American History*. New Haven, CT: Yale University Press, 2000.

Dolin, Eric Jay. *Fur, Fortune, and Empire: The Epic History of the Fur Trade in America*. New York: W. W. Norton, 2011.

Donald, David. *Lincoln at Home*. New York: Simon and Schuster, 2003.

Dorrien, Gary J. *The Making of American Liberal Theology: Imagining Progressive Religion, 1805–1900*. Louisville, KY: Westminster John Knox Press, 2001.

Doss, Erika. *Memorial Mania: Public Feeling in America*. Chicago: University of Chicago Press, 2012.

Douglas, Ann. *The Feminization of American Culture*. New York: Knopf, 1977.

Douglass, Frederick. *Narrative of the Life of Frederick Douglass, an American Slave*. New York: Penguin, 1982.

Doyno, Victor. "Samuel Clemens as Family Man and Father." In *Constructing Mark Twain: New Directions in Scholarship*, edited by Laura E. Skandera Trombley and Michael J. Kiskis, 28–49. Columbia: University of Missouri Press, 2001.

Du Bois, William Edward Burghardt. *The Autobiography of W. E. B. DuBois: A Soliloquy on Viewing My Life from the Last Decade of Its First Century*. New York: International Publishers, 1968.

———. *Darkwater: Voices from within the Veil*. New York: Harcourt, Brace and Howe, 1920.

———. *Prayers for Dark People*. Edited by Herbert Aptheker. Amherst: University of Massachusetts Press, 1980.

———. *The Souls of Black Folk*. New York: Penguin, 1903.

Dunn, James D. G., and John William Rogerson, eds. *Eerdmans Commentary on the Bible*. Grand Rapids, MI: Eerdmans, 2003.

Edwards, Tim. "The Real Prayer and the Imagined: The War against Romanticism in Twain, Howells, and Bierce." *Journal of Transnational American Studies* 1, no. 1 (2009): 71–74.

Ely, Richard T. *The Social Aspects of Christianity*. New York: Crowell, 1889.

Emerson, Everett. *Mark Twain: A Literary Life*. Philadelphia: University of Pennsylvania Press, 2000.

Emerson, Ralph Waldo. "Experience." In *Essays and Lectures*. Edited by Joel Porte. New York: Library of America, 1983.

Ensor, Allison. "Mark Twain's 'The War Prayer': Its Ties to Howells and Hymnology." *Modern Fiction Studies* 16 (1970): 535–39.

Erikson, Erik H. *Childhood and Society*. New York: W. W. Norton, 1950.

Erikson, Kai. *Everything in Its Path*. New York: Simon and Schuster, 1976.

———. "Notes on Trauma and Community." In *Trauma: Explorations in Memory*, edited by Cathy Caruth, 183–99. Baltimore: Johns Hopkins University Press, 1999.

Eyerman, Ron. *Cultural Trauma and the Formation of African American Identity*. New York: Cambridge University Press, 2001.

Farrell, James J. *Inventing the American Way of Death, 1830–1920*. Philadelphia: Temple University Press, 1980.

Faulkner, William. *Requiem for a Nun*. New York: Random House, 2011.

Faust, Drew Gilpin. *This Republic of Suffering*. New York: Knopf, 2008.

Felman, Shoshana. "Education and Crisis." In *Trauma: Explorations in Memory*, edited by Cathy Caruth, 13–60. Baltimore: Johns Hopkins University Press, 1999.

Ferguson, Robert A. *The Trial in American Life*. Chicago: University of Chicago Press, 2008.

Fern, Fanny. *Ruth Hall*. New York: Penguin, 1997.

Fields, Annie, ed. *Life and Letters of Harriet Beecher Stowe*. Boston: Houghton Mifflin, 1897.

Florian, Victor. "Meaning and Purpose in the Life of Bereaved Parents Whose Son Fell during Active Military Service." *Omega* 17 (1989): 91–102.

Fornieri, Joseph R. *Abraham Lincoln's Political Faith*. DeKalb: Northern Illinois University Press, 2003.

Foster, Charles H. *The Rungless Ladder: Harriet Beecher Stowe and New England Puritanism*. Durham, NC: Duke University Press, 1954.

Frederickson, George M. *The Black Image in the White Mind: The Debate on Afro-American Character and Destiny, 1817–1914*. New York: Harper and Row, 1971.

———. *The Inner Civil War*. Urbana: University of Illinois Press, 1993.

Frost, Robert. "Acquainted with the Night." In *The Poetry of Robert Frost: The Collected Poems*. New York: Henry Holt, 1969.

Frye, Northrop. *The Great Code: The Bible and Literature*. Toronto: University of Toronto Press, 2006.

Fulton, Joe B. *The Reverend Mark Twain: Theological Burlesque, Form, and Content*. Columbus: Ohio State University Press, 2006.

Gamble, Richard M. *The War for Righteousness: Progressive Christianity, the Great War, and the Rise of the Messianic Nation*. Wilmington, DE: ISI Books, 2003.

Gatta, John. *American Madonna: Images of the Divine Woman in Literary Culture*. New York: Oxford University Press, 1997.

Gerrish, R. A. "The Place of Calvin in Christian Theology." In *The Cambridge Companion to John Calvin*, edited by D. K. McKim, 289–304. Cambridge: Cambridge University Press, 2004.

Gladden, Washington. *Recollections*. Boston: Houghton Mifflin, 1909.

Goldfield, David. *America Aflame: How the Civil War Created a Nation*. New York: Bloomsbury, 2011.

Gooding-Williams, Robert. *In the Shadow of Du Bois: Afro-Modern Political Thought in America*. Cambridge, MA: Harvard University Press, 2010.

Goodman, Susan, and Charles Dawson. *William Dean Howells: A Writer's Life*. Berkeley: University of California Press, 2005.

Greene, John C. *The Death of Adam: Evolution and Its Impact on Western Thought*. Ames: Iowa State University Press, 1959.

Gribben, Alan. *Mark Twain's Library: A Reconstruction*. Boston: G. K. Hall, 1980.

Grossman, Jay. *Reconstituting the American Renaissance: Emerson, Whitman, and the Politics of Representation*. Durham, NC: Duke University Press, 2003.

Guelzo, Allen C. *Abraham Lincoln: Redeemer President*. Grand Rapids, MI: Eerdmans, 1999.

———. *Lincoln's Emancipation Proclamation: The End of Slavery in America*. New York: Simon and Schuster, 2005.

Guthrie, Steve. *Creator Spirit: The Holy Spirit and the Art of Becoming Human*. Grand Rapids, MI: Baker Academic, 2011.

Hale, Grace Elizabeth. *Making Whiteness: The Culture of Segregation in the South, 1890–1940*. New York: Pantheon Books, 1998.

Haltunnen, Karen. *Confidence Men and Painted Women*. New Haven, CT: Yale University Press, 1983.

Harris, Susan K., ed. *God's Arbiters: Americans and the Philippines*. New York: Oxford University Press, 2011.

Hart, David Bentley. *The Doors of the Sea: Where Was God in the Tsunami?* Grand Rapids, MI: Eerdmans, 2005.

Hatch, Nathan. *The Democratization of American Christianity*. New Haven, CT: Yale University Press, 1989.

Hay, John. *Addresses of John Hay*. New York: Century, 1906.

———. *At Lincoln's Side: John Hay's Civil War Correspondence and Selected Writings*. Edited by Michael Burlingame. Carbondale: Southern Illinois University Press, 2000.

Hay, John, and John Nicolay. *Abraham Lincoln: A History*. New York: Century, 1914.

Hedrick, Joan D. *Harriet Beecher Stowe: A Life*. New York: Oxford University Press, 1994.

———. "'Peaceable Fruits': The Ministry of Harriet Beecher Stowe." *American Quarterly* 40, no. 3 (1988): 307–32.

Henry, Matthew. *Commentary on the Whole Bible*. Peabody, MA: Hendrickson, 1991.

Herman, Judith Lewis. *Trauma and Recovery*. New York: Basic Books, 1997.

Hertz, Emanuel. *The Hidden Lincoln, from the Letters and Papers of William H. Herndon*. New York: Viking Press, 1938.

Higginson, Thomas Wentworth. *Army Life in a Black Regiment*. New York: W. W. Norton, 1962.

Hill, Patricia. "*Uncle Tom's Cabin* as a Religious Text." *Departments of History and American Studies*, Wesleyan University, http://utc.iath.virginia.edu/interpret/exhibits/hill/hill.html, accessed April 29, 2015.

Hodge, Charles. "Professor Park's Remarks on the Princeton Review." *Princeton Review* 23 (1851): 313.

Hovet, Theodore R. "Christian Revolution: Harriet Beecher Stowe's Response to Slavery and the Civil War." *New England Quarterly* 47, no. 4 (1974): 535–49.

———. "Modernization and the American Fall into Slavery in *Uncle Tom's Cabin*." *New England Quarterly* 54, no. 4 (1981): 499–518.

Howells, William Dean. "Bibliographical." In *A Hazard of New Fortunes*. Eds. David J. Nordloh et al. Bloomington, IN: Indiana University Press, 1993.

______. "A Counsel of Consolation." In *In After Days: Thoughts on the Future Life*. New York: Harper and Brothers, 1910.

———. *Criticism and Fiction*. New York: Harper, 1892.

———. "Editha." In *The Heath Anthology of American Literature*. Edited by Paul Lauter et al. Cengage Learning, 2010.

———. "Editor's Easy Chair." *Harper's Monthly* (February 1915).

———. "Editor's Study." *Harper's Monthly* (February 1890).

———. *A Hazard of New Fortunes*. Eds. David J. Nordloh et al. Bloomington, IN: Indiana University Press, 1993.

———. "Lyof N. Tolstoi." *North American Review* (1908).

———. *Selected Letters*. Boston: Twayne Publishers, 1979.

———. *Stops of Various Quills*. New York: Harper, 1895.

———. *Winifred Howells*. Privately printed, 1891.

Howells, Winifred. "Past." *Century Magazine* (April 1886): 838.

Hutchison, William R. *The Modernist Impulse in American Protestantism*. Durham, NC: Duke University Press, 1992.

Ingersoll, Robert. *The Ghosts, and Other Lectures*. Peoria, IL: C. P. Farrell, 1878.

———. "On Abraham Lincoln." In *The Works of Robert G. Ingersoll*. New York: C. P. Farrell, 1894.

Jalland, Patricia. *Death in the Victorian Family*. New York: Oxford University Press, 1996.

James, Henry, and William Dean Howells. *Letters, Fictions, Lives: Henry James and William Dean Howells*. Edited by Michael Anesko. New York: Oxford University Press, 1997.

James, William. *The Will to Believe and Other Essays in Popular Philosophy*. Cambridge, MA: Harvard University Press, 1979.

Jasper, David. *The Sacred Body: Asceticism in Religion, Literature, Art, and Culture*. Waco, TX: Baylor University Press, 2009.

Jenkins, Thomas E. *The Character of God: Recovering the Lost Literary Power of American Protestantism*. New York: Oxford University Press, 1997.

Johnson, Terrence. *Tragic Soul-Life: W. E. B. Du Bois and the Moral Crisis Facing American Democracy*. New York: Oxford University Press, 2012.

Jones, Edgar. *Lincoln and the Preachers*. New York: Harper, 1948.

Jones, Serene. *Trauma and Grace: Theology in a Ruptured World*. Louisville, KY: Westminster John Knox, 2009.

Kahn, Jonathan S. *Divine Discontent: The Religious Imagination of W. E. B. Du Bois*. New York: Oxford University Press, 2009.

Kaplan, Amy. *The Social Construction of American Realism*. Chicago: University of Chicago Press, 1989.

Keckley, Elizabeth. *Behind the Scenes; or, Thirty Years a Slave and Four Years in the White House*. New York: Oxford University Press, 1988.

Kellehear, Allan. *A Social History of Dying*. Cambridge: Cambridge University Press, 2007.

Kete, Mary. *Sentimental Collaborations: Mourning and Middle-Class Identity in Nineteenth-Century America*. Durham, NC: Duke University Press, 2000.

Kirschke, Amy Helene. *Art in Crisis: W. E. B. Du Bois and the Struggle for African American Identity and Memory*. Bloomington: Indiana University Press, 2007.

Klass, Dennis. *The Spiritual Lives of Bereaved Parents*. Philadelphia: Brunner/Mazel, 1999.

Klass, Dennis, Phyllis Silverman, and Steven Nickman, eds. *Continuing Bonds: New Understandings of Grief*. Washington, DC: Taylor and Francis, 1996.

Koester, Nancy. *Harriet Beecher Stowe: A Spiritual Life*. Grand Rapids, MI: Eerdmans, 2014.

Koselleck, Reinhart. *The Practice of Conceptual History: Timing History, Spacing Concepts*. Stanford, CA: Stanford University Press, 2002.

Kuklick, Bruce. *Churchmen and Philosophers: From Jonathan Edwards to John Dewey*. New Haven, CT: Yale University Press, 1985.

Laderman, Gary. *The Sacred Remains: American Attitudes toward Death, 1799–1883*. New Haven, CT: Yale University Press, 1999.

Landy, Joshua, and Michael T. Saler. *The Re-Enchantment of the World: Secular Magic in a Rational Age*. Stanford, CA: Stanford University Press, 2009.

Larsen, Timothy. *Crisis of Doubt: Honest Faith in Nineteenth-Century England*. New York: Oxford University Press, 2007.

Lears, T. Jackson. *No Place of Grace: Antimodernism and the Transformation of American Culture, 1880–1920*. Chicago: University of Chicago Press, 1981.

LeMaster, J. R., and James D. Wilson, eds. *The Mark Twain Encyclopedia*. New York: Garland, 1995.

Lewis, David Levering. *W. E .B. Du Bois: Biography of a Race, 1868–1919*. New York: Henry Holt, 1993.

Lewis, David Levering, and Deborah Willis. *A Small Nation of People*. New York: Harper Collins, 2010.

Lincoln, Abraham. *The Collected Works of Abraham Lincoln*. Edited by Roy P. Basler. 8 Volumes. New Brunswick, NJ: Rutgers University Press, 1953–55.

Little, David. "Calvinism and American National Identity." In *John Calvin's American Legacy*, edited by Thomas J. Davis, 43–64. New York: Oxford University Press, 2010.

Long, Thomas. *What Shall We Say?: Evil, Suffering, and the Crisis of Faith*. Grand Rapids, MI: Eerdmans, 2011.

Lovin, Robin W. *Reinhold Niebuhr and Christian Realism*. New York: Cambridge University Press, 1995.

Lowell, James Russell. "Abraham Lincoln." In *Political Essays*, 178–208. Cambridge, MA: Riverside Press, 1891.

Luciano, Dana. *Arranging Grief: Sacred Time and the Body in Nineteenth-Century America*. New York: New York University Press, 2007.

Lundin, Roger. "Nimble Believing: Dickinson and the Conflict of Interpretations." In *There Before Us: Religion, Literature, and Culture from Emerson to Wendell Berry*, 80–109. Grand Rapids, MI: Eerdmans, 2007.

Lynn, Kenneth S. *William Dean Howells: An American Life*. New York: Harcourt, Brace, Jovanovich, 1971.

Madsen, Valden J. "Social Guilt and Private Suffering in W. D. Howells's *Stops of Various Quills*." *Markham Review* 5 (1976).

Mansfield, Stephen. *Lincoln's Battle with God: A President's Struggle with Faith and What It Meant for America*. Nashville: Thomas Nelson, 2012.

McAdams, Dan P. "The Redemptive Self: Generativity and the Stories Americans Live By." *Research in Human Development* 3, no. 2–3 (2006): 81–100.

McAdams, Dan P., and Regina L. Logan. "What Is Generativity?" American Psychological Association, 2004.

McFarland, Philip. *Loves of Harriet Beecher Stowe*. New York: Grove Press, 2008.

McIntosh, James. *Nimble Believing: Emily Dickinson and the Unknown*. Ann Arbor: University of Michigan Press, 2000.

McLoughlin, William. *Revivals, Awakenings, and Reform*. Chicago: University of Chicago Press, 1978.

McPherson, James. *Crossroads of Freedom: Antietam*. New York: Oxford University Press, 2002.

Menand, Louis. *The Metaphysical Club*. New York: Farrar, Strauss and Giroux, 2001.

Messent, Peter. *Mark Twain and Male Friendship: The Twichell, Howells, and Rogers Friendships*. New York: Oxford University Press, 2009.

Miller, Randall M., Harry S. Stout, and Charles Reagan Wilson, eds. Introduction to *Religion and the American Civil War*. New York: Oxford University Press, 1998.

Milton, John. *Lycidas*. New York: Macmillan, 1898.

Mitford, Jessica. *The American Way of Death*. New York: Simon and Schuster, 1963.

Moltmann, Jürgen. *In the End—The Beginning: The Life of Hope*. Minneapolis: Fortress Press, 2004.

———. *Theology of Hope: On the Ground and the Implications of a Christian Eschatology*. Translated by James W. Leitch. New York: Harper and Row, 1967.

Moody, Lisa. "Religion and Realism in Late Nineteenth-Century American Literature." PhD diss., Louisiana State University, 2009.

Morel, Lucas E. *Lincoln's Sacred Effort: Defining Religion's Role in American Self-Government*. Lanham, MD: Lexington Books, 2000.

Morley, John. *Death, Heaven, and the Victorians*. London: Studio Vista, 1971.

Morris, Linda. "When Did Susy Become Mark Twain's Favorite Daughter?" Unpublished paper presented at the American Literature Association Conference, Boston, May 2011.

Neeley, Mark E. *The Last, Best Hope of Earth: Abraham Lincoln and the Promise of America*. Cambridge, MA: Harvard University Press, 1995.

Neiman, Susan. *Evil in Modern Thought: An Alternative History of Philosophy*. Princeton, NJ: Princeton University Press, 2004.

Neimeyer, Robert A., ed. *Meaning Reconstruction and the Experience of Loss*. Washington, DC: American Psychological Association, 2001.

Niebuhr, Reinhold. *The Irony of American History*. New York: Scribner's Sons, 1952.

———. *Moral Man and Immoral Society: A Study of Ethics and Politics*. New York: Scribner's Sons, 1932.

———. *The Nature and Destiny of Man: A Christian Interpretation*. New York: Scribner's Sons, 1943.

———. "The Religion of Abraham Lincoln." In *Lincoln and the Gettysburg Address*, edited by Allan Nevins. Urbana: University of Illinois Press, 1964.

Nietzsche, Friedrich. *The Portable Nietzsche*. New York: Penguin, 1977.

Noble, Marianne. "The Ecstasies of Sentimental Wounding in *Uncle Tom's Cabin*." *Yale Journal of Criticism* 10, no. 2 (1997): 295–320.

Noll, Mark A. *America's God: From Jonathan Edwards to Abraham Lincoln*. New York: Oxford University Press, 2002.

———. "'Both . . . Pray to the Same God': The Singularity of Lincoln's Faith in the Era of the Civil War." *Journal of the Abraham Lincoln Association* (1997): 1–26.

———. *The Civil War as a Theological Crisis*. Chapel Hill: University of North Carolina Press, 2006.

Oggel, Terry. "Speaking Out about Race: 'The United States of Lyncherdom' Clemens Really Wrote." In *Prospects: An Annual of American Cultural Studies*, 115–58. Cambridge: Cambridge University Press, 2000.

Palmer, Phoebe. *Promise of the Father*. New York: Garland, 1985.

Parrillo, Nicholas. "Lincoln's Calvinist Transformation: Emancipation and War." *Civil War History* 46, no. 3 (2000): 227–53.

Percoco, James A. *Summers with Lincoln: Looking for the Man in the Monuments*. New York: Fordham University Press, 2008.

Phipps, William E. *Mark Twain's Religion*. Macon, GA: Mercer University Press, 2003.

Pine, Vanderlyn R., and Carolyn Brauer. "Parental Grief: A Synthesis of Theory, Research, and Intervention." In *Parental Loss of a Child*, edited by Therese A. Rando, 59–96. Champaign, IL: Research Press, 1986.

Plantinga, Cornelius. *Not the Way It's Supposed to Be: A Breviary of Sin*. Grand Rapids, MI: Eerdmans, 1995.

Provenzo, Eugene F., Jr., ed. *Du Bois on Education*. Lanham, MD: Altamira Press, 2002.

Puskar, Jason. *Accident Society: Fiction, Collectivity, and the Production of Chance*. Stanford, CA: Stanford University Press. 2012.

———. "William Dean Howells and the Insurance of the Real." *American Literary History* 18, no. 1 (2006): 29–58.

Quirk, Tom. *Nothing Abstract: Investigation in the American Literary Imagination*. Columbia: University of Missouri Press, 2001.

Rambo, Shelly. *Spirit and Trauma: A Theology of Remaining*. Louisville, KY: Westminster John Knox, 2010.

Reed, James A. "The Later Life and Religious Sentiments of Abraham Lincoln." *Scribner's Monthly* (July 1873).

Reynolds, David S. *Mightier Than the Sword: Uncle Tom's Cabin and the Battle for America*. New York: W. W. Norton, 2011.

Roberts, Jon H. *Darwinism and the Divine in America: Protestant Intellectuals and Organic Evolution, 1859–1900*. Madison: University of Wisconsin Press, 1988.

Roof, Wade Clarke. *Spiritual Marketplace: Baby Boomers and the Remaking of American Religion*. Princeton, NJ: Princeton University Press, 2001.

Rose, Anne C. *Victorian America and the Civil War*. Cambridge: Cambridge University Press, 1992.

Rosenberg, Charles. "Cholera Epidemics." *Ohio History Central*, http://ohiohistorycentral.org/w/Cholera_Epidemics?rec=487, accessed April 29, 2015.

———. *The Cholera Years: The United States in 1832, 1849, and 1866*. Chicago: University of Chicago Press, 2009.

Rosenblatt, Paul C. *Bitter, Bitter Tears: Nineteenth-Century Diarists and Twentieth-Century Grief Theories*. Minneapolis: University of Minnesota Press, 1983.

Rusling, James. "Lincoln and Sickles." May 5, 1910. Parish Memorabilia of the Asylum Hill Congregational Church, Connecticut State Library.

Russett, Cynthia Eagle. *Darwin in America: The Intellectual Response, 1865–1912*. San Francisco: W. H. Freeman, 1976.

Ryan, Ann M. "Mark Twain and the Cosmopolitan Ideal." In *Cosmopolitan Twain*, edited by Ann Ryan and Joseph McCullough. Columbia: University of Missouri Press, 2008.

Saum, Lewis O. *The Popular Mood of America, 1860–1890*. Lincoln: University of Nebraska Press, 1990.

Savelsberg, Joachim J., and Ryan D. King. *American Memories: Atrocities and the Law*. New York: Russell Sage Foundation, 2011.

Schantz, Mark S. *Awaiting the Heavenly Country: The Civil War and America's Culture of Death*. Ithaca, NY: Cornell University Press, 2013.

Scharnhorst, Gary, ed. *Mark Twain: The Complete Interviews*. Tuscaloosa: University of Alabama Press, 2006.

Schmidt, Leigh Eric. *Restless Souls: The Making of American Spirituality*. Berkeley: University of California Press, 2012.

Schneider, Ryan. "How to Be a (Sentimental) Race Man: Mourning and Passing in W. E. B. Du Bois's *The Souls of Black Folk*." *Boys Don't Cry: Rethinking Narrative of Masculinity and Emotion in the US* (2002): 106–23.

———. *The Public Intellectualism of Ralph Waldo Emerson and W. E. B. Du Bois: Emotional Dimensions of Race and Reform*. New York: Palgrave Macmillan, 2010.

Schwartz, Thomas D. "Mark Twain and Robert Ingersoll: The Freethought Connection." *American Literature* 48 (1976): 183–93.

Shelden, Michael. *Mark Twain, Man in White: The Grand Adventure of His Final Years*. New York: Random House, 2010.

Shenk, Joshua Wolf. "Eureka Dept.: The Suicide Poem." *New Yorker*, June 14, 2004.

———. *Lincoln's Melancholy: How Depression Challenged a President and Fueled His Greatness*. New York: Mariner, 2006.

Shi, David E. *Facing Facts: Realism in American Thought and Culture, 1850–1920*. New York: Oxford University Press, 1995.

Shurr, William. *Rappacini's Children: American Writers in a Calvinist World*. Lexington: University of Kentucky P, 1981.

Smith, Christian. *The Bible Made Impossible: Why Biblicism Is Not a Truly Evangelical Reading of Scripture*. Grand Rapids, MI: Baker Books, 2012.

Smith, Shawn Michelle. *Photography on the Color Line: W. E. B. Du Bois, Race, and Visual Culture*. Durham, NC: Duke University Press, 2004.

Smith, Timothy L. *Revivalism and Social Reform in Mid-Nineteenth-Century America*. New York: Abington, 1957.

Snedecor, Barbara E. "'He Was So Rarely Beautiful': Langdon Clemens." *American Literary Realism* 45, no. 1 (2012): 60–69.

SoRelle, James M. "The 'Waco Horror': The Lynching of Jesse Washington." *Southwestern Historical Quarterly* 86 (April 1983): 517–36.

Stauffer, John. *Giants: The Parallel Lives of Frederick Douglass and Abraham Lincoln*. New York: Twelve, 2008.

Stedman, Edmund Clarence, ed. *An American Anthology*. Boston: Houghton Mifflin, 1900.

Stephenson, Nathaniel. *Lincoln*. Indianapolis: Bobbs-Merrill, 1922.

Stout, Harry S. *Upon the Altar of the Nation: A Moral History of the Civil War*. New York: Penguin, 2007.

Stowe, Charles Edward, and Lyman Beecher Stowe. *Harriet Beecher Stowe: The Story of Her Life*. Boston: Houghton Mifflin, 1911.

Stowe, Harriet Beecher. "Abraham Lincoln." *The Living Age*, February 6, 1864.

———. "The Interior or Hidden Life." *New York Evangelist*, April 17, 1845.

———. *The Key to "Uncle Tom's Cabin."* In *Uncle Tom's Cabin: A Norton Critical Edition*. Edited by Elizabeth Ammons. New York: W. W. Norton, 1994.

———. *The Minister's Wooing*. Edited by Susan K. Harris. New York: Penguin, 1999.

———. *Oldtown Folks*. New York: Library of America, 1982.

———. "On the Ministration of Departed Spirits in the World." *New York Evangelist*, January 25, 1849.

———. "To Sarah Beecher, July 29, 1849." Stowe-Day Memorial Library, Hartford, Connecticut.

Stroebe, Margaret. "Bereavement Research and Theory: Retrospective and Prospective." *American Behavioral Scientist* 44, no. 5 (2001): 854–65.

———. "Coping with Bereavement: A Review of the Grief Work Hypothesis." *Omega* 26 (1992–93): 19–42.

Stuckey, P. Sterling. "Afterword: Frederick Douglass and W. E. B. Du Bois on the Consciousness of the Enslaved." *Journal of African American History* (2006): 451–58.

Synan, Vinson. *The Holiness-Pentecostal Movement in the United States*. Grand Rapids, MI: Eerdmans, 1971.

Szasz, Ferenc Morton. *The Divided Mind of Protestant America, 1880–1930*. Tuscaloosa: University of Alabama Press, 1982.

Tackach, James. *Lincoln's Moral Vision: The Second Inaugural Address*. Jackson: University Press of Mississippi, 2002.

Tallon, Philip. *The Poetics of Evil: Toward an Aesthetic Theodicy*. New York: Oxford University Press, 2012.

Taylor, Charles. *A Secular Age*. Cambridge, MA: Belknap Press of Harvard University Press, 2007.

Taylor, Isaac. *Physical Theory of Another Life*. London: Bell and Daldy, 1871.

Tennyson, Alfred Tennyson, Baron. *The Complete Works of Alfred, Lord Tennyson, Poet Laureate*. New York: Grosset and Dunlap, 1913.

Thomas, Christopher. *The Lincoln Memorial and American Life*. Princeton, NJ: Princeton University Press, 2002.

Thuesen, Peter J. "Geneva's Crystalline Clarity: Harriet Beecher Stowe and Max Weber on Calvinism and the American Character." In *John Calvin's Ameri-*

can Legacy, edited by Thomas J. Davis, 219–38. New York: Oxford University Press, 2010.

Till-Mobley, Mamie, and Christopher Benson. *Death of Innocence: The Story of the Hate Crime That Changed America*. New York: Random House, 2004.

Tirman, John. *The Deaths of Others: The Fate of Civilians in America's Wars*. New York: Oxford University Press, 2011.

Trueblood, Elton. *Abraham Lincoln: Theologian of American Anguish*. New York: Harper and Row, 1973.

Trueman, Carl R. "Calvin and Calvinism." In *The Cambridge Companion to John Calvin*, edited by Donald K. McKim, 225–44. Cambridge: Cambridge University Press, 2005.

Tuckey, John S. Introduction to *The Devil's Race-Track: Mark Twain's "Great Dark" Writings: The Best from "Which Was the Dream?" and "The Fables of Man."* Berkeley: University of California Press, 1980.

Turner, Francis, ed. *Golden Treasury of Songs and Poems*. London: Macmillan, 1894.

Turner, James. *Without God, Without Creed: The Origins of Unbelief in America*. Baltimore: Johns Hopkins University Press, 1985.

Twain, Mark. *Autobiography of Mark Twain*. Edited by Harriet Smith. Berkeley: University of California Press, 2010.

———. *A Connecticut Yankee in King Arthur's Court*. Edited by Bernard L. Stein. Berkeley: University of California Press, 1983.

______. *Mark Twain's Letters Volume 5: 1872–73*. Edited by Lin Salamo and Harriet Elinor Smith. Berkeley: University of California Press, 1997.

———. "The United States of Lyncherdom." *Prospects* 25 (2000): 139–50.

———. "The War Prayer." In *Collected Tales, Sketches, Speeches, and Essays, 1891–1910*. Edited by Louis J. Budd. New York: Library of America, 1992.

———. "Which Was the Dream?" In *Mark Twain's Which Was the Dream?, and Other Symbolic Writings of the Later Years*, edited by John S. Tuckey, 33–73. Berkeley: University of California Press, 1968.

Twichell, Joseph. *Journals*. Joseph Hopkins Twichell Papers. Beinecke Rare Book and Manuscript Library, Yale University.

Valentine, Christine. *Bereavement Narratives: Continuing Bonds in the Twenty-First Century*. New York: Routledge, 2008.

Valeri, Mark. "Calvin and the Social Order in Early America: Moral Ideals and Transatlantic Empire." In *John Calvin's American Legacy*, edited by Thomas J. Davis, 19–41. New York: Oxford University Press, 2010.

Vollaro, Daniel R. "Lincoln, Stowe, and the 'Little Woman/Great War' Story: The Making, and Breaking, of a Great American Anecdote." *Journal of the Abraham Lincoln Association* 30, no. 1 (2009): 18–34.

Webb, Stephen H. *American Providence: A Nation with a Mission*. New York: Continuum, 2004.

Weik, Jesse William. *Herndon's Lincoln*. Urbana: University of Illinois Press, 2006.

Weinstein, Cindy. *Family, Kinship, and Sympathy in Nineteenth-Century American Literature*. Cambridge: Cambridge University Press, 2004.

Welles, Gideon. *Diary of Gideon Welles*. Boston: Houghton Mifflin, 1911.

Wheatley, Richard. *The Life and Letters of Phoebe Palmer*. New York: W. C. Palmer Jr., 1876.

Wheeler, Inese. "The Role of Meaning and Purpose in Life in Bereaved Parents Associated with a Self-Help Group: Compassionate Friends." *Omega* 28 (1993–94): 261–71.

White, Charles Edward. *The Beauty of Holiness: Phoebe Palmer as Theologian, Revivalist, Feminist, and Humanitarian*. Grand Rapids, MI: Zondervan, 1986.

White, Ronald. *Lincoln's Greatest Speech: The Second Inaugural*. New York: Simon and Schuster, 2002.

Whittier, John Greenleaf, et al. *Voices of the True-Hearted*. Philadelphia: Merrihew and Thompson, 1846.

Wigglesworth, Edward, and Thomas Gamaliel Bradford. *Encyclopedia Americana: A Popular Dictionary of Arts, Sciences, Literature, History, Politics, and Biography*. Boston: B. B. Mussey, 1854.

Williamson, Joel. "Wounds Not Scars: Lynching, the National Conscience, and the American Historian." *Journal of American History* 83, no. 4 (1997): 1221–53.

Willis, Resa. *Mark and Livy: The Love Story of Mark Twain and the Woman Who (Almost) Tamed Him*. New York: TV Books, 1992.

Wills, Garry. "Lincoln's Greatest Speech?" *Atlantic Monthly* (September 1999): 60–70.

Winger, Stewart. *Lincoln, Religion, and Romantic Cultural Politics*. DeKalb: Northern Illinois University Press, 2003.

Wolf, William. *Lincoln's Religion*. Boston: Pilgrim, 1959.

Wolterstorff, Nicholas. *Until Justice and Peace Embrace*. Grand Rapids, MI: Eerdmans, 1983.

Woodress, James Leslie. *Howells and Italy*. Westport, CT: Greenwood, 1969.

Wortham, Thomas. "William Dean Howells's Spiritual Quest(ioning) in a 'World Come of Age.'" *Renascence* 65 (Spring 2013): 206–24.

Wright, Nicholas Thomas. *Jesus and the Victory of God*. Minneapolis: Fortress Press, 1996.

———. *Surprised by Hope: Rethinking Heaven, the Resurrection, and the Mission of the Church*. New York: Harper One, 2008.

Wright, Richard. *Black Boy: A Record of Childhood and Youth*. New York: Random House, 2000.

Wuthnow, Robert. *After Heaven: Spirituality in America Since the 1950s*. Berkeley: University of California Press, 1998.

Zwarg, Christina. "Fathering and Blackface in *Uncle Tom's Cabin*." In *Uncle Tom's Cabin: A Norton Critical Edition*. Edited by Elizabeth Ammons, 568–84. New York: W. W. Norton, 1994.

Zwick, Jim, ed. *Mark Twain's Weapons of Satire: Anti-Imperialist Writings on the Philippine-American War*. Syracuse, NY: Syracuse University Press, 1992.

Index